Praise for *Practical Modern JavaScript*

Practical Modern JavaScript brings a whole ton of new syntax and semantics that makes your code more expressive and declarative. Nicolás does an amazing job of distilling this with simple examples so you can get up to speed quickly.

—*Kent C. Dodds (PayPal, TC39)*

Nicolás demystifies the massive ES6 specification with a pragmatic and practical dive into the features that are redefining modern JavaScript development.

—*Rod Vagg (NodeSource, Node.js TSC)*

Nicolás has an amazing ability to break down highly complex technical topics into easy-to-understand prose and sample code.

—*Mathias Bynens (Google, TC39)*

JavaScript is a tough language to master, and the 2015 edition adds a lot of new features. *Practical Modern JavaScript* helps break them down and explains use cases, conceptual models, and best practices, with simple examples—making these new patterns much easier to grasp.

—*Jordan Harband (Airbnb, TC39)*

ES6 brought significant changes to the language—changes that take time to grasp even for advanced JavaScript developers. You'll need a guide on this journey, and Nicolás' book is one of the best you can get.

—*Ingvar Stepanyan (CloudFlare)*

When I created JavaScript in 1995, I had no definite idea that it would become the most widely used programming language on the Internet. This Modular JavaScript book series fulfills my hope for an incremental and straightforward pedagogy about JavaScript. I encourage you to dive in, to discover and embrace JavaScript, and to contribute to developing a better web for everyone.

—*Brendan Eich (creator of JavaScript)*

Practical Modern JavaScript

Nicolás Bevacqua

Beijing · Boston · Farnham · Sebastopol · Tokyo

Practical Modern JavaScript

by Nicolás Bevacqua

Printed in the United States of America.

Published by O'Reilly Media, Inc., 1005 Gravenstein Highway North, Sebastopol, CA 95472.

O'Reilly books may be purchased for educational, business, or sales promotional use. Online editions are also available for most titles (*http://oreilly.com/safari*). For more information, contact our corporate/institutional sales department: 800-998-9938 or *corporate@oreilly.com*.

Editor: Allyson MacDonald	**Indexer:** Wendy Catalano
Production Editor: Melanie Yarbrough	**Interior Designer:** David Futato
Copyeditor: Kim Cofer	**Cover Designer:** Karen Montgomery
Proofreader: Molly Ives Brower	**Illustrator:** Rebecca Demarest

June 2017:   First Edition

Revision History for the First Edition
2017-06-26:   First Release

See *http://oreilly.com/catalog/errata.csp?isbn=9781491943533* for release details.

978-1-491-94353-3

[LSI]

Table of Contents

Foreword

When I created JavaScript in 1995 at Netscape, I had no definite idea that it would become the most widely used programming language on the Internet. I did know that I had very little time to get it into "minimum viable shipping" state, and so I made it extensible and mutable from global object on down, even to base-level meta-object protocol hooks (e.g., `toString` and `valueOf`, styled after Java's methods of the same names).

Yet in spite of its ongoing evolution and still-rising popularity, JavaScript always benefits from an incremental and careful teaching approach that puts first things first. I think this follows inevitably from the hurried design and intentional extensibility. I overloaded two kernel elements, functions and objects, so that programmers could use them in various ways as general workalikes for individual tools in a larger Swiss army knife. This meant that students would need to learn which tool was best to use for a specific task, and how precisely to wield that particular blade.

Netscape was a whirlwind for me, and I think for anyone there from early 1995 on. It was rushing toward an initial public offering predicated on competing with Microsoft via the infamous "Netscape + Java kills Windows" formula repeated by Marc Andreessen on the IPO roadshow that year. Java was the big-brother or "Batman" programming language to little-brother, "Robin the boy hostage" sidekick "scripting language," JavaScript.

But I knew while I was writing the first version (code-named "Mocha") that JavaScript and not Java would be integrated deeply with the Netscape browser and the Document Object Model I created at the same time. There was no way across the Netscape/Sun organizational boundary, or the browser/JVM code bases, to embed Java other than as a plugin.

So I did have a vague sense that JavaScript would either succeed over time and do well, or else fade quickly in the shadow of something else. I remember telling my friend and cubicle-mate Jeff Weinstein, when he asked me what I'd be doing in 20 years, that it would be "JavaScript or bust." Even then I felt a sense of deep obligation to JavaScript's users that was inherent in the "two-blade Swiss army knife" design I had chosen under the dual constraints of extremely short schedule and "make it look like Java" management edict.

The Modular JavaScript book series fulfills my hope for an incremental and straightforward pedagogy, starting with easily applicable code examples and scaling through design patterns to entire module-based applications. This series nicely covers best testing practices and winning techniques for deploying JavaScript applications. It is another jewel in O'Reilly's crown of books on JavaScript.

I am delighted to support Nicolás' endeavor because his book looks exactly like what people who are coming to JavaScript with fresh eyes need. I first met Nicolás at a dinner in Paris and got to know him a bit there, and over time online. His pragmatism combined with empathy for newcomers to the language and a great sense of humor convinced me to review this book in draft form. The finished work is easy to digest and fun. I encourage you to dive in, to discover and embrace JavaScript, and to contribute to developing a better web for everyone.

— Brendan Eich, Inventor of
JavaScript, CEO and cofounder
of Brave Software

Preface

Back in 1998, when I was using FrontPage for all my web development needs at school, if someone had told me that I'd end up working on the web for a living, I would've probably chuckled. JavaScript has grown along with us in all the years since, and it's hard to imagine how the web could've thrived without it. Bit by bit, this book will give you a comprehensive picture of the modern JavaScript landscape.

Who Should Read This Book

This book is meant for web developers, enthusiasts, and professionals with a working knowledge of plain JavaScript. These developers and anyone looking to further their understanding of the JavaScript language shall benefit from reading *Practical Modern JavaScript*.

Why Modern JavaScript?

The goal of this book is to provide an approachable way of learning the latest developments in JavaScript: ES6 and later. ES6 was a huge update to the language, and it came out around the same time as a streamlined specification development process. Around this time I wrote quite a few blog posts about the different features in ES6, which became a bit popular. There are quite a few other books on ES6 out there, but they're a little different from what I had in mind for a book on ES6 and beyond. This book tries to explain features in detail without getting caught up in the specification, its implementation details, or unlikely corner cases that would almost certainly need to be researched online if happened upon.

Instead of extreme thoroughness, the book places its utmost focus in the learning process, having sorted its material in such an incremental way that you don't have to scan ahead in the book for the definition of something else. Armed with practical examples, *Practical Modern JavaScript* goes beyond ES6 to capture the changes to the language since June 2015—when the ES6 specification was finalized —including async functions, object destructuring, dynamic imports, `Promise#finally`, and async generators.

Lastly, this book has the goal of establishing a baseline we can take for granted in the rest of the Modular JavaScript series. After having learned the latest language features in this first book, we'll be all set to discuss modular design, testing, and deployment, without having to diverge into language features whenever they're used in a code example. This incremental and modular approach is meant to be pervasive across the series, each book, each chapter, and each section.

How Is This Book Organized?

In Chapter 1, we open with an introduction to JavaScript and its standards development process, how it has evolved over the years, where it is now, and where it's going. You'll also get a short introduction to Babel and ESLint, modern tools that can aid us in the process of discovering modern JavaScript.

Chapter 2 covers all of the absolutely essential changes in ES6, including arrow functions, destructuring, `let` and `const`, template literals, and a few other syntax embellishments.

In Chapter 3, we'll discuss the new `class` syntax for declaring object prototypes, a new primitive type known as `Symbol`, and a few new `Object` methods.

Chapter 4 goes over all of the new ways we can deal with flow control starting in ES6. We discuss Promises, iterators, generators, and async functions in great detail and with heaps of accompanying examples, uncovering the synergistic properties between all the different techniques. You won't only learn how to use these flow control techniques but how to best reason about them so that they truly simplify your code.

Chapter 5 describes the new collection built-ins found in ES6, which we can use to create object maps and unique sets. You'll find usage examples for each of these collection types.

Chapter 6 covers the new `Proxy` and `Reflect` built-ins. We'll learn all about how we can use proxies and the reasons why we need to be careful when choosing to do so.

Chapter 7 is dedicated to the rest of built-in improvements that can be found in ES6. Particularly around `Array`, `Math`, numbers, strings, Unicode, and regular expressions.

Chapter 8 is devoted to native JavaScript Modules and, briefly, the history that led to their inception. We'll then discuss their syntax implications at length.

Chapter 9, the last chapter—dubbed "Practical Considerations"—is somewhat unconventional for books about programming languages. Rather than spreading my personal views throughout the book, I condensed them into the last chapter. Here you'll find reasoning behind how to decide when to use which kind of variable declaration or string literal quotation mark, advice on handling asynchronous code flows and whether using classes or proxies is a good idea, and a few more nuggets of insight.

For those of you who are already somewhat familiar with ES6 and comfortable jumping around the pages in a book, I recommend reading Chapter 4 in detail, as you should find the insight into flow control most valuable. Chapters 7 and 8 are also a must, since they provide details around the areas of ES6 that are less often discussed in the open. The last chapter will indubitably—regardless of whether you agree with the views expressed therein—challenge you to think deeply about what works and what doesn't in the context of Java-Script applications written under the wild new world order that is modern JavaScript.

Conventions Used in This Book

The following typographical conventions are used in this book:

Italic
    Indicates new terms, URLs, email addresses, filenames, and file extensions.

Constant width

Used for program listings, as well as within paragraphs to refer to program elements such as variable or function names, databases, data types, environment variables, statements, and keywords.

 This icon signifies a tip, suggestion, or general note.

 This icon indicates a warning or caution.

O'Reilly Safari

 *Safari* (formerly Safari Books Online) is a membership-based training and reference platform for enterprise, government, educators, and individuals.

Members have access to thousands of books, training videos, Learning Paths, interactive tutorials, and curated playlists from over 250 publishers, including O'Reilly Media, Harvard Business Review, Prentice Hall Professional, Addison-Wesley Professional, Microsoft Press, Sams, Que, Peachpit Press, Adobe, Focal Press, Cisco Press, John Wiley & Sons, Syngress, Morgan Kaufmann, IBM Redbooks, Packt, Adobe Press, FT Press, Apress, Manning, New Riders, McGraw-Hill, Jones & Bartlett, and Course Technology, among others.

For more information, please visit *http://oreilly.com/safari*.

How to Contact Us

Please address comments and questions concerning this book to the publisher:

> O'Reilly Media, Inc.
> 1005 Gravenstein Highway North
> Sebastopol, CA 95472
> 800-998-9938 (in the United States or Canada)
> 707-829-0515 (international or local)
> 707-829-0104 (fax)

We have a web page for this book, where we list errata, examples, and any additional information. You can access this page at *http://www.oreilly.com/catalog/0636920047124*.

To comment or ask technical questions about this book, send email to *bookquestions@oreilly.com*.

For more information about our books, courses, conferences, and news, see our website at *http://www.oreilly.com*.

Find us on Facebook: *http://facebook.com/oreilly*

Follow us on Twitter: *http://twitter.com/oreillymedia*

Watch us on YouTube: *http://www.youtube.com/oreillymedia*

Acknowledgments

Like virtually every human task ever carried out, *Practical Modern JavaScript* was made possible only by building upon the work of others. I want to thank Nan Barber, my editor at O'Reilly, for her fantastic support along the ride of writing this book. Ally MacDonald, another editor at O'Reilly, helped me out in the early days of the project and is the foremost reason why Modular JavaScript became a book series, as she helped me conjure up a modular approach to teaching JavaScript.

This book had a phenomenal ensemble of technical reviewers. Many of these folks are on TC39, the technical committee devoted to pushing JavaScript forward, and it's deeply humbling that they gave up some of their time to help future-proof this book. As always, Mathias Bynens (ex-Opera) proved instrumental to proofing everything in the book with regards to Unicode standards and held my work to a high degree of consistency in terms of code snippets. Kent C. Dodds (TC39, PayPal) ingeniously offered video reviews where he identified weak spots and helped improve the book. Jordan Harband (TC39, Airbnb) came through with deep technical commentary about many of the JavaScript features discussed in the book, and along with Alex Russell (TC39, Google) helped me iron out the history of JavaScript and its standards body for the first chapter. Ingvar Stepanyan (Cloudflare) was also a sharp eye in identifying code issues and pinpointed mistakes around low-level aspects of the specification. Brian Terlson (TC39 editor, Microsoft) also helped out with timelines and details around TC39. Rod Vagg (Node.js) provided insight that lead to better code examples and more consistent code style throughout the book.

Brendan Eich (TC39, Brave CEO) provided a trove of insight into the early days of JavaScript and TC39, which proved essential to the development of the first chapter. And naturally, if not for him, you wouldn't be holding this book in your hands.

Lastly, I'd like to thank my wife, Marianela, for her sacrifices and putting up with me through the development of the first book in a long series. Marian, I couldn't do this without you!

ECMAScript and the Future of JavaScript

JavaScript has gone from being a 1995 marketing ploy to gain a tactical advantage to becoming the core programming experience in the world's most widely used application runtime platform in 2017. The language doesn't merely run in browsers anymore, but is also used to create desktop and mobile applications, in hardware devices, and even in space suit design at NASA.

How did JavaScript get here, and where is it going next?

1.1 A Brief History of JavaScript Standards

Back in 1995, Netscape envisioned a dynamic web beyond what HTML could offer. Brendan Eich was initially brought into Netscape to develop a language that was functionally akin to Scheme, but for the browser. Once he joined, he learned that upper management wanted it to look like Java, and a deal to that effect was already underway.

Brendan created the first JavaScript prototype in 10 days, taking Scheme's first-class functions and Self's prototypes as its main ingredients. The initial version of JavaScript was code-named Mocha. It didn't have array or object literals, and every error resulted in an alert. The lack of exception handling is why, to this day, many operations result in NaN or undefined. Brendan's work on DOM level 0 and the first edition of JavaScript set the stage for standards work.

This revision of JavaScript was marketed as LiveScript when it started shipping with a beta release of Netscape Navigator 2.0, in September 1995. It was rebranded as JavaScript (trademarked by Sun, now owned by Oracle) when Navigator 2.0 beta 3 was released in December 1995. Soon after this release, Netscape introduced a server-side JavaScript implementation for scripting in Netscape Enterprise Server, and named it LiveWire.[1] JScript, Microsoft's reverse-engineered implementation of JavaScript, was bundled with IE3 in 1996. JScript was available for Internet Information Server (IIS) in the server side.

The language started being standardized under the ECMAScript name (ES) into the ECMA-262 specification in 1996, under a technical committee at ECMA known as TC39. Sun wouldn't transfer ownership of the JavaScript trademark to ECMA, and while Microsoft offered JScript, other member companies didn't want to use that name, so ECMAScript stuck.

Disputes by competing implementations, JavaScript by Netscape and JScript by Microsoft, dominated most of the TC39 standards committee meetings at the time. Even so, the committee was already bearing fruit: backward compatibility was established as a golden rule, bringing about strict equality operators (=== and !==) instead of breaking existing programs that relied on the loose Equality Comparison Algorithm.

The first edition of ECMA-262 was released June 1997. A year later, in June 1998, the specification was refined under the ISO/IEC 16262 international standard, after much scrutiny from national ISO bodies, and formalized as the second edition.

By December 1999 the third edition was published, standardizing regular expressions, the `switch` statement, `do/while`, `try/catch`, and `Object#hasOwnProperty`, among a few other changes. Most of these features were already available in the wild through Netscape's JavaScript runtime, SpiderMonkey.

---

1 A booklet from 1998 (*https://mjavascript.com/out/livewire*) explains the intricacies of server-side JavaScript with LiveWire.

Drafts for an ES4 specification were soon afterwards published by TC39. This early work on ES4 led to JScript.NET in mid-2000[2] and, eventually, to ActionScript 3 for Flash in 2006.[3]

Conflicting opinions on how JavaScript was to move forward brought work on the specification to a standstill. This was a delicate time for web standards: Microsoft had all but monopolized the web and they had little interest in standards development.

As AOL laid off 50 Netscape employees in 2003,[4] the Mozilla Foundation was formed. With over 95% of web-browsing market share now in the hands of Microsoft, TC39 was disbanded.

It took two years until Brendan, now at Mozilla, had ECMA resurrect work on TC39 by using Firefox's growing market share as leverage to get Microsoft back in the fold. By mid-2005, TC39 started meeting regularly once again. As for ES4, there were plans for introducing a module system, classes, iterators, generators, destructuring, type annotations, proper tail calls, algebraic typing, and an assortment of other features. Due to how ambitious the project was, work on ES4 was repeatedly delayed.

By 2007 the committee was split in two: ES3.1, which hailed a more incremental approach to ES3; and ES4, which was overdesigned and underspecified. It wouldn't be until August 2008[5] when ES3.1 was agreed upon as the way forward, but later rebranded as ES5. Although ES4 would be abandoned, many of its features eventually made its way into ES6 (which was dubbed Harmony at the time of this resolution), while some of them still remain under consideration and a few others have been abandoned, rejected, or withdrawn. The ES3.1 update served as the foundation on top of which the ES4 specification could be laid in bits and pieces.

---

2 You can read the original announcement at the Microsoft website (*https://mjava script.com/out/jscript-net*) (July, 2000).

3 Listen to Brendan Eich in the JavaScript Jabber podcast, talking about the origin of JavaScript (*https://mjavascript.com/out/brendan-devchat*).

4 You can read a news report from *The Mac Observer* (*https://mjavascript.com/out/aol-netscape*), July 2003.

5 Brendan Eich sent an email to the es-discuss mailing list in 2008 where he summarized the situation (*https://mjavascript.com/out/harmony*), almost 10 years after ES3 had been released.

In December 2009, on the 10-year anniversary since the publication of ES3, the fifth edition of ECMAScript was published. This edition codified de facto extensions to the language specification that had become common among browser implementations, adding `get` and `set` accessors, functional improvements to the `Array` prototype, reflection and introspection, as well as native support for JSON parsing and strict mode.

A couple of years later, in June 2011, the specification was once again reviewed and edited to become the third edition of the international standard ISO/IEC 16262:2011, and formalized under ECMAScript 5.1.

It took TC39 another four years to formalize ECMAScript 6, in June 2015. The sixth edition is the largest update to the language that made its way into publication, implementing many of the ES4 proposals that were deferred as part of the Harmony resolution. Throughout this book, we'll be exploring ES6 in depth.

In parallel with the ES6 effort, in 2012 the WHATWG (a standards body interested in pushing the web forward) set out to document the differences between ES5.1 and browser implementations, in terms of compatibility and interoperability requirements. The task force standardized `String#substr`, which was previously unspecified; unified several methods for wrapping strings in HTML tags, which were inconsistent across browsers; and documented `Object.prototype` properties like `__proto__` and `__defineGetter__`, among other improvements.[6] This effort was condensed into a separate Web ECMAScript specification, which eventually made its way into Annex B in 2015. Annex B was an informative section of the core ECMAScript specification, meaning implementations weren't required to follow its suggestions. Jointly with this update, Annex B was also made normative and required for web browsers.

The sixth edition is a significant milestone in the history of JavaScript. Besides the dozens of new features, ES6 marks a key inflection point where ECMAScript would become a rolling standard.

---

6 For the full set of changes made when merging the Web ECMAScript specification upstream, see the WHATWG blog (*https://mjavascript.com/out/javascript-standard*).

1.2 ECMAScript as a Rolling Standard

Having spent 10 years without observing significant change to the language specification after ES3, and 4 years for ES6 to materialize, it was clear the TC39 process needed to improve. The revision process used to be deadline-driven. Any delay in arriving at consensus would cause long wait periods between revisions, which led to feature creep, causing more delays. Minor revisions were delayed by large additions to the specification, and large additions faced pressure to finalize so that the revision would be pushed through, avoiding further delays.

Since ES6 came out, TC39 has streamlined[7] its proposal revisioning process and adjusted it to meet modern expectations: the need to iterate more often and consistently, and to democratize specification development. At this point, TC39 moved from an ancient Word-based flow to using Ecmarkup (an HTML superset used to format ECMAScript specifications) and GitHub pull requests, greatly increasing the number of proposals[8] being created as well as external participation by nonmembers. The new flow is continuous and thus, more transparent: while previously you'd have to download a Word doc or its PDF version from a web page, the latest draft of the specification (*https://mjavascript.com/out/spec-draft*) is now always available.

Firefox, Chrome, Edge, Safari, and Node.js all offer over 95% compliance of the ES6 specification,[9] but we've been able to use the features as they came out in each of these browsers rather than having to wait until the flip of a switch when their implementation of ES6 was 100% finalized.

---

7 Check out the presentation "Post-ES6 Spec Process" (*https://mjavascript.com/out/tc39-improvement*) from September 2013 that led to the streamlined proposal revisioning process here.

8 Check out all of the proposals being considered by TC39 (*https://mjavascript.com/out/tc39-proposals*).

9 Check out this detailed table reporting ES6 compatibility across browsers (*https://mjavascript.com/out/es6-compat*).

The new process involves four different maturity stages.[10] The more mature a proposal is, the more likely it is to eventually make it into the specification.

Any discussion, idea, or proposal for a change or addition that has not yet been submitted as a formal proposal is considered to be an aspirational "strawman" proposal (stage 0), but only TC39 members can create strawman proposals. At the time of this writing, there are over a dozen active strawman proposals.[11]

At stage 1 a proposal is formalized and expected to address cross-cutting concerns, interactions with other proposals, and implementation concerns. Proposals at this stage should identify a discrete problem and offer a concrete solution to the problem. A stage 1 proposal often includes a high-level API description, illustrative usage examples, and a discussion of internal semantics and algorithms. Stage 1 proposals are likely to change significantly as they make their way through the process.

Proposals in stage 2 offer an initial draft of the specification. At this point, it's reasonable to begin experimenting with actual implementations in runtimes. The implementation could come in the form of a polyfill, user code that mangles the runtime into adhering to the proposal; an engine implementation, natively providing support for the proposal; or compiled into something existing engines can execute, using build-time tools to transform source code.

Proposals in stage 3 are candidate recommendations. In order for a proposal to advance to this stage, the specification editor and designated reviewers must have signed off on the final specification. Implementors should've expressed interest in the proposal as well. In practice, proposals move to this level with at least one browser implementation, a high-fidelity polyfill, or when supported by a build-time compiler like Babel. A stage 3 proposal is unlikely to change beyond fixes to issues identified in the wild.

In order for a proposal to attain stage 4 status, two independent implementations need to pass acceptance tests. Proposals that make

---

10 Take a look at the TC39 proposal process documentation (*https://mjavascript.com/out/ tc39-process*).

11 You can track strawman proposals (*https://mjavascript.com/out/tc39-stage0*).

---

their way through to stage 4 will be included in the next revision of ECMAScript.

New releases of the specification are expected to be published every year from now on. To accommodate the yearly release schedule, versions will now be referred to by their publication year. Thus ES6 becomes ES2015, then we have ES2016 instead of ES7, ES2017, and so on. Colloquially, ES2015 hasn't taken and is still largely regarded as ES6. ES2016 had been announced before the naming convention changed, thus it is sometimes still referred to as ES7. When we leave out ES6 due to its pervasiveness in the community, we end up with: ES6, ES2016, ES2017, ES2018, and so on.

The streamlined proposal process combined with the yearly cut into standardization translates into a more consistent publication process, and it also means specification revision numbers are becoming less important. The focus is now on proposal stages, and we can expect references to specific revisions of the ECMAScript standard to become more uncommon.

1.3 Browser Support and Complementary Tooling

A stage 3 candidate recommendation proposal is most likely to make it into the specification in the next cut, provided two independent implementations land in JavaScript engines. Effectively, stage 3 proposals are considered safe to use in real-world applications, be it through an experimental engine implementation, a polyfill, or using a compiler. Stage 2 and earlier proposals are also used in the wild by JavaScript developers, tightening the feedback loop between implementors and consumers.

Babel and similar compilers that take code as input and produce output native to the web platform (HTML, CSS, or JavaScript) are often referred to as *transpilers*, which are considered to be a subset of compilers. When we want to leverage a proposal that's not widely implemented in JavaScript engines in our code, compilers like Babel can transform the portions of code using that new proposal into something that's more widely supported by existing JavaScript implementations.

This transformation can be done at build time, so that consumers receive code that's well supported by their JavaScript runtime of choice. This mechanism improves the runtime support baseline, giving JavaScript developers the ability to take advantage of new language features and syntax sooner. It is also significantly beneficial to specification writers and implementors, as it allows them to collect feedback regarding viability, desirability, and possible bugs or corner cases.

A transpiler can take the ES6 source code we write and produce ES5 code that browsers can interpret more consistently. This is the most reliable way of running ES6 code in production today: using a build step to produce ES5 code that most old browsers, as well as modern browsers, can execute.

The same applies to ES7 and beyond. As new versions of the language specification are released every year, we can expect compilers to support ES2017 input, ES2018 input, and so on. Similarly, as browser support becomes better, we can also expect compilers to reduce complexity in favor of ES6 output, then ES7 output, and so on. In this sense, we can think of JavaScript-to-JavaScript transpilers as a moving window that takes code written using the latest available language semantics and produces the most modern code they can output without compromising browser support.

Let's talk about how you can use Babel as part of your workflow.

1.3.1 Introduction to the Babel Transpiler

Babel can compile modern JavaScript code that relies on ES6 features into ES5. It produces human-readable code, making it more welcoming when we don't have a firm grasp on all of the new features we're using.

The online Babel REPL (Read-Evaluate-Print Loop) (*https://mjava script.com/out/babel-repl*) is an excellent way of jumping right into learning ES6, without any of the hassle of installing Node.js and the `babel` CLI, and manually compiling source code.

The REPL provides us with a source code input area that gets automatically compiled in real time. We can see the compiled code to the right of our source code.

Let's write some code into the REPL. You can use the following code snippet to get started:

```
var double = value => value * 2
console.log(double(3))
// <- 6
```

To the right of the source code we've entered, you'll see the transpiled ES5 equivalent, as shown in Figure 1-1. As you update your source code, the transpiled result is also updated in real time.

Figure 1-1. The online Babel REPL in action—a great way to dive right into an interactive ES6 session

The Babel REPL is an effective companion as a way of trying out some of the features introduced in this book. However, note that Babel doesn't transpile new built-ins, such as `Symbol`, `Proxy`, and `WeakMap`. Those references are instead left untouched, and it's up to the runtime executing the Babel output to provide those built-ins. If we want to support runtimes that haven't yet implemented these built-ins, we could import the `babel-polyfill` package in our code.

In older versions of JavaScript, semantically correct implementations of these features are hard to accomplish or downright impossible. Polyfills may mitigate the problem, but they often can't cover all use cases and thus some compromises need to be made. We need to be careful and test our assumptions before we release transpiled code that relies on built-ins or polyfills into the wild.

Given the situation, it might be best to wait until browsers support new built-ins holistically before we start using them. It is suggested that you consider alternative solutions that don't rely on built-ins. At the same time, it's important to learn about these features, as to not fall behind in our understanding of the JavaScript language.

Modern browsers like Chrome, Firefox, and Edge now support a large portion of ES2015 and beyond, making their developer tools useful when we want to take the semantics of a particular feature for a spin, provided it's supported by the browser. When it comes to production-grade applications that rely on modern JavaScript features, a transpilation build-step is advisable so that your application supports a wider array of JavaScript runtimes.

Besides the REPL, Babel offers a command-line tool written as a Node.js package. You can install it through npm, the package manager for Node.

 Download Node.js (*https://mjavascript.com/out/ node*). After installing node, you'll also be able to use the npm command-line tool in your terminal.

Before getting started we'll make a project directory and a *package.json* file, which is a manifest used to describe Node.js applications. We can create the *package.json* file through the npm CLI:

```
mkdir babel-setup
cd babel-setup
npm init --yes
```

 Passing the --yes flag to the init command configures *package.json* using the default values provided by npm, instead of asking us any questions.

Let's also create a file named *example.js*, containing the following bits of ES6 code. Save it to the *babel-setup* directory you've just created, under a *src* subdirectory:

```
var double = value => value * 2
console.log(double(3))
// <- 6
```

To install Babel, enter the following couple of commands into your favorite terminal:

```
npm install babel-cli@6 --save-dev
npm install babel-preset-env@6 --save-dev
```

Packages installed by npm will be placed in a *node_modules* directory at the project root. We can then access these packages by creating npm scripts or by using require statements in our application.

Using the --save-dev flag will add these packages to our *package.json* manifest as development dependencies, so that when copying our project to new environments we can reinstall every dependency just by running npm install.

The @ notation indicates we want to install a specific version of a package. Using @6 we're telling npm to install the latest version of babel-cli in the 6.x range. This preference is handy to future-proof our applications, as it would never install 7.0.0 or later versions, which might contain breaking changes that could not have been foreseen at the time of this writing.

For the next step, we'll replace the value of the scripts property in *package.json* with the following. The babel command-line utility provided by babel-cli can take the entire contents of our *src* directory, compile them into the desired output format, and save the results to a *dist* directory, while preserving the original directory structure under a different root:

```
{
  "scripts": {
    "build": "babel src --out-dir dist"
  }
}
```

Together with the packages we've installed in the previous step, a minimal *package.json* file could look like the code in the following snippet:

```
{
  "scripts": {
    "build": "babel src --out-dir dist"
  },
  "devDependencies": {
    "babel-cli": "^6.24.0",
    "babel-preset-env": "^1.2.1"
  }
}
```

Any commands enumerated in the scripts object can be executed through npm run <name>, which temporarily modifies the $PATH environment variable so that we can run the command-line executables found in babel-cli without installing babel-cli globally on our system.

If you execute npm run build in your terminal now, you'll note that a *dist/example.js* file is created. The output file will be identical to our original file, because Babel doesn't make assumptions, and we have to configure it first. Create a *.babelrc* file next to *package.json*, and write the following JSON in it:

```
{
  "presets": ["env"]
}
```

The env preset, which we installed earlier via npm, adds a series of plugins to Babel that transform different bits of ES6 code into ES5. Among other things, this preset transforms arrow functions like the one in our *example.js* file into ES5 code. The env Babel preset works by convention, enabling Babel transformation plugins according to feature support in the latest browsers. This preset is configurable, meaning we can decide how far back we want to cover browser support. The more browsers we support, the larger our transpiled bundle. The fewer browsers we support, the fewer customers we can satisfy. As always, research is of the essence to identify what the correct configuration for the Babel env preset is. By default, every transform is enabled, providing broad runtime support.

Once we run our build script again, we'll observe that the output is now valid ES5 code:

```
» npm run build
» cat dist/example.js
"use strict"

var double = function double(value) {
  return value * 2
}
console.log(double(3))
// <- 6
```

Let's jump into a different kind of tool, the eslint code linter, which can help us establish a code quality baseline for our applications.

1.3.2 Code Quality and Consistency with ESLint

As we develop a codebase we factor out snippets that are redundant or no longer useful, write new pieces of code, delete features that are no longer relevant or necessary, and shift chunks of code around while accommodating a new architecture. As the codebase grows, the team working on it changes as well: at first it may be a handful of people or even one person, but as the project grows in size so might the team.

A lint tool can be used to identify syntax errors. Modern linters are often customizable, helping establish a coding style convention that works for everyone on the team. By adhering to a consistent set of style rules and a quality baseline, we bring the team closer together in terms of coding style. Every team member has different opinions about coding styles, but those opinions can be condensed into style rules once we put a linter in place and agree upon a configuration.

Beyond ensuring a program can be parsed, we might want to prevent `throw` statements throwing string literals as exceptions, or disallow `console.log` and `debugger` statements in production code. However, a rule demanding that every function call must have exactly one argument is probably too harsh.

While linters are effective at defining and enforcing a coding style, we should be careful when devising a set of rules. If the lint step is too stringent, developers may become frustrated to the point where productivity is affected. If the lint step is too lenient, it may not yield a consistent coding style across our codebase.

In order to strike the right balance, we may consider avoiding style rules that don't improve our programs in the majority of cases when they're applied. Whenever we're considering a new rule, we should ask ourselves whether it would noticeably improve our existing codebase, as well as new code going forward.

ESLint is a modern linter that packs several plugins, sporting different rules, allowing us to pick and choose which ones we want to enforce. We decide whether failing to stick by these rules should result in a warning being printed as part of the output, or a halting error. To install `eslint`, we'll use `npm` just like we did with `babel` in the previous section:

```
npm install eslint@3 --save-dev
```

Next, we need to configure ESLint. Since we installed `eslint` as a local dependency, we'll find its command-line tool in *node_modules/.bin*. Executing the following command will guide us through configuring ESLint for our project for the first time. To get started, indicate you want to use a popular style guide and choose Standard,[12] then pick JSON format for the configuration file:

```
./node_modules/.bin/eslint --init
? How would you like to configure ESLint?
  Use a popular style guide
? Which style guide do you want to follow? Standard
? What format do you want your config file to be in? JSON
```

Besides individual rules, `eslint` allows us to extend predefined sets of rules, which are packaged up as Node.js modules. This is useful when sharing configuration across multiple projects, and even across a community. After picking Standard, we'll notice that ESLint adds a few dependencies to *package.json*, namely the packages that define the predefined Standard ruleset; and then creates a configuration file, named *.eslintrc.json*, with the following contents:

```
{
  "extends": "standard",
  "plugins": [
    "standard",
    "promise"
  ]
}
```

Referencing the *node_modules/.bin* directory, an implementation detail of how npm works, is far from ideal. While we used it when initializing our ESLint configuration, we shouldn't keep this reference around nor type it out whenever we lint our codebase. To solve this problem, we'll add the `lint` script in the next code snippet to our *package.json*:

```
{
  "scripts": {
    "lint": "eslint ."
  }
}
```

---

12 Note that Standard is just a self-proclamation, and not actually standardized in any official capacity. It doesn't really matter which style guide you follow as long as you follow it consistently. Consistency helps reduce confusion while reading a project's codebase. The Airbnb style guide is also fairly popular and it doesn't omit semicolons by default, unlike Standard.

As you might recall from the Babel example, npm run adds *node_modules* to the PATH when executing scripts. To lint our codebase, we can execute npm run lint and npm will find the ESLint CLI embedded deep in the *node_modules* directory.

Let's consider the following *example.js* file, which is purposely riddled with style issues, to demonstrate what ESLint does:

```
var goodbye='Goodbye!'

function hello(){
  return goodbye}

if(false){}
```

When we run the lint script, ESLint describes everything that's wrong with the file, as shown in Figure 1-2.

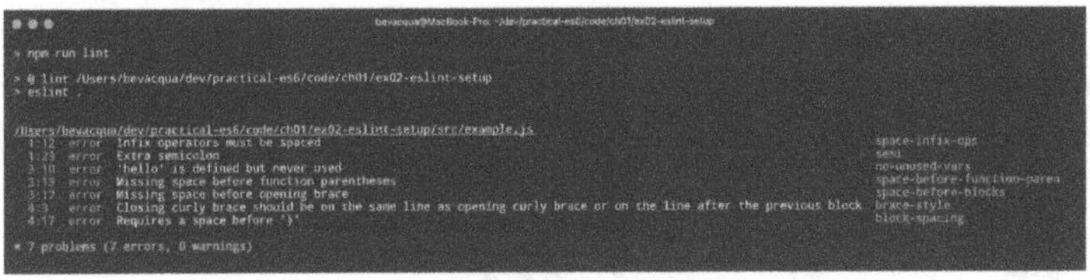

Figure 1-2. The ESLint tool is a great way to keep your code free of syntax errors and, optionally, inconsistent coding style

ESLint is able to fix most style problems automatically if we pass in a --fix flag. Add the following script to your *package.json*:

```
{
  "scripts": {
    "lint-fix": "eslint . --fix"
  }
}
```

When we run lint-fix we'll only get a pair of errors: hello is never used and false is a constant condition. Every other error has been fixed in place, resulting in the following bit of source code. The remaining errors weren't fixed because ESLint avoids making assumptions about our code, and prefers not to incur semantic changes. In doing so, --fix becomes a useful tool to resolve code style wrinkles without risking a broken program as a result.

```
var goodbye = 'Goodbye!'

function hello() {
  return goodbye
}

if (false) {}
```

 A similar kind of tool can be found in `prettier` (*https://mjavascript.com/out/prettier*), which can be used to automatically format your code. Prettier can be configured to automatically overwrite our code ensuring it follows preferences such as a given amount of spaces for indentation, single or double quotes, trailing commas, or a maximum line length.

Now that you know how to compile modern JavaScript into something every browser understands, and how to properly lint and format your code, let's jump into ES6 feature themes and the future of JavaScript.

1.4 Feature Themes in ES6

ES6 is big: the language specification went from 258 pages in ES5.1 to over double that amount in ES6, at 566 pages. Each change to the specification falls in some of a few different categories:

- Syntactic sugar
- New mechanics
- Better semantics
- More built-ins and methods
- Nonbreaking solutions to existing limitations

Syntactic sugar is one of the most significant drivers in ES6. The new version offers a shorter way of expressing object inheritance, using the new class syntax; functions, using a shorthand syntax known as arrow functions; and properties, using property value shorthands. Several other features we'll explore, such as destructuring, rest, and spread, also offer semantically sound ways of writing programs. Chapters 2 and 3 attack these aspects of ES6.

We get several new mechanics to describe asynchronous code flows in ES6: *promises*, which represent the eventual result of an operation; *iterators*, which represent a sequence of values; and *generators*, a special kind of iterator that can produce a sequence of values. In ES2017, async/await builds on top of these new concepts and constructs, letting us write asynchronous routines that appear synchronous. We'll evaluate all of these iteration and flow control mechanisms in Chapter 4.

There's a common practice in JavaScript where developers use plain objects to create hash maps with arbitrary string keys. This can lead to vulnerabilities if we're not careful and let user input end up defining those keys. ES6 introduces a few different native built-ins to manage sets and maps, which don't have the limitation of using string keys exclusively. These collections are explored in Chapter 9.

Proxy objects redefine what can be done through JavaScript reflection. Proxy objects are similar to proxies in other contexts, such as web traffic routing. They can intercept any interaction with a JavaScript object such as defining, deleting, or accessing a property. Given the mechanics of how proxies work, they are impossible to polyfill holistically: polyfills exist, but they have limitations making them incompatible with the specification in some use cases. We'll devote Chapter 6 to understanding proxies.

Besides new built-ins, ES6 comes with several updates to Number, Math, Array, and strings. In Chapter 7 we'll go over a plethora of new instance and static methods added to these built-ins.

We are getting a new module system that's native to JavaScript. After going over the CommonJS module format that's used in Node.js, Chapter 8 explains the semantics we can expect from native JavaScript modules.

Due to the sheer amount of changes introduced by ES6, it's hard to reconcile its new features with our pre-existing knowledge of JavaScript. We'll spend all of Chapter 9 analyzing the merits and importance of different individual features in ES6, so that you have a practical grounding upon which you can start experimenting with ES6 right away.

1.5 Future of JavaScript

The JavaScript language has evolved from its humble beginnings in 1995 to the formidable language it is today. While ES6 is a great step forward, it's not the finish line. Given we can expect new specification updates every year, it's important to learn how to stay up-to-date with the specification.

Having gone over the rolling standard specification development process in Section 1.2, "ECMAScript as a Rolling Standard," on page 5, one of the best ways to keep up with the standard is by periodically visiting the TC39 proposals repository.[13] Keep an eye on candidate recommendations (stage 3), which are likely to make their way into the specification.

Describing an ever-evolving language in a book can be challenging, given the rolling nature of the standards process. An effective way of keeping up-to-date with the latest JavaScript updates is by watching the TC39 proposals repository, subscribing to weekly email newsletters[14], and reading JavaScript blogs.[15]

At the time of this writing, the long awaited Async Functions proposal has made it into the specification and is slated for publication in ES2017. There are several candidates at the moment, such as dynamic `import()`, which enables asynchronous loading of native JavaScript modules, and a proposal to describe object property enumerations using the new rest and spread syntax that was first introduced for parameter lists and arrays in ES6.

While the primary focus in this book is on ES6, we'll also learn about important candidate recommendations such as the aforementioned async functions, dynamic `import()` calls, or object rest/spread, among others.

---

13 Check out all of the proposals being considered by TC39 (*https://mjavascript.com/out/tc39-proposals*).

14 There are many newsletters, including Pony Foo Weekly (*https://mjavascript.com/out/pfw*) and JavaScript Weekly (*https://mjavascript.com/out/jsw*).

15 Many of the articles on Pony Foo (*https://mjavascript.com/out/pf*) and by Axel Rauschmayer (*https://mjavascript.com/out/ar*) focus on ECMAScript development.

CHAPTER 2

ES6 Essentials

The sixth edition of the language comes with a plethora of nonbreaking syntax improvements, most of which we'll tackle throughout this chapter. Many of these changes are syntactic sugar; that is, they could be represented in ES5, albeit using more complicated pieces of code. There are also changes that aren't merely syntactic sugar but a completely different way of declaring variables using let and const, as we'll see toward the end of the chapter.

Object literals get a few syntax changes in ES6, and they're a good place to start.

2.1 Object Literals

An *object literal* is any object declaration using the {} shorthand syntax, such as the following example:

```
var book = {
  title: 'Modular ES6',
  author: 'Nicolas',
  publisher: 'O´Reilly'
}
```

ES6 brings a few improvements to object literal syntax: property value shorthands, computed property names, and method definitions. Let's go through them and describe their use cases as well.

2.1.1 Property Value Shorthands

Sometimes we declare objects with one or more properties whose values are references to variables by the same name. For example, we might have a `listeners` collection, and in order to assign it to a property called `listeners` of an object literal, we have to repeat its name. The following snippet has a typical example where we have an object literal declaration with a couple of these repetitive properties:

```
var listeners = []
function listen() {}
var events = {
  listeners: listeners,
  listen: listen
}
```

Whenever you find yourself in this situation, you can omit the property value and the colon by taking advantage of the new property value shorthand syntax in ES6. As shown in the following example, the new ES6 syntax makes the assignment implicit:

```
var listeners = []
function listen() {}
var events = { listeners, listen }
```

As we'll further explore in the second part of the book, property value shorthands help de-duplicate the code we write without diluting its meaning. In the following snippet, I reimplemented part of `localStorage`, a browser API for persistent storage, as an in-memory ponyfill.[1] If it weren't for the shorthand syntax, the `storage` object would be more verbose to type out:

```
var store = {}
var storage = { getItem, setItem, clear }
function getItem(key) {
  return key in store ? store[key] : null
}
function setItem(key, value) {
```

---

1 Like polyfills, ponyfills (*https://mjavascript.com/out/ponyfills*) are user-land implementations of features that aren't available in every JavaScript runtime. While polyfills try to patch the runtime environment so that it behaves as if the feature was indeed available on the runtime, ponyfills implement the missing functionality as standalone modules that don't pollute the runtime environment. This has the benefit of not breaking expectations third-party libraries (that don't know about your polyfill) may have about the environment.

```
    store[key] = value
  }
  function clear() {
    store = {}
  }
```

That's the first of many ES6 features that are aimed toward reducing complexity in the code you have to maintain. Once you get used to the syntax, you'll notice that code readability and developer productivity get boosts as well.

2.1.2 Computed Property Names

Sometimes you have to declare objects that contain properties with names based on variables or other JavaScript expressions, as shown in the following piece of code written in ES5. For this example, assume that expertise is provided to you as a function parameter, and is not a value you know beforehand:

```
var expertise = 'journalism'
var person = {
  name: 'Sharon',
  age: 27
}
person[expertise] = {
  years: 5,
  interests: ['international', 'politics', 'internet']
}
```

Object literals in ES6 aren't constrained to declarations with static names. With computed property names, you can wrap any expression in square brackets, and use that as the property name. When the declaration is reached, your expression is evaluated and used as the property name. The following example shows how the piece of code we just saw could declare the person object in a single step, without having to resort to a second statement adding the person's expertise.

```
var expertise = 'journalism'
var person = {
  name: 'Sharon',
  age: 27,
  [expertise]: {
    years: 5,
    interests: ['international', 'politics', 'internet']
  }
}
```

You can't combine the property value shorthands with computed property names. Value shorthands are simple compile-time syntactic sugar that helps avoid repetition, while computed property names are evaluated at runtime. Given that we're trying to mix these two incompatible features, the following example would throw a syntax error. In most cases this combination would lead to code that's hard to interpret for other humans, so it's probably a good thing that you can't combine the two.

```
var expertise = 'journalism'
var journalism = {
  years: 5,
  interests: ['international', 'politics', 'internet']
}
var person = {
  name: 'Sharon',
  age: 27,
  [expertise] // this is a syntax error!
}
```

A common scenario for computed property names is when we want to add an entity to an object map that uses the entity.id field as its keys, as shown next. Instead of having to have a third statement where we add the grocery to the groceries map, we can inline that declaration in the groceries object literal itself.

```
var grocery = {
  id: 'bananas',
  name: 'Bananas',
  units: 6,
  price: 10,
  currency: 'USD'
}
var groceries = {
  [grocery.id]: grocery
}
```

Another case may be whenever a function receives a parameter that it should then use to build out an object. In ES5 code, you'd need to allocate a variable declaring an object literal, then add the dynamic property, and then return the object. The following example shows exactly that, when creating an envelope that could later be used for Ajax messages that follow a convention: they have an error property with a description when something goes wrong, and a success property when things turn out okay:

```
function getEnvelope(type, description) {
  var envelope = {
```

```
    data: {}
  }
  envelope[type] = description
  return envelope
}
```

Computed property names help us write the same function more concisely, using a single statement:

```
function getEnvelope(type, description) {
  return {
    data: {},
    [type]: description
  }
}
```

The last enhancement coming to object literals is about functions.

2.1.3 Method Definitions

Typically, you can declare methods on an object by adding properties to it. In the next snippet, we're creating a small event emitter that supports multiple kinds of events. It comes with an emitter#on method that can be used to register event listeners, and an emit ter#emit method that can be used to raise events:

```
var emitter = {
  events: {},
  on: function (type, fn) {
    if (this.events[type] === undefined) {
      this.events[type] = []
    }
    this.events[type].push(fn)
  },
  emit: function (type, event) {
    if (this.events[type] === undefined) {
      return
    }
    this.events[type].forEach(function (fn) {
      fn(event)
    })
  }
}
```

Starting in ES6, you can declare methods on an object literal using the new method definition syntax. In this case, we can omit the colon and the function keyword. This is meant as a terse alternative to traditional method declarations where you need to use the function keyword. The following example shows how our `emitter` object looks when using method definitions.

```
var emitter = {
  events: {},
  on(type, fn) {
    if (this.events[type] === undefined) {
      this.events[type] = []
    }
    this.events[type].push(fn)
  },
  emit(type, event) {
    if (this.events[type] === undefined) {
      return
    }
    this.events[type].forEach(function (fn) {
      fn(event)
    })
  }
}
```

Arrow functions are another way of declaring functions in ES6, and they come in several flavors. Let's investigate what arrow functions are, how they can be declared, and how they behave semantically.

2.2 Arrow Functions

In JavaScript you typically declare functions using code like the following, where you have a name, a list of parameters, and a function body.

```
function name(parameters) {
  // function body
}
```

You could also create anonymous functions, by omitting the name when assigning the function to a variable, a property, or a function call.

```
var example = function (parameters) {
  // function body
}
```

Starting with ES6, you can use arrow functions as another way of writing anonymous functions. Keep in mind, there are several slightly different ways of writing them. The following piece of code shows an arrow function that's very similar to the anonymous function we just saw. The only difference seems to be the missing `func` `tion` keyword and the `=>` arrow to the right of the parameter list.

```
var example = (parameters) => {
  // function body
}
```

While arrow functions look very similar to your typical anonymous function, they are fundamentally different: arrow functions can't be named explicitly, although modern runtimes can infer a name based on the variable they're assigned to; they can't be used as constructors nor do they have a `prototype` property, meaning you can't use `new` on an arrow function; and they are bound to their lexical scope, which is the reason why they don't alter the meaning of `this`.

Let's dig into their semantic differences with traditional functions, the many ways to declare an arrow function, and practical use cases.

2.2.1 Lexical Scoping

In the body of an arrow function, `this`, `arguments`, and `super` point to the containing scope, since arrow functions don't create a new scope. Consider the following example. We have a `timer` object with a `seconds` counter and a `start` method defined using the syntax we learned about earlier. We then start the timer, wait for a few seconds, and log the current amount of elapsed seconds:

```
var timer = {
  seconds: 0,
  start() {
    setInterval(() => {
      this.seconds++
    }, 1000)
  }
}
timer.start()
setTimeout(function () {
  console.log(timer.seconds)
}, 3500)
// <- 3
```

If we had defined the function passed to `setInterval` as a regular anonymous function instead of using an arrow function, `this` would've been bound to the context of the anonymous function, instead of the context of the `start` method. We could have implemented `timer` with a declaration like `var self = this` at the beginning of the `start` method, and then referencing `self` instead of `this`. With arrow functions, the added complexity of keeping context references around fades away and we can focus on the functionality of our code.

In a similar fashion, lexical binding in ES6 arrow functions also means that function calls won't be able to change the this context when using .call, .apply, .bind, etc. That limitation is usually more useful than not, as it ensures that the context will always be preserved and constant.

Let's now shift our attention to the following example. What do you think the console.log statement will print?

```
function puzzle() {
  return function () {
    console.log(arguments)
  }
}
puzzle('a', 'b', 'c')(1, 2, 3)
```

The answer is that arguments refers to the context of the anonymous function, and thus the arguments passed to that function will be printed. In this case, those arguments are 1, 2, 3.

What about in the following case, where we use an arrow function instead of the anonymous function in the previous example?

```
function puzzle() {
  return () => console.log(arguments)
}
puzzle('a', 'b', 'c')(1, 2, 3)
```

In this case, the arguments object refers to the context of the puzzle function, because arrow functions don't create a closure. For this reason, the printed arguments will be 'a', 'b', 'c'.

I've mentioned there are several flavors of arrow functions, but so far we've only looked at their fully fleshed version. What are the other ways to represent an arrow function?

2.2.2 Arrow Function Flavors

Let's look one more time at the arrow function syntax we've learned so far:

```
var example = (parameters) => {
  // function body
}
```

An arrow function with exactly one parameter can omit the parentheses. This is optional. It's useful when passing the arrow function to another method, as it reduces the amount of parentheses involved, making it easier for some humans to parse the code:

```
var double = value => {
  return value * 2
}
```

Arrow functions are heavily used for simple functions, such as the double function we just saw. The following flavor of arrow functions does away with the function body. Instead, you provide an expression such as value * 2. When the function is called, the expression is evaluated and its result is returned. The return statement is implicit, and there's no need for curly braces denoting the function body anymore, as you can only use a single expression:

```
var double = (value) => value * 2
```

Note that you can combine implicit parentheses and implicit return, making for concise arrow functions:

```
var double = value => value * 2
```

Implicitly Returning Object Literals

When you need to implicitly return an object literal, you'll need to wrap that object literal expression in parentheses. Otherwise, the compiler would interpret your curly braces as the start and the end of the function block.

```
var objectFactory = () => ({ modular: 'es6' })
```

In the following example, JavaScript interprets the curly braces as the body of our arrow function. Furthermore, number is interpreted as a label[2] and then figures out we have a value expression that doesn't do anything. Since we're in a block and not returning anything, the mapped values will be undefined:

```
[1, 2, 3].map(value => { number: value })
// <- [undefined, undefined, undefined]
```

---

2 Labels (*https://mjavascript.com/out/label*) are used as a way of identifying instructions. Labels can be used by goto statements, to indicate what instruction we should jump to; break statements, to indicate the sequence we want to break out of; and continue statements, to indicate the sequence we want to advance.

If our attempt at implicitly returning an object literal had more than a single property, then the compiler wouldn't be able to make sense of the second property, and it'd throw a SyntaxError:

```
[1, 2, 3].map(value => { number: value, verified: true })
// <- SyntaxError
```

Wrapping the expression in parentheses fixes these issues, because the compiler would no longer interpret it as a function block. Instead, the object declaration becomes an expression that evaluates to the object literal we want to return implicitly:

```
[1, 2, 3].map(value => ({ number: value, verified: true }))
/* <- [
  { number: 1, verified: true },
  { number: 2, verified: true },
  { number: 3, verified: true }]
*/
```

Now that you understand arrow functions, let's ponder about their merits and where they might be a good fit.

2.2.3 Merits and Use Cases

As a rule of thumb, you shouldn't blindly adopt ES6 features wherever you can. Instead, it's best to reason about each case individually and see whether adopting the new feature actually improves code readability and maintainability. ES6 features are not strictly better than what we had all along, and it's a bad idea to treat them as such.

There are a few situations where arrow functions may not be the best tool. For example, if you have a large function comprised of several lines of code, replacing function with => is hardly going to improve your code. Arrow functions are often most effective for short routines, where the function keyword and syntax boilerplate make up a significant portion of the function expression.

Properly naming a function adds context to make it easier for humans to interpret them. Arrow functions can't be explicitly named, but they can be named implicitly by assigning them to a variable. In the following example, we assign an arrow function to the throwError variable. When calling this function results in an error, the stack trace properly identifies the arrow function as throw Error:

```
var throwError = message => {
  throw new Error(message)
}
throwError('this is a warning')
<- Uncaught Error: this is a warning
   at throwError
```

Arrow functions are neat when it comes to defining anonymous functions that should probably be lexically bound anyway, and they can definitely make your code more terse in some situations. They are particularly useful in most functional programming situations, such as when using .map, .filter, or .reduce on collections, as shown in the following example:

```
[1, 2, 3, 4]
  .map(value => value * 2)
  .filter(value => value > 2)
  .forEach(value => console.log(value))
// <- 4
// <- 6
// <- 8
```

2.3 Assignment Destructuring

This is one of the most flexible and expressive features in ES6. It's also one of the simplest. It binds properties to as many variables as you need. It works with objects, arrays, and even in function parameter lists. Let's go step by step, starting with objects.

2.3.1 Destructuring Objects

Imagine you had a program with some comic book characters, Bruce Wayne being one of them, and you want to refer to properties in the object that describes him. Here's the example object we'll be using for Batman:

```
var character = {
  name: 'Bruce',
  pseudonym: 'Batman',
  metadata: {
    age: 34,
    gender: 'male'
  },
  batarang: ['gas pellet', 'bat-mobile control', 'bat-cuffs']
}
```

If you wanted a pseudonym variable referencing character.pseudo nym, you could write the following bit of ES5 code. This is commonplace when, for instance, you'll be referencing pseudonym in several places in your codebase and you'd prefer to avoid typing out charac ter.pseudonym each time:

```
var pseudonym = character.pseudonym
```

With destructuring in assignment, the syntax becomes a bit more clear. As you can see in the next example, you don't have to write pseudonym twice, while still clearly conveying intent. The following statement is equivalent to the previous one written in ES5 code:

```
var { pseudonym } = character
```

Just like you could declare multiple comma-separated variables with a single var statement, you can also declare multiple variables within the curly braces of a destructuring expression:

```
var { pseudonym, name } = character
```

In a similar fashion, you could mix and match destructuring with regular variable declarations in the same var statement. While this might look a bit confusing at first, it'll be up to any JavaScript coding style guides you follow to determine whether it's appropriate to declare several variables in a single statement. In any case, it goes to show the flexibility offered by destructuring syntax:

```
var { pseudonym } = character, two = 2
```

If you want to extract a property named pseudonym but would like to declare it as a variable named alias, you can use the following destructuring syntax, known as *aliasing*. Note that you can use alias or any other valid variable name:

```
var { pseudonym: alias } = character
console.log(alias)
// <- 'Batman'
```

While aliases don't look any simpler than the ES5 flavor, alias = character.pseudonym, they start making sense when you consider the fact that destructuring supports deep structures, as in the following example:

```
var { metadata: { gender } } = character
```

In cases like the previous one, where you have deeply nested properties being destructured, you might be able to convey a property name more clearly if you choose an alias. Consider the next snippet, where a property named code wouldn't have been as indicative of its contents as colorCode could be:

```
var { metadata: { gender: characterGender } } = character
```

The scenario we just saw repeats itself frequently, because properties are often named in the context of their host object. While palette.color.code is perfectly descriptive, code on its own could mean a wide variety of things, and aliases such as colorCode can help you bring context back into the variable name while still using destructuring.

Whenever you access a nonexistent property in ES5 notation, you get a value of undefined:

```
console.log(character.boots)
// <- undefined
console.log(character['boots'])
// <- undefined
```

With destructuring, the same behavior prevails. When declaring a destructured variable for a property that's missing, you'll get back undefined as well.

```
var { boots } = character
console.log(boots)
// <- undefined
```

A destructured declaration accessing a nested property of a parent object that's null or undefined will throw an Exception, just like regular attempts to access properties of null or undefined would, in other cases.

```
var { boots: { size } } = character
// <- Exception
var { missing } = null
// <- Exception
```

When you think of that piece of code as the equivalent ES5 code shown next, it becomes evident why the expression must throw, given that destructuring is mostly syntactic sugar.

```
var nothing = null
var missing = nothing.missing
// <- Exception
```

As part of destructuring, you can provide default values for those cases where the value is undefined. The default value can be anything you can think of: numbers, strings, functions, objects, a reference to another variable, etc.

```
var { boots = { size: 10 } } = character
console.log(boots)
// <- { size: 10 }
```

Default values can also be provided in nested property destructuring.

```
var { metadata: { enemy = 'Satan' } } = character
console.log(enemy)
// <- 'Satan'
```

For use in combination with aliases, you should place the alias first, and then the default value, as shown next.

```
var { boots: footwear = { size: 10 } } = character
```

It's possible to use the computed property names syntax in destructuring patterns. In this case, however, you're required to provide an alias to be used as the variable name. That's because computed property names allow arbitrary expressions and thus the compiler wouldn't be able to infer a variable name. In the following example we use the `value` alias, and a computed property name to extract the boots property from the `character` object.

```
var { ['boo' + 'ts']: characterBoots } = character
console.log(characterBoots)
// <- true
```

This flavor of destructuring is probably the least useful, as `charac terBoots = character[type]` is usually simpler than `{ [type]: characterBoots } = character`, as it's a more sequential statement. That being said, the feature is useful when you have properties you want to declare in the object literal, as opposed to using subsequent assignment statements.

That's it, as far as objects go, in terms of destructuring. What about arrays?

2.3.2 Destructuring Arrays

The syntax for destructuring arrays is similar to that of objects. The following example shows a `coordinates` object that's destructured into two variables: x and y. Note how the notation uses square brackets instead of curly braces; this denotes we're using array destructuring instead of object destructuring. Instead of having to sprinkle your code with implementation details like x = coordinates[0], with destructuring you can convey your meaning clearly and without explicitly referencing the indices, naming the values instead.

```
var coordinates = [12, -7]
var [x, y] = coordinates
console.log(x)
// <- 12
```

When destructuring arrays, you can skip uninteresting properties or those that you otherwise don't need to reference.

```
var names = ['James', 'L.', 'Howlett']
var [ firstName, , lastName ] = names
console.log(lastName)
// <- 'Howlett'
```

Array destructuring allows for default values just like object destructuring.

```
var names = ['James', 'L.']
var [ firstName = 'John', , lastName = 'Doe' ] = names
console.log(lastName)
// <- 'Doe'
```

In ES5, when you have to swap the values of two variables, you typically resort to a third, temporary variable, as in the following snippet.

```
var left = 5
var right = 7
var aux = left
left = right
right = aux
```

Destructuring helps you avoid the aux declaration and focus on your intent. Once again, destructuring helps us convey intent more tersely and effectively for the use case.

```
var left = 5
var right = 7
[left, right] = [right, left]
```

The last area of destructuring we'll be covering is function parameters.

2.3.3 Function Parameter Defaults

Function parameters in ES6 enjoy the ability of specifying default values as well. The following example defines a default exponent with the most commonly used value.

```
function powerOf(base, exponent = 2) {
  return Math.pow(base, exponent)
}
```

Defaults can be applied to arrow function parameters as well. When we have default values in an arrow function we must wrap the parameter list in parentheses, even when there's a single parameter.

```
var double = (input = 0) => input * 2
```

Default values aren't limited to the rightmost parameters of a function, as in a few other programming languages. You could provide default values for any parameter, in any position.

```
function sumOf(a = 1, b = 2, c = 3) {
  return a + b + c
}
console.log(sumOf(undefined, undefined, 4))
// <- 1 + 2 + 4 = 7
```

In JavaScript it's not uncommon to provide a function with an options object, containing several properties. You could determine a default options object if one isn't provided, as shown in the next snippet.

```
var defaultOptions = { brand: 'Volkswagen', make: 1999 }
function carFactory(options = defaultOptions) {
  console.log(options.brand)
  console.log(options.make)
}
carFactory()
// <- 'Volkswagen'
// <- 1999
```

The problem with this approach is that as soon as the consumer of carFactory provides an options object, you lose all of your defaults.

```
carFactory({ make: 2000 })
// <- undefined
// <- 2000
```

We can mix function parameter default values with destructuring, and get the best of both worlds.

2.3.4 Function Parameter Destructuring

A better approach than merely providing a default value might be to destructure options entirely, providing default values for each property, individually, within the destructuring pattern. This approach also lets you reference each option without going through an options object, but you lose the ability to reference options directly, which might represent an issue in some situations.

```
function carFactory({ brand = 'Volkswagen', make = 1999 }) {
  console.log(brand)
  console.log(make)
}
carFactory({ make: 2000 })
// <- 'Volkswagen'
// <- 2000
```

In this case, however, we've once again lost the default value for the case where the consumer doesn't provide any options. Meaning car Factory() will now throw when an options object isn't provided. This can be remedied by using the syntax shown in the following snippet of code, which adds a default options value of an empty object. The empty object is then filled, property by property, with the default values on the destructuring pattern.

```
function carFactory({
  brand = 'Volkswagen',
  make = 1999
} = {}) {
  console.log(brand)
  console.log(make)
}
carFactory()
// <- 'Volkswagen'
// <- 1999
```

Besides default values, you can use destructuring in function parameters to describe the shape of objects your function can handle. Consider the following code snippet, where we have a car object with several properties. The car object describes its owner, what kind of car it is, who manufactured it, when, and the owner's preferences when he purchased the car.

```
var car = {
  owner: {
    id: 'e2c3503a4181968c',
    name: 'Donald Draper'
  },
```

```
  brand: 'Peugeot',
  make: 2015,
  model: '208',
  preferences: {
    airbags: true,
    airconditioning: false,
    color: 'red'
  }
}
```

If we wanted to implement a function that only takes into account certain properties of a parameter, it might be a good idea to reference those properties explicitly by destructuring up front. The upside is that we become aware of every required property upon reading the function's signature.

When we destructure everything up front, it's easy to spot when input doesn't adhere to the contract of a function. The following example shows how every property we need could be specified in the parameter list, laying bare the shape of the objects we can handle in the getCarProductModel API.

```
var getCarProductModel = ({ brand, make, model }) => ({
  sku: brand + ':' + make + ':' + model,
  brand,
  make,
  model
})
getCarProductModel(car)
```

Besides default values and filling an options object, let's explore what else destructuring is good at.

2.3.5 Use Cases for Destructuring

Whenever there's a function that returns an object or an array, destructuring makes it much terser to interact with. The following example shows a function that returns an object with some coordinates, where we grab only the ones we're interested in: x and y. We're avoiding an intermediate point variable declaration that often gets in the way without adding a lot of value to the readability of your code.

```
function getCoordinates() {
  return { x: 10, y: 22, z: -1, type: '3d' }
}
var { x, y } = getCoordinates()
```

The case for default option values bears repeating. Imagine you have a `random` function that produces random integers between a `min` and a `max` value, and that it should default to values between 1 and 10. This is particularly interesting as an alternative to named parameters in languages with strong typing features, such as Python and C#. This pattern, where you're able to define default values for options and then let consumers override them individually, offers great flexibility.

```
function random({ min = 1, max = 10 } = {}) {
  return Math.floor(Math.random() * (max - min)) + min
}
console.log(random())
// <- 7
console.log(random({ max: 24 }))
// <- 18
```

Regular expressions are another great fit for destructuring. Destructuring empowers you to name groups from a match without having to resort to index numbers. Here's an example `RegExp` that could be used for parsing simple dates, and an example of destructuring those dates into each of their components. The first entry in the resulting array is reserved for the raw input string, and we can discard it.

```
function splitDate(date) {
  var rdate = /(\d+).(\d+).(\d+)/
  return rdate.exec(date)
}
var [ , year, month, day] = splitDate('2015-11-06')
```

You'll want to be careful when the regular expression doesn't match, as that returns `null`. Perhaps a better approach would be to test for the failure case before destructuring, as shown in the following bit of code.

```
var matches = splitDate('2015-11-06')
if (matches === null) {
  return
}
var [, year, month, day] = matches
```

Let's turn our attention to spread and rest operators next.

2.4 Rest Parameter and Spread Operator

Before ES6, interacting with an arbitrary amount of function parameters was complicated. You had to use `arguments`, which isn't an

---

array but has a `length` property. Usually you'd end up casting the `arguments` object into an actual array using `Array#slice.call`, and going from there, as shown in the following snippet.

```
function join() {
  var list = Array.prototype.slice.call(arguments)
  return list.join(', ')
}
join('first', 'second', 'third')
// <- 'first, second, third'
```

ES6 has a better solution to the problem, and that's rest parameters.

2.4.1 Rest Parameters

You can now precede the last parameter in any JavaScript function with three dots, converting it into a special "rest parameter." When the rest parameter is the only parameter in a function, it gets all arguments passed to the function: it works just like the `.slice` solution we saw earlier, but you avoid the need for a complicated construct like `arguments`, and it's specified in the parameter list.

```
function join(...list) {
  return list.join(', ')
}
join('first', 'second', 'third')
// <- 'first, second, third'
```

Named parameters before the rest parameter won't be included in the `list`.

```
function join(separator, ...list) {
  return list.join(separator)
}
join('; ', 'first', 'second', 'third')
// <- 'first; second; third'
```

Note that arrow functions with a rest parameter must include parentheses, even when it's the only parameter. Otherwise, a `SyntaxError` would be thrown. The following piece of code is a beautiful example of how combining arrow functions and rest parameters can yield concise functional expressions.

```
var sumAll = (...numbers) => numbers.reduce(
  (total, next) => total + next
)
console.log(sumAll(1, 2, 5))
// <- 8
```

Compare that with the ES5 version of the same function. Granted, it's all in the complexity. While terse, the sumAll function can be confusing to readers unused to the .reduce method, or because it uses two arrow functions. This is a complexity trade-off that we'll cover in the second part of the book.

```
function sumAll() {
  var numbers = Array.prototype.slice.call(arguments)
  return numbers.reduce(function (total, next) {
    return total + next
  })
}
console.log(sumAll(1, 2, 5))
// <- 8
```

Next up we have the spread operator. It's also denoted with three dots, but it serves a slightly different purpose.

2.4.2 Spread Operator

The spread operator can be used to cast any iterable object into an array. Spreading effectively expands an expression onto a target such as an array literal or a function call. The following example uses ...arguments to cast function parameters into an array literal.

```
function cast() {
  return [...arguments]
}
cast('a', 'b', 'c')
// <- ['a', 'b', 'c']
```

We could use the spread operator to split a string into an array with each code point that makes up the string.

```
[...'show me']
// <- ['s', 'h', 'o', 'w', ' ', 'm', 'e']
```

You can place additional elements to the left and to the right of a spread operation and still get the result you would expect.

```
function cast() {
  return ['left', ...arguments, 'right']
}
cast('a', 'b', 'c')
// <- ['left', 'a', 'b', 'c', 'right']
```

Spread is an useful way of combining multiple arrays. The following example shows how you can spread arrays anywhere into an array literal, expanding their elements into place.

```
var all = [1, ...[2, 3], 4, ...[5], 6, 7]
console.log(all)
// <- [1, 2, 3, 4, 5, 6, 7]
```

Note that the spread operator isn't limited to arrays and `arguments`. The spread operator can be used with any iterable object. Iterable is a protocol in ES6 that allows you to turn any object into something that can be iterated over. We'll research the iterable protocol in Chapter 4.

Shifting and Spreading

When you want to extract an element or two from the beginning of an array, the common approach is to use `.shift`. While functional, the following snippet of code can be hard to understand at a glance, because it uses `.shift` twice to grab a different item from the beginning of the `list` each time. The focus is, like in many other pre-ES6 situations, placed on getting the language to do what we want.

```
var list = ['a', 'b', 'c', 'd', 'e']
var first = list.shift()
var second = list.shift()
console.log(first)
// <- 'a'
```

In ES6, you can combine spread with array destructuring. The following piece of code is similar to the preceding one, except we're using a single line of code, and that single line is more descriptive of what we're doing than repeatedly calling `list.shift()` in the previous example.

```
var [first, second, ...other] = ['a', 'b', 'c', 'd', 'e']
console.log(other)
// <- ['c', 'd', 'e']
```

Using the spread operator you can focus on implementing the functionality you need while the language stays out of the way. Improving expressiveness and decreasing time spent working around language limitations is a common pattern we can observe in ES6 features.

Before ES6, whenever you had a dynamic list of arguments that needed to be applied to a function call, you'd use `.apply`. This is inelegant because `.apply` also takes a context for `this`, which, in this scenario, you don't want to concern yourself with.

```
fn.apply(null, ['a', 'b', 'c'])
```

Besides spreading onto arrays, you can also spread items onto function calls. The following example shows how you could use the spread operator to pass an arbitrary number of arguments to the `multiply` function.

```
function multiply(left, right) {
  return left * right
}
var result = multiply(...[2, 3])
console.log(result)
// <- 6
```

Spreading arguments onto a function call can be combined with regular arguments as much as necessary, just like with array literals. The next example calls `print` with a couple of regular arguments and a couple of arrays being spread over the parameter list. Note how conveniently the rest `list` parameter matches all the provided arguments. Spread and rest can help make code intent more clear without diluting your codebase.

```
function print(...list) {
  console.log(list)
}
print(1, ...[2, 3], 4, ...[5])
// <- [1, 2, 3, 4, 5]
```

Another limitation of `.apply` is that combining it with the `new` keyword, when instantiating an object, becomes very verbose. Here's an example of combining `new` and `.apply` to create a `Date` object. Ignore for a moment that months in JavaScript dates are zero-based, turning 11 into December, and consider how much of the following line of code is spent bending the language in our favor, just to instantiate a `Date` object.

```
new (Date.bind.apply(Date, [null, 2015, 11, 31]))
// <- Thu Dec 31 2015
```

As shown in the next snippet, the spread operator strips away all the complexity and we're only left with the important bits. It's a `new` instance, it uses `...` to spread a dynamic list of arguments over the function call, and it's a `Date`. That's it.

```
new Date(...[2015, 11, 31])
// <- Thu Dec 31 2015
```

The following table summarizes the use cases we've discussed for the spread operator.

Use case	ES5	ES6
Concatenation	`[1, 2].concat(more)`	`[1, 2, ...more]`
Push an array onto list	`list.push.apply(list, items)`	`list.push(...items)`
Destructuring	`a = list[0], other = list.slice(1)`	`[a, ...other] = list`
new and apply	`new (Date.bind.apply(Date, [null,2015,31,8]))`	`new Date(... [2015,31,8])`

2.5 Template Literals

Template literals are a vast improvement upon regular JavaScript strings. Instead of using single or double quotes, template literals are declared using backticks, as shown next.

```
var text = `This is my first template literal`
```

Given that template literals are delimited by backticks, you're now able to declare strings with both ' and " quotation marks in them without having to escape either, as shown here.

```
var text = `I'm "amazed" at these opportunities!`
```

One of the most appealing features of template literals is their ability to interpolate JavaScript expressions.

2.5.1 String Interpolation

With template literals, you're able to interpolate any JavaScript expressions inside your templates. When the template literal expression is reached, it's evaluated and you get back the compiled result. The following example interpolates a name variable into a template literal.

```
var name = 'Shannon'
var text = `Hello, ${ name }!`
console.log(text)
// <- 'Hello, Shannon!'
```

We've already established that you can use any JavaScript expressions, and not just variables. You can think of each expression in a template literal as defining a variable before the template runs, and then concatenating each variable with the rest of the string. However, the code becomes easier to maintain because it doesn't involve manually concatenating strings and JavaScript expressions. The variables you use in those expressions, the functions you call, and so on, should all be available to the current scope.

It will be up to your coding style guides to decide how much logic you want to cram into the interpolation expressions. The following code snippet, for example, instantiates a Date object and formats it into a human-readable date inside a template literal.

```
`The time and date is ${ new Date().toLocaleString() }.`
// <- 'the time and date is 8/26/2015, 3:15:20 PM'
```

You could interpolate mathematical operations.

```
`The result of 2+3 equals ${ 2 + 3 }`
// <- 'The result of 2+3 equals 5'
```

You could even nest template literals, as they are also valid Java-Script expressions.

```
`This template literal ${ `is ${ 'nested' }` }!`
// <- 'This template literal is nested!'
```

Another perk of template literals is their multiline string representation support.

2.5.2 Multiline Template Literals

Before template literals, if you wanted to represent strings in multiple lines of JavaScript, you had to resort to escaping, concatenation, arrays, or even elaborate hacks using comments. The following snippet summarizes some of the most common multiline string representations prior to ES6.

```
var escaped =
'The first line\n\
A second line\n\
Then a third line'

var concatenated =
'The first line\n' `
'A second line\n' `
'Then a third line'

var joined = [
'The first line',
'A second line',
'Then a third line'
].join('\n')
```

Under ES6, you could use backticks instead. Template literals support multiline strings by default. Note how there are no \n escapes, no concatenation, and no arrays involved.

```
var multiline =
`The first line
A second line
Then a third line`
```

Multiline strings really shine when you have, for instance, a chunk of HTML you want to interpolate some variables into. If you need to display a list within the template, you could iterate the list, mapping its items into the corresponding markup, and then return the joined result from an interpolated expression. This makes it a breeze to declare subcomponents within your templates, as shown in the following piece of code.

```
var book = {
  title: 'Modular ES6',
  excerpt: 'Here goes some properly sanitized HTML',
  tags: ['es6', 'template-literals', 'es6-in-depth']
}
var html = `<article>
  <header>
    <h1>${ book.title }</h1>
  </header>
  <section>${ book.excerpt }</section>
  <footer>
    <ul>
      ${
        book.tags
          .map(tag => `<li>${ tag }</li>`)
          .join('\n      ')
      }
    </ul>
  </footer>
</article>`
```

The template we've just prepared would produce output like what's shown in the following snippet of code. Note how spacing was preserved,[3] and how <li> tags are properly indented thanks to how we joined them together using a few spaces.

---

3 When using multiline template literals, spacing isn't preserved automatically. However, in many cases we can provide just enough indentation to make it work. Be wary of indented code blocks that may result in undesired indentation due to our code block being nested.

```
<article>
  <header>
    <h1>Modular ES6</h1>
  </header>
  <section>Here goes some properly sanitized HTML</section>
  <footer>
    <ul>
      <li>es6</li>
      <li>template-literals</li>
      <li>es6-in-depth</li>
    </ul>
  </footer>
</article>
```

A downside when it comes to multiline template literals is indentation. The following example shows a typically indented piece of code with a template literal contained in a function. While we may have expected no indentation, the string has four spaces of indentation.

```
function getParagraph() {
  return `
    Dear Rod,

    This is a template literal string that's indented
    four spaces. However, you may have expected for it
    to be not indented at all.

    Nico
  `
}
```

While not ideal, we could get away with a utility function to remove indentation from each line in the resulting string.

```
function unindent(text) {
  return text
    .split('\n')
    .map(line => line.slice(4))
    .join('\n')
    .trim()
}
```

Sometimes, it might be a good idea to pre-process the results of interpolated expressions before inserting them into your templates. For these advanced kinds of use cases, it's possible to use another feature of template literals called *tagged templates*.

2.5.3 Tagged Templates

By default, JavaScript interprets \ as an escape character with special meaning. For example, \n is interpreted as a newline, \u00f1 is interpreted as ñ, etc. You could avoid these rules using the String.raw tagged template. The next snippet shows a template literal using String.raw, which prevents \n from being interpreted as a newline.

```
var text = String.raw`"\n" is taken literally.
It'll be escaped instead of interpreted.`
console.log(text)
// "\n" is taken literally.
// It'll be escaped instead of interpreted.
```

The String.raw prefix we've added to our template literal is a tagged template. It's used to parse the template. Tagged templates receive a parameter with an array containing the static parts of the template, as well as the result of evaluating each expression, each in its own parameter.

As an example, consider the tagged template literal in the next code snippet.

```
tag`Hello, ${ name }. I am ${ emotion } to meet you!`
```

That tagged template expression would, in practice, be translated into the following function call.

```
tag(
  ['Hello, ', '. I am ', ' to meet you!'],
  'Maurice',
  'thrilled'
)
```

The resulting string is built by taking each part of the template and placing one of the expressions next to it, until there are no more parts of the template left. It might be hard to interpret the argument list without looking at a potential implementation of the default template literal tag, so let's do that.

The following snippet of code shows a possible implementation of the default tag. It provides the same functionality as a template literal does when a tagged template isn't explicitly provided. It reduces the parts array into a single value, the result of evaluating the template literal. The result is initialized with the first part, and then each other part of the template is preceded by one of the values.

We've used the rest parameter syntax for `...values` in order to make it easier to grab the result of evaluating each expression in the template. We're using an arrow function with an implicit `return` statement, given that its expression is relatively simple.

```
function tag(parts, ...values) {
  return parts.reduce(
    (all, part, index) => all + values[index - 1] + part
  )
}
```

You can try the `tag` template using code like in the following snippet. You'll notice you get the same output as if you omitted `tag`, since we're copying the default behavior.

```
var name = 'Maurice'
var emotion = 'thrilled'
var text = tag`Hello, ${ name }. I am ${ emotion } to meet you!`
console.log(text)
// <- 'Hello Maurice, I am thrilled to meet you!'
```

Multiple use cases apply to tagged templates. One possible use case might be to make user input uppercase, making the string sound satirical. That's what the following piece of code does. We've modified `tag` slightly so that any interpolated strings are uppercased.

```
function upper(parts, ...values) {
  return parts.reduce((all, part, index) =>
    all + values[index - 1].toUpperCase() + part
  )
}
var name = 'Maurice'
var emotion = 'thrilled'
upper`Hello, ${ name }. I am ${ emotion } to meet you!`
// <- 'Hello MAURICE, I am THRILLED to meet you!'
```

A decidedly more useful use case would be to sanitize expressions interpolated into your templates, automatically, using a tagged template. Given a template where all expressions are considered user input, we could use a hypothetical `sanitize` library to remove HTML tags and similar hazards, preventing cross-site scripting (XSS) attacks where users might inject malicious HTML into our websites.

```
function sanitized(parts, ...values) {
  return parts.reduce((all, part, index) =>
    all + sanitize(values[index - 1]) + part
  )
}
```

```
var comment = 'Evil comment<iframe src="http://evil.corp">
    </iframe>'
var html = sanitized`<div>${ comment }</div>`
console.log(html)
// <- '<div>Evil comment</div>'
```

Phew, that malicious <iframe> almost got us. Rounding out ES6 syntax changes, we have the let and const statements.

2.6 let and const Statements

The let statement is one of the most well-known features in ES6. It works like a var statement, but it has different scoping rules.

JavaScript has always had a complicated ruleset when it comes to scoping, driving many programmers crazy when they were first trying to figure out how variables work in JavaScript. Eventually, you discover hoisting, and JavaScript starts making a bit more sense to you. *Hoisting* means that variables get pulled from anywhere they were declared in user code to the top of their scope. For example, see the following code.

```
function isItTwo(value) {
  if (value === 2) {
    var two = true
  }
  return two
}
isItTwo(2)
// <- true
isItTwo('two')
// <- undefined
```

JavaScript code like this works, even though two was declared in a code branch and then accessed outside of said branch. That behavior is due to the fact that var bindings are bound to the enclosing scope, be it a function or the global scope. That, coupled with hoisting, means that the code we've written earlier will be interpreted as if it were written in a similar way to the next piece of code.

```
function isItTwo(value) {
  var two
  if (value === 2) {
    two = true
  }
  return two
}
```

Whether we like it or not, hoisting is more confusing than having block-scoped variables would be. Block scoping works on the curly braces level, rather than the function level.

2.6.1 Block Scoping and let Statements

Instead of having to declare a new function if we want a deeper scoping level, block scoping allows you to just leverage existing code branches like those in if, for, or while statements; you could also create new {} blocks arbitrarily. As you may or may not know, the JavaScript language allows us to create an indiscriminate number of blocks, just because we want to.

```
{{{{{ var deep = 'This is available from outer scope.'; }}}}}
console.log(deep)
// <- 'This is available from outer scope.'
```

With var, because of lexical scoping, one could still access the deep variable from outside those blocks, and not get an error. Sometimes it can be very useful to get errors in these situations, particularly if one or more of the following is true:

- Accessing the inner variable breaks some sort of encapsulation principle in our code
- The inner variable doesn't belong in the outer scope at all
- The block in question has many siblings that would also want to use the same variable name
- One of the parent blocks already has a variable with the name we need, but the name is still appropriate to use in the inner block

The let statement is an alternative to var. It follows block scoping rules instead of the default lexical scoping rules. With var, the only way of getting a deeper scope is to create a nested function, but with let you can just open another pair of curly braces. This means you don't need entirely new functions to get a new scope; a simple {} block will do.

```
let topmost = {}
{
  let inner = {}
  {
    let innermost = {}
  }
```

```
  // attempts to access innermost here would throw
}
// attempts to access inner here would throw
// attempts to access innermost here would throw
```

One useful aspect of let statements is that you can use them when declaring a for loop, and variables will be scoped to the contents of the loop, as shown next.

```
for (let i = 0; i < 2; i++) {
  console.log(i)
  // <- 0
  // <- 1
}
console.log(i)
// <- i is not defined
```

Given let variables declared in a loop are scoped to each step in the loop, the bindings would work as expected in combination with an asynchronous function call, as opposed to what we're used to with var. Let's look at concrete examples.

First, we'll look at the typical example of how var scoping works. The i binding is scoped to the printNumbers function, and its value increases all the way to 10 as each timeout callback is scheduled. By the time each callback runs—one every 100 milliseconds—i has a value of 10 and thus that's what's printed every single time.

```
function printNumbers() {
  for (var i = 0; i < 10; i++) {
    setTimeout(function () {
      console.log(i)
    }, i * 100)
  }
}
printNumbers()
```

Using let, in contrast, binds the variable to the block's scope. Indeed, each step in the loop still increases the value of the variable, but a new binding is created each step of the way, meaning that each timeout callback will hold a reference to the binding holding the value of i at the point when the callback was scheduled, printing every number from 0 through 9 as expected.

```
function printNumbers() {
  for (let i = 0; i < 10; i++) {
    setTimeout(function () {
      console.log(i)
    }, i * 100)
```

```
      }
    }
    printNumbers()
```

One more thing of note about `let` is a concept called the "Temporal Dead Zone."

2.6.2 Temporal Dead Zone

In so many words: if you have code such as the following code snippet, it'll throw. Once execution enters a scope, and until a `let` statement is reached, attempting to access the variable for said `let` statement will throw. This is known as the Temporal Dead Zone (TDZ).

```
    {
      console.log(name)
      // <- ReferenceError: name is not defined
      let name = 'Stephen Hawking'
    }
```

If your code tries to access `name` in any way before the `let name` statement is reached, the program will throw. Declaring a function that references `name` before it's defined is okay, as long as the function doesn't get executed while `name` is in the TDZ, and `name` will be in the TDZ until the `let name` statement is reached. This snippet won't throw because `return name` isn't executed until after `name` leaves the TDZ.

```
    function readName() {
      return name
    }
    let name = 'Stephen Hawking'
    console.log(readName())
    // <- 'Stephen Hawking'
```

But the following snippet will, because access to `name` occurs before leaving the TDZ for `name`.

```
    function readName() {
      return name
    }
    console.log(readName())
    // ReferenceError: name is not defined
    let name = 'Stephen Hawking'
```

Note that the semantics for these examples don't change when `name` isn't actually assigned a value when initially declared. The next snippet throws as well, as it still tries to access name before leaving the TDZ.

```
function readName() {
  return name
}
console.log(readName())
// ReferenceError: name is not defined
let name
```

The following bit of code works because it leaves the TDZ before accessing name in any way.

```
function readName() {
  return name
}
let name
console.log(readName())
// <- undefined
```

The only tricky part to remember is that it's okay to declare functions that access a variable in the TDZ as long as the statements accessing TDZ variables aren't reached before the let declaration is reached.

The whole point of the TDZ is to make it easier to catch errors where accessing a variable before it's declared in user code leads to unexpected behavior. This happened a lot before ES6 due both to hoisting and poor coding conventions. In ES6 it's easier to avoid. Keep in mind that hoisting still applies for let as well. That means variables will be created when we enter the scope, and the TDZ will be born, but they will be inaccessible until code execution hits the place where the variable was actually declared, at which point we leave the TDZ and are allowed to access the variable.

We made it through the Temporal Dead Zone! It's now time to cover const, a similar statement to let but with a few major differences.

2.6.3 Const Statements

The const statement is block scoped like let, and it follows TDZ semantics as well. In fact, TDZ semantics were implemented because of const, and then TDZ was also applied to let for consistency. The reason why const needed TDZ semantics is that it would otherwise have been possible to assign a value to a hoisted const variable before reaching the const declaration, meaning that the declaration itself would throw. The temporal dead zone defines a solution that solves the problem of making const assignment possible only at declaration time, helps avoid potential issues when using let, and also makes it easy to eventually implement other features that benefit from TDZ semantics.

The following snippet shows how const follows block scoping rules exactly like let.

```
const pi = 3.1415
{
  const pi = 6
  console.log(pi)
  // <- 6
}
console.log(pi)
// <- 3.1415
```

We've mentioned major differences between let and const. The first one is that const variables must be declared using an initializer. A const declaration must be accompanied by an initializer, as shown in the following snippet.

```
const pi = 3.1415
const e // SyntaxError, missing initializer
```

Besides the assignment when initializing a const, variables declared using a const statement can't be assigned to. Once a const is initialized, you can't change its value. Under strict mode, attempts to change a const variable will throw. Outside of strict mode, they'll fail silently, as demonstrated by the following piece of code.

```
const people = ['Tesla', 'Musk']
people = []
console.log(people)
// <- ['Tesla', 'Musk']
```

Note that creating a const variable doesn't mean that the assigned value becomes immutable. This is a common source of confusion, and it is strongly recommended that you pay attention when reading the following warning.

Variables Declared Using const Are Not Immutable

Using const only means that the variable will always have a reference to the same object or primitive value, because that reference can't change. The reference itself is immutable, but the value held by the variable does not become immutable.

The following example shows that even though the `people` reference couldn't be changed, the array itself can indeed be modified. If the array were immutable, this wouldn't be possible.

```
const people = ['Tesla', 'Musk']
people.push('Berners-Lee')
console.log(people)
// <- ['Tesla', 'Musk', 'Berners-Lee']
```

A `const` statement only prevents the variable binding from referencing a different value. Another way of representing that difference is the following piece of code, where we create a `people` variable using `const`, and later assign that variable to a plain `var` `humans` binding. We can reassign the `humans` variable to reference something else, because it wasn't declared using `const`. However, we can't reassign `people` to reference something else, because it was created using `const`.

```
const people = ['Tesla', 'Musk']
var humans = people
humans = 'evil'
console.log(humans)
// <- 'evil'
```

If our goal was to make the value immutable, then we'd have to use a function such as `Object.freeze`. Using `Object.freeze` prevents extensions to the provided object, as represented in the following code snippet.

```
const frozen = Object.freeze(
  ['Ice', 'Icicle', 'Ice cube']
)
frozen.push('Water')
// Uncaught TypeError: Can't add property 3
// object is not extensible
```

Let's take a moment to discuss the merits of `const` and `let`.

2.6.4 Merits of const and let

New features should never be used for the sake of using new features. ES6 features should be used where they genuinely improve code readability and maintainability. The `let` statement is able to, in many cases, simplify pieces of code where you'd otherwise declare `var` statements at the top of a function just so that hoisting doesn't produce unexpected results. Using the `let` statement you'd be able to place your declarations at the top of a code block, instead of the top of the whole function, reducing the latency in mental trips to the top of the scope.

Using the const statement is a great way to prevent accidents. The following piece of code is a plausibly error-prone scenario where we pass a reference to an items variable off to a checklist function, which then returns a todo API that in turn interacts with said items reference. When the items variable is changed to reference another list of items, we're in for a world of hurt—the todo API still works with the value items used to have, but items is referencing something else now.

```
var items = ['a', 'b', 'c']
var todo = checklist(items)
todo.check()
console.log(items)
// <- ['b', 'c']
items = ['d', 'e']
todo.check()
console.log(items)
// <- ['d', 'e'], would be ['c'] if items had been constant
function checklist(items) {
  return {
    check: () => items.shift()
  }
}
```

This type of problem is hard to debug because it might take a while until you figure out that the reference was modified. The const statement helps prevent this scenario by producing a runtime error (under strict mode), which should help capture the bug soon after it's introduced.

A similar benefit of using the const statement is its ability to visually identify variables that aren't reassigned. The const cue signals that the variable binding is read-only and thus we have one less thing to worry about when reading a piece of code.

If we choose to default to using const and use let for variables that need to be reassigned, all variables will follow the same scoping rules, which makes code easier to reason about. The reason why const is sometimes proposed as the "default" variable declaration type is that it's the one that does the least: const prevents reassignment, follows block scoping, and the declared binding can't be accessed before the declaration statement is executed. The let statement allows reassignment, but behaves like const, so it naturally follows to choose let when we're in need of a reassignable variable.

On the counter side, var is a more complex declaration because it is hard to use in code branches due to function scoping rules, it allows reassignment, and it can be accessed before the declaration statement is reached. The var statement is inferior to const and let, which do less, and is thus less prominent in modern JavaScript codebases.

Throughout this book, we'll follow the practice of using const by default and let when reassignment is desirable. You can learn more about the rationale behind this choice in Chapter 9.

CHAPTER 3

Classes, Symbols, Objects, and Decorators

Now that we've covered the basic improvements to the syntax, we're in good shape to take aim at a few other additions to the language: classes and symbols. Classes provide syntax to represent prototypal inheritance under the traditional class-based programming paradigm. Symbols are a new primitive value type in JavaScript, like strings, Booleans, and numbers. They can be used for defining protocols, and in this chapter we'll investigate what that means. When we're done with classes and symbols, we'll discuss a few new static methods added to the `Object` built-in in ES6.

3.1 Classes

JavaScript is a prototype-based language, and classes are mostly syntactic sugar on top of prototypal inheritance. The fundamental difference between prototypal inheritance and classes is that classes can `extend` other classes, making it possible for us to extend the `Array` built-in—something that was very convoluted before ES6.

The `class` keyword acts, then, as a device that makes JavaScript more inviting to programmers coming from other paradigms, who might not be all that familiar with prototype chains.

3.1.1 Class Fundamentals

When learning about new language features, it's always a good idea to look at existing constructs first, and then see how the new feature improves those use cases. We'll start by looking at a simple prototype-based JavaScript constructor and then compare that with the newer classes syntax in ES6.

The following code snippet represents a fruit using a constructor function and adding a couple of methods to the prototype. The constructor function takes a `name` and the amount of `calories` for a fruit, and defaults to the fruit being in a single piece. There's a `.chop` method that will slice another piece of fruit, and then there's a `.bite` method. The `person` passed into `.bite` will eat a piece of fruit, getting satiety equal to the remaining calories divided by the amount of fruit pieces left.

```
function Fruit(name, calories) {
  this.name = name
  this.calories = calories
  this.pieces = 1
}
Fruit.prototype.chop = function () {
  this.pieces++
}
Fruit.prototype.bite = function (person) {
  if (this.pieces < 1) {
    return
  }
  const calories = this.calories / this.pieces
  person.satiety += calories
  this.calories -= calories
  this.pieces--
}
```

While fairly simple, the piece of code we just put together should be enough to note a few things. We have a constructor function that takes a couple of parameters, a pair of methods, and a number of properties. The next snippet codifies how one should create a `Fruit` and a `person` that chops the fruit into four slices and then takes three bites.

```
const person = { satiety: 0 }
const apple = new Fruit('apple', 140)
apple.chop()
apple.chop()
apple.chop()
apple.bite(person)
```

```
apple.bite(person)
apple.bite(person)
console.log(person.satiety)
// <- 105
console.log(apple.pieces)
// <- 1
console.log(apple.calories)
// <- 35
```

When using `class` syntax, as shown in the following code listing, the `constructor` function is declared as an explicit member of the `Fruit` class, and methods follow the object literal method definition syntax. When we compare the `class` syntax with the prototype-based syntax, you'll notice we're reducing the amount of boilerplate code quite a bit by avoiding explicit references to `Fruit.prototype` while declaring methods. The fact that the entire declaration is kept inside the `class` block also helps the reader understand the scope of this piece of code, making our classes' intent clearer. Lastly, having the constructor explicitly as a method member of `Fruit` makes the `class` syntax easier to understand when compared with the prototype-based flavor of class syntax.

```
class Fruit {
  constructor(name, calories) {
    this.name = name
    this.calories = calories
    this.pieces = 1
  }
  chop() {
    this.pieces++
  }
  bite(person) {
    if (this.pieces < 1) {
      return
    }
    const calories = this.calories / this.pieces
    person.satiety += calories
    this.calories -= calories
    this.pieces--
  }
}
```

A not-so-minor detail you might have missed is that there aren't any commas in between method declarations of the `Fruit` class. That's not a mistake our copious copyeditors missed, but rather part of the `class` syntax. The distinction can help avoid mistakes where we treat plain objects and classes as interchangeable even though they're not, and at the same time it makes classes better suited for future improvements to the syntax such as public and private class fields.

The class-based solution is equivalent to the prototype-based piece of code we wrote earlier. Consuming a fruit wouldn't change in the slightest; the API for Fruit remains unchanged. The previous piece of code where we instantiated an apple, chopped it into smaller pieces, and ate most of it would work well with our class-flavored Fruit as well.

It's worth noting that class declarations aren't hoisted to the top of their scope, unlike function declarations. That means you won't be able to instantiate, or otherwise access, a class before its declaration is reached and executed.

```
new Person() // <- ReferenceError: Person is not defined
class Person {
}
```

Besides the class declaration syntax presented earlier, classes can also be declared as expressions, just like with function declarations and function expressions. You may omit the name for a class expression, as shown in the following bit of code.

```
const Person = class {
  constructor(name) {
    this.name = name
  }
}
```

Class expressions could be easily returned from a function, making it possible to create a factory of classes with minimal effort. In the following example we create a JakePerson class dynamically in an arrow function that takes a name parameter and then feeds that to the parent Person constructor via super().

```
const createPersonClass = name => class extends Person {
  constructor() {
    super(name)
  }
}
const JakePerson = createPersonClass('Jake')
const jake = new JakePerson()
```

We'll dig deeper into class inheritance later. Let's take a more nuanced look at properties and methods first.

3.1.2 Properties and Methods in Classes

It should be noted that the `constructor` method declaration is an optional member of a `class` declaration. The following bit of code shows an entirely valid `class` declaration that's comparable to an empty constructor function by the same name.

```
class Fruit {
}
function Fruit() {
}
```

Any arguments passed to `new Log()` will be received as parameters to the `constructor` method for `Log`, as depicted next. You can use those parameters to initialize instances of the class.

```
class Log {
  constructor(...args) {
    console.log(args)
  }
}
new Log('a', 'b', 'c')
// <- ['a' 'b' 'c']
```

The following example shows a class where we create and initialize an instance property named `count` upon construction of each instance. The `get next` method declaration indicates instances of our `Counter` class will have a `next` property that will return the results of calling its method, whenever that property is accessed.

```
class Counter {
  constructor(start) {
    this.count = start
  }
  get next() {
    return this.count++
  }
}
```

In this case, you could consume the `Counter` class as shown in the next snippet. Each time the `.next` property is accessed, the count raises by one. While mildly useful, this sort of use case is usually better suited by methods than by magical `get` property accessors, and we need to be careful not to abuse property accessors, as consuming an object that abuses of accessors may become very confusing.

```
const counter = new Counter(2)
console.log(counter.next)
// <- 2
```

```
console.log(counter.next)
// <- 3
console.log(counter.next)
// <- 4
```

When paired with setters, though, accessors may provide an interesting bridge between an object and its underlying data store. Consider the following example where we define a class that can be used to store and retrieve JSON data from localStorage using the provided storage key.

```
class LocalStorage {
  constructor(key) {
    this.key = key
  }
  get data() {
    return JSON.parse(localStorage.getItem(this.key))
  }
  set data(data) {
    localStorage.setItem(this.key, JSON.stringify(data))
  }
}
```

Then you could use the LocalStorage class as shown in the next example. Any value that's assigned to ls.data will be converted to its JSON object string representation and stored in localStorage. Then, when the property is read from, the same key will be used to retrieve the previously stored contents, parse them as JSON into an object, and returned.

```
const ls = new LocalStorage('groceries')
ls.data = ['apples', 'bananas', 'grapes']
console.log(ls.data)
// <- ['apples', 'bananas', 'grapes']
```

Besides getters and setters, you can also define regular instance methods, as we've explored earlier when creating the Fruit class. The following code example creates a Person class that's able to eat Fruit instances as we had declared them earlier. We then instantiate a fruit and a person, and have the person eat the fruit. The person ends up with a satiety level equal to 40, because he ate the whole fruit.

```
class Person {
  constructor() {
    this.satiety = 0
  }
  eat(fruit) {
    while (fruit.pieces > 0) {
```

```
      fruit.bite(this)
    }
  }
}
const plum = new Fruit('plum', 40)
const person = new Person()
person.eat(plum)
console.log(person.satiety)
// <- 40
```

Sometimes it's necessary to add static methods at the class level, rather than members at the instance level. Using syntax available before ES6, instance members have to be explicitly added to the prototype chain. Meanwhile, static methods should be added to the constructor directly.

```
function Person() {
  this.hunger = 100
}
Person.prototype.eat = function () {
  this.hunger--
}
Person.isPerson = function (person) {
  return person instanceof Person
}
```

JavaScript classes allow you to define static methods like `Person.isPerson` using the `static` keyword, much like you would use `get` or `set` as a prefix to a method definition that's a getter or a setter.

The following example defines a `MathHelper` class with a static `sum` method that's able to calculate the sum of all numbers passed to it in a function call, by taking advantage of the `Array#reduce` method.

```
class MathHelper {
  static sum(...numbers) {
    return numbers.reduce((a, b) => a + b)
  }
}
console.log(MathHelper.sum(1, 2, 3, 4, 5))
// <- 15
```

Finally, it's worth mentioning that you could also declare static property accessors, such as getters or setters (`static get`, `static set`). These might come in handy when maintaining global configuration state for a class, or when a class is used under a singleton pattern. Of course, you're probably better off using plain old JavaScript objects at that point, rather than creating a class you never intend to instantiate or only intend to instantiate once. This is JavaScript, a highly dynamic language, after all.

3.1.3 Extending JavaScript Classes

You could use plain JavaScript to extend the Fruit class, but as you will notice by reading the next code snippet, declaring a subclass involves esoteric knowledge such as Parent.call(this) in order to pass in parameters to the parent class so that we can properly initialize the subclass, and setting the prototype of the subclass to an instance of the parent class's prototype. As you can readily find heaps of information about prototypal inheritance around the web, we won't be delving into detailed minutia about prototypal inheritance.

```
function Banana() {
  Fruit.call(this, 'banana', 105)
}
Banana.prototype = Object.create(Fruit.prototype)
Banana.prototype.slice = function () {
  this.pieces = 12
}
```

Given the ephemeral knowledge one has to remember, and the fact that Object.create was only made available in ES5, JavaScript developers have historically turned to libraries to resolve their prototype inheritance issues. One such example is util.inherits in Node.js, which is usually favored over Object.create for legacy support reasons.

```
const util = require('util')
function Banana() {
  Fruit.call(this, 'banana', 105)
}
util.inherits(Banana, Fruit)
Banana.prototype.slice = function () {
  this.pieces = 12
}
```

Consuming the Banana constructor is no different than how we used Fruit, except that the banana has a name and calories already assigned to it, and they come with an extra slice method we can use to promptly chop the banana instance into 12 pieces. The following piece of code shows the Banana in action as we take a bite.

```
const person = { satiety: 0 }
const banana = new Banana()
```

```
banana.slice()
banana.bite(person)
console.log(person.satiety)
// <- 8.75
console.log(banana.pieces)
// <- 11
console.log(banana.calories)
// <- 96.25
```

Classes consolidate prototypal inheritance, which up until recently had been highly contested in user-space by several libraries trying to make it easier to deal with prototypal inheritance in JavaScript.

The Fruit class is ripe for inheritance. In the following code snippet we create the Banana class as an extension of the Fruit class. Here, the syntax clearly signals our intent and we don't have to worry about thoroughly understanding prototypal inheritance in order to get to the results that we want. When we want to forward parameters to the underlying Fruit constructor, we can use super. The super keyword can also be used to call functions in the parent class, such as super.chop, and it's not just limited to the constructor for the parent class.

```
class Banana extends Fruit {
  constructor() {
    super('banana', 105)
  }
  slice() {
    this.pieces = 12
  }
}
```

Even though the class keyword is static we can still leverage JavaScript's flexible and functional properties when declaring classes. Any expression that returns a constructor function can be fed to extends. For example, we could have a constructor function factory and use that as the base class.

The following piece of code has a createJuicyFruit function where we forward the name and calories for a fruit to the Fruit class using a super call, and then all we have to do to create a Plum is extend the intermediary JuicyFruit class.

```
const createJuicyFruit = (...params) =>
  class JuicyFruit extends Fruit {
    constructor() {
      this.juice = 0
      super(...params)
```

```
      }
      squeeze() {
        if (this.calories <= 0) {
          return
        }
        this.calories -= 10
        this.juice += 3
      }
    }
    class Plum extends createJuicyFruit('plum', 30) {
    }
```

Let's move onto Symbol. While not an iteration or flow control mechanism, learning about Symbol is crucial to shaping an understanding of iteration protocols, which are discussed at length later in the chapter.

3.2 Symbols

Symbols are a new primitive type in ES6, and the seventh type in JavaScript. It is a unique value type, like strings and numbers. Unlike strings and numbers, symbols don't have a literal representation such as 'text' for strings, or 1 for numbers. The purpose of symbols is primarily to implement protocols. For example, the iterable protocol uses a symbol to define how objects are iterated, as we'll learn in Section 4.2, "Iterator Protocol and Iterable Protocol," on page 108.

There are three flavors of symbols, and each flavor is accessed in a different way. These are: local symbols, created with the Symbol built-in wrapper object and accessed by storing a reference or via reflection; global symbols, created using another API and shared across code realms; and "well-known" symbols, built into JavaScript and used to define internal language behavior.

We'll explore each of these, looking into possible use cases along the way. Let's begin with local symbols.

3.2.1 Local Symbols

Symbols can be created using the Symbol wrapper object. In the following piece of code, we create our first symbol.

```
const first = Symbol()
```

While you can use the new keyword with Number and String, the new operator throws a TypeError when we try it on Symbol. This avoids mistakes and confusing behavior like new Number(3) !== Number(3). The following snippet shows the error being thrown.

```
const oops = new Symbol()
// <- TypeError, Symbol is not a constructor
```

For debugging purposes, you can create symbols using a description.

```
const mystery = Symbol('my symbol')
```

Like numbers or strings, symbols are immutable. Unlike other value types, however, symbols are unique. As shown in the next piece of code, descriptions don't affect that uniqueness. Symbols created using the same description are also unique and thus different from each other.

```
console.log(Number(3) === Number(3))
// <- true
console.log(Symbol() === Symbol())
// <- false
console.log(Symbol('my symbol') === Symbol('my symbol'))
// <- false
```

Symbols are of type symbol, new in ES6. The following snippet shows how typeof returns the new type string for symbols.

```
console.log(typeof Symbol())
// <- 'symbol'
console.log(typeof Symbol('my symbol'))
// <- 'symbol'
```

Symbols can be used as property keys on objects. Note how you can use a computed property name to avoid an extra statement just to add a weapon symbol key to the character object, as shown in the following example. Note also that, in order to access a symbol property, you'll need a reference to the symbol that was used to create said property.

```
const weapon = Symbol('weapon')
const character = {
  name: 'Penguin',
  [weapon]: 'umbrella'
}
console.log(character[weapon])
// <- 'umbrella'
```

Keep in mind that symbol keys are hidden from many of the traditional ways of pulling keys from an object. The next bit of code shows how `for..in`, `Object.keys`, and `Object.getOwnProperty Names` fail to report on symbol properties.

```
for (let key in character) {
  console.log(key)
  // <- 'name'
}
console.log(Object.keys(character))
// <- ['name']
console.log(Object.getOwnPropertyNames(character))
// <- ['name']
```

This aspect of symbols means that code that was written before ES6 and without symbols in mind won't unexpectedly start stumbling upon symbols. In a similar fashion, as shown next, symbol properties are discarded when representing an object as JSON.

```
console.log(JSON.stringify(character))
// <- '{"name":"Penguin"}'
```

That being said, symbols are by no means a safe mechanism to conceal properties. Even though you won't stumble upon symbol properties when using reflection or serialization methods, symbols are revealed by a dedicated method as shown in the next snippet of code. In other words, symbols are not nonenumerable, but hidden in plain sight. Using `Object.getOwnPropertySymbols` we can retrieve all symbols used as property keys on any given object.

```
console.log(Object.getOwnPropertySymbols(character))
// <- [Symbol(weapon)]
```

Now that we've established how symbols work, what can we use them for?

3.2.2 Practical Use Cases for Symbols

Symbols could be used by a library to map objects to DOM elements. For example, a library that needs to associate the API object for a calendar to the provided DOM element. Before ES6, there wasn't a clear way of mapping DOM elements to objects. You could add a property to a DOM element pointing to the API, but polluting DOM elements with custom properties is a bad practice. You have to be careful to use property keys that won't be used by other libraries, or worse, by the language itself in the future. That leaves you with using an array lookup table containing an entry for each

DOM/API pair. That, however, might be slow in long-running applications where the array lookup table might grow in size, slowing down the lookup operation over time.

Symbols, on the other hand, don't have this problem. They can be used as properties that don't have a risk of clashing with future language features, as they're unique. The following code snippet shows how a symbol could be used to map DOM elements into calendar API objects.

```
const cache = Symbol('calendar')
function createCalendar(el) {
  if (cache in el) { // does the symbol exist in the element?
    return el[cache] // use the cache to avoid re-instantiation
  }
  const api = el[cache] = {
    // the calendar API goes here
  }
  return api
}
```

There is an ES6 built-in—the WeakMap—that can be used to uniquely map objects to other objects without using arrays or placing foreign properties on the objects we want to be able to look up. In contrast with array lookup tables, WeakMap lookups are constant in time or O(1). We'll explore WeakMap in Chapter 5, alongside other ES6 collection built-ins.

Defining protocols through symbols

Earlier, we posited that a use case for symbols is to define protocols. A protocol is a communication contract or convention that defines behavior. In less abstract terms, a library could use a symbol that could then be used by objects that adhere to a convention from the library.

Consider the following bit of code, where we use the special toJSON method to determine the object serialized by JSON.stringify. As you can see, stringifying the character object produces a serialized version of the object returned by toJSON.

```
const character = {
  name: 'Thor',
  toJSON: () => ({
    key: 'value'
  })
}
```

```
console.log(JSON.stringify(character))
// <- '"{"key":"value"}"'
```

In contrast, if toJSON was anything other than a function, the original character object would be serialized, including the toJSON property, as shown next. This sort of inconsistency ensues from relying on regular properties to define behavior.

```
const character = {
  name: 'Thor',
  toJSON: true
}
console.log(JSON.stringify(character))
// <- '"{"name":"Thor","toJSON":true}"'
```

The reason why it would be better to implement the toJSON modifier as a symbol is that that way it wouldn't interfere with other object keys. Given that symbols are unique, never serialized, and never exposed unless explicitly requested through Object.getOwn PropertySymbols, they would represent a better choice when defining a contract between JSON.stringify and how objects want to be serialized. Consider the following piece of code with an alternative implementation of toJSON using a symbol to define serialization behavior for a stringify function.

```
const json = Symbol('alternative to toJSON')
const character = {
  name: 'Thor',
  [json]: () => ({
    key: 'value'
  })
}
stringify(character)
function stringify(target) {
  if (json in target) {
    return JSON.stringify(target[json]())
  }
  return JSON.stringify(target)
}
```

Using a symbol means we need to use a computed property name to define the json behavior directly on an object literal. It also means that the behavior won't clash with other user-defined properties or upcoming language features we couldn't foresee. Another difference is that the json symbol should be available to consumers of the stringify function, so that they can define their own behavior. We could easily add the following line of code to expose the json symbol directly through `stringify`, as shown next. That'd also tie the `stringify` function with the symbol that modifies its behavior.

```
stringify.as = json
```

By exposing the `stringify` function we'd be exposing the `string ify.as` symbol as well, allowing consumers to tweak behavior by minimally modifying objects, using the custom symbol.

When it comes to the merits of using a symbol to describe behavior, as opposed to an option passed to the `stringify` function, there are a few considerations to keep in mind. First, adding option parameters to a function changes its public API, whereas changing the internal implementation of the function to support another symbol wouldn't affect the public API. Using an `options` object with different properties for each option mitigates this effect, but it's not always convenient to require an `options` object in every function call.

A benefit of defining behavior via symbols is that you could augment and customize the behavior of objects without changing anything other than the value assigned to a symbol property and perhaps the internal implementation of the piece of code that leverages that behavior. The benefit of using symbols over properties is that you're not subject to name clashes when new language features are introduced.

Besides local symbols, there's also a global symbol registry, accessible from across code realms. Let's look into what that means.

3.2.3 Global Symbol Registry

A code realm is any JavaScript execution context, such as the page your application is running in, an `<iframe>` within that page, a script running through `eval`, or a worker of any kind—such as web workers, service workers, or shared workers.[1] Each of these execution contexts has its own global object. Global variables defined on the `window` object of a page, for example, aren't available to a `Serv iceWorker`. In contrast, the global symbol registry is shared across all code realms.

---

1 Workers are a way of executing background tasks in browsers. The initiator can communicate with their workers (*https://mjavascript.com/out/workers*), which run in a different execution context, via messaging.

There are two methods that interact with the runtime-wide global symbol registry: `Symbol.for` and `Symbol.keyFor`. What do they do?

Getting symbols with Symbol.for(key)

The `Symbol.for(key)` method looks up key in the runtime-wide symbol registry. If a symbol with the provided key exists in the global registry, that symbol is returned. If no symbol with that key is found in the registry, one is created and added to the registry under the provided key. That's to say, `Symbol.for(key)` is idempotent: it looks for a symbol under a key, creates one if it didn't already exist, and then returns the symbol.

In the following code snippet, the first call to `Symbol.for` creates a symbol identified as `'example'`, adds it to the registry, and returns it. The second call returns that same symbol because the key is already in the registry—and associated to the symbol returned by the first call.

```
const example = Symbol.for('example')
console.log(example === Symbol.for('example'))
// <- true
```

The global symbol registry keeps track of symbols by their key. Note that the key will also be used as a `description` when the symbols that go into the registry are created. Considering these symbols are global on a runtime-wide level, you might want to prefix symbol keys in the global registry with a value that identifies your library or component, mitigating potential name clashes.

Using Symbol.keyFor(symbol) to retrieve symbol keys

Given a symbol `symbol`, `Symbol.keyFor(symbol)` returns the key that was associated with `symbol` when the symbol was added to the global registry. The next example shows how we can grab the key for a symbol using `Symbol.keyFor`.

```
const example = Symbol.for('example')
console.log(Symbol.keyFor(example))
// <- 'example'
```

Note that if the symbol isn't in the global runtime registry, then the method returns `undefined`.

```
console.log(Symbol.keyFor(Symbol()))
// <- undefined
```

Also keep in mind that it's not possible to match symbols in the global registry using local symbols, even when they share the same description. The reason for that is that local symbols aren't part of the global registry, as shown in the following piece of code.

```
const example = Symbol.for('example')
console.log(Symbol.keyFor(Symbol('example')))
// <- undefined
```

Now that you've learned about the API for interacting with the global symbol registry, let's take some considerations into account.

Best practices and considerations

A runtime-wide registry means the symbols are accessible across code realms. The global registry returns a reference to the same object in any realm the code runs in. In the following example, we demonstrate how the Symbol.for API returns the same symbol in a page and within an <iframe>.

```
const d = document
const frame = d.body.appendChild(d.createElement('iframe'))
const framed = frame.contentWindow
const s1 = window.Symbol.for('example')
const s2 = framed.Symbol.for('example')
console.log(s1 === s2)
// <- true
```

There are trade-offs in using widely available symbols. On the one hand, they make it easy for libraries to expose their own symbols, but on the other hand they could also expose their symbols on their own API, using local symbols. The symbol registry is obviously useful when symbols need to be shared across any two code realms; for example, ServiceWorker and a web page. The API is also convenient when you don't want to bother storing references to the symbols. You could use the registry directly for that, since every call with a given key is guaranteed to return the same symbol. You'll have to keep in mind, though, that these symbols are shared across the runtime and that might lead to unwanted consequences if you use generic symbol names like each or contains.

There's one more kind of symbol: built-in well-known symbols.

3.2.4 Well-Known Symbols

So far we've covered symbols you can create using the Symbol function and those you can create through Symbol.for. The third and last kind of symbols we're going to cover are the well-known symbols. These are built into the language instead of created by JavaScript developers, and they provide hooks into internal language behavior, allowing you to extend or customize aspects of the language that weren't accessible prior to ES6.

A great example of how symbols can add extensibility to the language without breaking existing code is the Symbol.toPrimitive well-known symbol. It can be assigned a function to determine how an object is cast into a primitive value. The function receives a hint parameter that can be 'string', 'number', or 'default', indicating what type of primitive value is expected.

```
const morphling = {
  [Symbol.toPrimitive](hint) {
    if (hint === 'number') {
      return Infinity
    }
    if (hint === 'string') {
      return 'a lot'
    }
    return '[object Morphling]'
  }
}
console.log(+morphling)
// <- Infinity
console.log(`That is ${ morphling }!`)
// <- 'That is a lot!'
console.log(morphling + ' is powerful')
// <- '[object Morphling] is powerful'
```

Another example of a well-known symbol is Symbol.match. A regular expression that sets Symbol.match to false will be treated as a string literal when passed to .startsWith, .endsWith, or .includes. These three functions are new string methods in ES6. First we have .startsWith, which can be used to determine if the string starts with another string. Then there's .endsWith, which finds out whether the string ends in another one. Lastly, the .includes method returns true if a string contains another one. The next snippet of code shows how Symbol.match can be used to compare a string with the string representation of a regular expression.

```
const text = '/an example string/'
const regex = /an example string/
regex[Symbol.match] = false
console.log(text.startsWith(regex))
// <- true
```

If the regular expression wasn't modified through the symbol, it would've thrown because the .startsWith method expects a string instead of a regular expression.

Shared across realms but not in the registry

Well-known symbols are shared across realms. The following example shows how Symbol.iterator is the same reference as that within the context of an <iframe> window.

```
const frame = document.createElement('iframe')
document.body.appendChild(frame)
Symbol.iterator === frame.contentWindow.Symbol.iterator
// <- true
```

Note that even though well-known symbols are shared across code realms, they're not in the global registry. The following bit of code shows that Symbol.iterator produces undefined when we ask for its key in the registry. That means the symbol isn't listed in the global registry.

```
console.log(Symbol.keyFor(Symbol.iterator))
// <- undefined
```

One of the most useful well-known symbols is Symbol.iterator, used by a few different language constructs to iterate over a sequence, as defined by a function assigned to a property using that symbol on any object. In the next chapter we'll go over Symbol.iterator in detail, using it extensively along with the iterator and iterable protocols.

3.3 Object Built-in Improvements

While we've already addressed syntax enhancements coming to object literals in Chapter 2, there are a few new static methods available to the Object built-in that we haven't addressed yet. It's time to take a look at what these methods bring to the table.

We've already looked at Object.getOwnPropertySymbols, but let's also take a look at Object.assign, Object.is, and Object.setPrototypeOf.

3.3.1 Extending Objects with Object.assign

The need to provide default values for a configuration object is not at all uncommon. Typically, libraries and well-designed component interfaces come with sensible defaults that cater to the most frequented use cases.

A Markdown library, for example, might convert Markdown into HTML by providing only an input parameter. That's its most common use case, simply parsing Markdown, and so the library doesn't demand that the consumer provides any options. The library might, however, support many different options that could be used to tweak its parsing behavior. It could have an option to allow <script> or <iframe> tags, or an option to highlight keywords in code snippets using CSS.

Imagine, for example, that you want to provide a set of defaults like the one shown next.

```
const defaults = {
  scripts: false,
  iframes: false,
  highlightSyntax: true
}
```

One possibility would be to use the defaults object as the default value for the options parameter, using destructuring. In this case, the users must provide values for every option whenever they decide to provide any options at all.

```
function md(input, options=defaults) {
}
```

The default values have to be merged with user-provided configuration, somehow. That's where Object.assign comes in, as shown in the following example. We start with an empty {} object—which will be mutated and returned by Object.assign—we copy the default values over to it, and then copy the options on top. The resulting config object will have all of the default values plus the user-provided configuration.

```
function md(input, options) {
  const config = Object.assign({}, defaults, options)
}
```

Understanding the Target of Object.assign

The `Object.assign` function mutates its first argument. Its signature is (`target, ...sources`). Every source is applied onto the target object, source by source and property by property.

Consider the following scenario, where we don't pass an empty object as the first argument of `Object.assign`, instead just providing it with the `defaults` and the `options`. We would be changing the contents of the `defaults` object, losing some of our default values—and obtaining some wrong ones—in the process of mutating the object. The first invocation would produce the same result as the previous example, but it would modify our defaults in the process, changing how subsequent calls to md work.

```
function md(input, options) {
  const config = Object.assign(defaults, options)
}
```

For this reason, it's generally best to pass a brand new object on the first position, every time.

For any properties that had a default value where the user also provided a value, the user-provided value will prevail. Here's how `Object.assign` works. First, it takes the first argument passed to it; let's call it `target`. It then iterates over all keys of each of the other arguments; let's call them `sources`. For each source in `sources`, all of its properties are iterated and assigned to `target`. The end result is that rightmost sources—in our case, the `options` object—overwrite any previously assigned values, as shown in the following bit of code.

```
const defaults = {
  first: 'first',
  second: 'second'
}
function applyDefaults(options) {
  return Object.assign({}, defaults, options)
}
applyDefaults()
// <- { first: 'first', second: 'second' }
applyDefaults({ third: 3 })
```

```
// <- { first: 'first', second: 'second', third: 3 }
applyDefaults({ second: false })
// <- { first: 'first', second: false }
```

Before `Object.assign` made its way into the language, there were numerous similar implementations of this technique in user-land JavaScript, with names like assign, or extend. Adding `Object.assign` to the language consolidates these options into a single method.

Note that `Object.assign` takes into consideration only own enumerable properties, including both string and symbol properties.

```
const defaults = {
  [Symbol('currency')]: 'USD'
}
const options = {
  price: '0.99'
}
Object.defineProperty(options, 'name', {
  value: 'Espresso Shot',
  enumerable: false
})
console.log(Object.assign({}, defaults, options))
// <- { [Symbol('currency')]: 'USD', price: '0.99' }
```

Note, however, that `Object.assign` doesn't cater to every need. While most user-land implementations have the ability to perform deep assignment, `Object.assign` doesn't offer a recursive treatment of objects. Object values are assigned as properties on `target` directly, instead of being recursively assigned key by key.

In the following bit of code you might expect the f property to be added to `target.a` while keeping b.c and b.d intact, but the b.c and b.d properties are lost when using `Object.assign`.

```
Object.assign({}, { a: { b: 'c', d: 'e' } }, { a: { f: 'g' } })
// <- { a: { f: 'g' } }
```

In the same vein, arrays don't get any special treatment either. If you expected recursive behavior in `Object.assign` the following snippet of code may also come as a surprise, where you may have expected the resulting object to have 'd' in the third position of the array.

```
Object.assign({}, { a: ['b', 'c', 'd'] }, { a: ['e', 'f'] })
// <- { a: ['e', 'f'] }
```

At the time of this writing, there's an ECMAScript stage 3 proposal[2] to implement spread in objects, similar to how you can spread iterable objects onto an array in ES6. Spreading an object onto another is equivalent to using an `Object.assign` function call.

The following piece of code shows a few cases where we're spreading the properties of an object onto another one, and their `Object.assign` counterpart. As you can see, using object spread is more succinct and should be preferred where possible.

```
const grocery = { ...details }
// Object.assign({}, details)
const grocery = { type: 'fruit', ...details }
// Object.assign({ type: 'fruit' }, details)
const grocery = { type: 'fruit', ...details, ...fruit }
// Object.assign({ type: 'fruit' }, details, fruit)
const grocery = { type: 'fruit', ...details, color: 'red' }
// Object.assign({ type: 'fruit' }, details, { color: 'red' })
```

As a counterpart to object spread, the proposal includes object rest properties, which is similar to the array rest pattern. We can use object rest whenever we're destructuring an object.

The following example shows how we could leverage object rest to get an object containing only properties that we haven't explicitly named in the parameter list. Note that the object rest property must be in the last position of destructuring, just like the array rest pattern.

```
const getUnknownProperties = ({ name, type, ...unknown }) =>
  unknown
getUnknownProperties({
  name: 'Carrot',
  type: 'vegetable',
  color: 'orange'
})
// <- { color: 'orange' }
```

We could take a similar approach when destructuring an object in a variable declaration statement. In the next example, every property that's not explicitly destructured is placed in a `meta` object.

```
const { name, type, ...meta } = {
  name: 'Carrot',
  type: 'vegetable',
```

---

2 You can find the proposal draft at GitHub (*https://mjavascript.com/out/proposal-promise-finally*).

```
    color: 'orange'
}
// <- name = 'Carrot'
// <- type = 'vegetable'
// <- meta = { color: 'orange' }
```

We dive deeper into object rest and spread in Chapter 9.

3.3.2 Comparing Objects with Object.is

The `Object.is` method is a slightly different version of the strict equality comparison operator, `===`. For the most part, `Object.is(a, b)` is equal to `a === b`. There are two differences: the case of `NaN` and the case of `-0` and `+0`. This algorithm is referred to as `SameValue` in the ECMAScript specification.

When `NaN` is compared to `NaN`, the strict equality comparison operator returns `false` because `NaN` is not equal to itself. The `Object.is` method, however, returns `true` in this special case.

```
NaN === NaN
// <- false
Object.is(NaN, NaN)
// <- true
```

Similarly, when `-0` is compared to `+0`, the `===` operator produces `true` while `Object.is` returns `false`.

```
-0 === +0
// <- true
Object.is(-0, +0)
// <- false
```

These differences may not seem like much, but dealing with `NaN` has always been cumbersome because of its special quirks, such as `typeof NaN` being `'number'` and it not being equal to itself.

3.3.3 Object.setPrototypeOf

The `Object.setPrototypeOf` method does exactly what its name conveys: it sets the prototype of an object to a reference to another object. It's considered the proper way of setting the prototype, as opposed to using `__proto__`, which is a legacy feature.

Before ES6, we were introduced to `Object.create` in ES5. Using that method, we could create an object based on any prototype passed into `Object.create`, as shown next.

```
const baseCat = { type: 'cat', legs: 4 }
const cat = Object.create(baseCat)
cat.name = 'Milanesita'
```

The `Object.create` method is, however, limited to newly created objects. In contrast, we could use `Object.setPrototypeOf` to change the prototype of an object that already exists, as shown in the following code snippet.

```
const baseCat = { type: 'cat', legs: 4 }
const cat = Object.setPrototypeOf(
  { name: 'Milanesita' },
  baseCat
)
```

Note however that there are serious performance implications when using `Object.setPrototypeOf` as opposed to `Object.create`, and some careful consideration is in order before you decide to go ahead and sprinkle `Object.setPrototypeOf` all over a codebase.

Performance Issues

Using `Object.setPrototypeOf` to change the prototype of an object is an expensive operation. Here is what the Mozilla Developer Network documentation has to say about the matter:

> Changing the prototype of an object is, by the nature of how modern JavaScript engines optimize property accesses, a very slow operation, in every browser and JavaScript engine. The effects on performance of altering inheritance are subtle and far-flung, and are not limited to simply the time spent in a `obj.__proto__ = …` statement, but may extend to any code that has access to any object whose prototype has been altered. If you care about performance you should avoid setting the prototype of an object. Instead, create a new object with the desired prototype using `Object.create()`.
>
> —Mozilla Developer Network

3.4 Decorators

Decorators are, as most things programming, definitely not a new concept. The pattern is fairly commonplace in modern programming languages: you have *attributes* in C#, they're called *annotations* in Java, there are *decorators* in Python, and the list goes on. There's a

JavaScript decorators proposal[3] in the works. It is currently sitting at stage 2 of the TC39 process.

3.4.1 A Primer on JavaScript Decorators

The syntax for JavaScript decorators is fairly similar to that of Python decorators. JavaScript decorators may be applied to classes and any statically defined properties, such as those found on an object literal declaration or in a `class` declaration—even if they are `get` accessors, `set` accessors, or `static` properties.

The proposal defines a *decorator* as an @ followed by a sequence of dotted identifiers[4] and an optional argument list. Here are a few examples:

- `@decorators.frozen` is a valid decorator
- `@decorators.frozen(true)` is a valid decorator
- `@decorators().frozen()` is a syntax error
- `@decorators['frozen']` is a syntax error

Zero or more decorators can be attached to `class` declarations and class members.

```
@inanimate
class Car {}

@expensive
@speed('fast')
class Lamborghini extends Car {}

class View {
  @throttle(200) // reconcile once every 200ms at most
  reconcile() {}
}
```

Decorators are implemented by way of functions. Member decorator functions take a member descriptor and return a member descriptor. Member descriptors are similar to property descriptors, but with a different shape. The following bit of code has the member descrip-

---

3 You can find the proposal draft online at GitHub (*https://mjavascript.com/out/decorators*).

4 Accessing properties via [ ] notation is disallowed due to the difficulty it would present when disambiguating grammar at the compiler level.

---

tor interface, as defined by the decorators proposal. An optional `fin`
`isher` function receives the class constructor, allowing us to perform
operations related to the class whose property is being decorated.

```
interface MemberDescriptor {
  kind: "Property"
  key: string,
  isStatic: boolean,
  descriptor: PropertyDescriptor,
  extras?: MemberDescriptor[]
  finisher?: (constructor): void;
}
```

In the following example we define a `readonly` member decorator
function that makes decorated members nonwritable. Taking advantage of the object rest parameter and object spread, we modify the
property descriptor to be non-writable while keeping the rest of the
member descriptor unchanged.

```
function readonly({ descriptor, ...rest }) {
  return {
    ...rest,
    descriptor: {
      ...descriptor,
      writable: false
    }
  }
}
```

Class decorator functions take a `ctor`, which is the class constructor
being decorated; a `heritage` parameter, containing the parent class
when the decorated class extends another class; and a `members` array,
with a list of member descriptors for the class being decorated.

We could implement a class-wide `readonlyMembers` decorator by
reusing the `readonly` member decorator on each member descriptor
for a decorated class, as shown next.

```
function readonlyMembers(ctor, heritage, members) {
  return members.map(member => readonly(member))
}
```

3.4.2 Stacking Decorators and a Warning About Immutability

With all the fluff around immutability you may be tempted to return
a new property descriptor from your decorators, without modifying
the original descriptor. While well-intentioned, this may have an

undesired effect, as it is possible to decorate the same `class` or class member several times.

If any decorators in a piece of code returned an entirely new `descriptor` without taking into consideration the `descriptor` parameter they receive, they'd effectively lose all the decoration that took place before the different descriptor was returned.

We should be careful to write decorators that take into account the supplied `descriptor`. Always create one that's based on the original `descriptor` that's provided as a parameter.

3.4.3 Use Case By Example: Attributes in C#

A long time ago, I was first getting acquainted with C# by way of an Ultima Online[5] server emulator written in open source C# code—RunUO. RunUO was one of the most beautiful codebases I've ever worked with, and it was written in C# to boot.

They distributed the server software as an executable and a series of .cs files. The `runuo` executable would compile those .cs scripts at runtime and dynamically mix them into the application. The result was that you didn't need the Visual Studio IDE (nor `msbuild`), or anything other than just enough programming knowledge to edit one of the "scripts" in those .cs files. All of the above made RunUO the perfect learning environment for the new developer.

RunUO relied heavily on reflection. RunUO's developers made significant efforts to make it customizable by players who were not necessarily invested in programming, but were nevertheless interested in changing a few details of the game, such as how much damage a dragon's fire breath inflicts or how often it shot fireballs. Great developer experience was a big part of their philosophy, and you could create a new kind of `Dragon` just by copying one of the monster files, changing it to inherit from the `Dragon` class, and overriding a few properties to change its color hue, its damage output, and so on.

Just as they made it easy to create new monsters—or "non-player characters" (*NPC* in gaming slang)--they also relied on reflection to provide functionality to in-game administrators. Administrators

---

5 Ultima Online is a decades-old fantasy role playing game based on the Ultima universe.

---

could run an in-game command and click on an item or a monster to visualize or change properties without ever leaving the game.

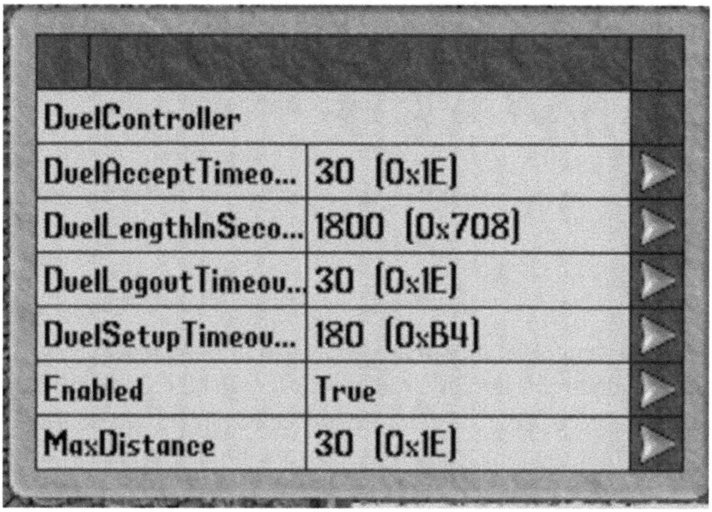

Figure 3-1. Modifying properties for a RunUO item in-game from the Ultima Online client

Not every property in a class is meant to be accessible in-game, though. Some properties are only meant for internal use, or not meant to be modified at runtime. RunUO had a `CommandPropertyAt tribute` decorator,[6] which defined that the property could be modified in-game and let you also specify the access level required to read and write that property. This decorator was used extensively throughout the RunUO codebase.[7]

The `PlayerMobile` class, which governed how a player's character works, is a great place to look at these attributes. `PlayerMobile` has several properties that are accessible in-game[8] to administrators and moderators. Here are a couple of getters and setters, but only the

---

6 The RunUO Git repository has the definition of `CommandPropertyAttribute` for RunUO (*https://mjavascript.com/out/runuo-attributes*).

7 Its use is widespread throughout the codebase, marking over 200 properties in the RunUO core alone (*https://mjavascript.com/out/runuo-commandprops*).

8 You can find quite a few usage examples of the `CommandProperty` attribute in the `Play erMobile.cs` class (*https://mjavascript.com/out/runuo-playermobile*).

first one has the `CommandProperty` attribute—making that property accessible to Game Masters in-game.

```
[CommandProperty(AccessLevel.GameMaster)]
public int Profession
{
  get{ return m_Profession }
  set{ m_Profession = value }
}

public int StepsTaken
{
  get{ return m_StepsTaken }
  set{ m_StepsTaken = value }
}
```

One interesting difference between C# attributes and JavaScript decorators is that reflection in C# allows us to pull all custom attributes from an object using `MemberInfo#getCustomAttributes`. RunUO leverages that method to pull up information about each property that should be accessible in-game when displaying the dialog that lets an administrator view or modify an in-game object's properties.

3.4.4 Marking Properties in JavaScript

In JavaScript, there's no such thing—not in the existing proposal draft, at least—to get the custom attributes on a property. That said, JavaScript is a highly dynamic language, and creating this sort of "labels" wouldn't be much of a hassle. Decorating a `Dog` with a "command property" wouldn't be all that different from RunUO and C#.

```
class Dog {
  @commandProperty('game-master')
  name;
}
```

The `commandProperty` function would need to be a little more sophisticated than its C# counterpart. Given that there is no reflection around JavaScript decorators[9], we could use a runtime-wide symbol to keep around an array of command properties for any given class.

---

9 Reflection around JavaScript decorators is not being considered for JavaScript at this time, as it'd involve engines keeping more metadata in memory. We can, however, use symbols and lists to get around the need for native reflection.

```
function commandProperty(writeLevel, readLevel = writeLevel) {
  return ({ key, ...rest }) => ({
    key,
    ...rest,
    finisher(ctor) {
      const symbol = Symbol.for('commandProperties')
      const commandPropertyDescriptor = {
        key,
        readLevel,
        writeLevel
      }
      if (!ctor[symbol]) {
        ctor[symbol] = []
      }
      ctor[symbol].push(commandPropertyDescriptor)
    }
  })
}
```

A `Dog` class could have as many command properties as we deemed necessary, and each would be listed behind a symbol property. To find the command properties for any given class, all we'd have to do is use the following function, which retrieves a list of command properties from the symbol property, and offers a default value of []. We always return a copy of the original list to prevent consumers from accidentally making changes to it.

```
function getCommandProperties(ctor) {
  const symbol = Symbol.for('commandProperties')
  const properties = ctor[symbol] || []
  return [...properties]
}
getCommandProperties(Dog)
// <- [{ key: 'name', readLevel: 'game-master',
// writeLevel: 'game-master' }]
```

We could then iterate over known safe command properties and render a way of modifying those during runtime, through a simple UI. Instead of maintaining long lists of properties that can be modified, relying on some sort of heuristics bound to break from time to time, or using some sort of restrictive naming convention, decorators are the cleanest way to implement a protocol where we mark properties as special for some particular use case.

In the following chapter we'll look at more features coming in ES6 and how they can be used to iterate over any JavaScript objects, as well as how to master flow control using promises and generators.

CHAPTER 4

Iteration and Flow Control

Having covered the essential aspects of ES6 in Chapter 2, and symbols in Chapter 3, we're now in great shape to understand promises, iterators, and generators. Promises offer a different way of attacking asynchronous code flows. Iterators dictate how an object is iterated, producing the sequence of values that gets iterated over. Generators can be used to write code that looks sequential but works asynchronously, in the background, as we'll learn toward the end of the chapter.

To kick off the chapter, we'll start by discussing promises. Promises have existed in user-land for a long time, but they're a native part of the language starting in ES6.

4.1 Promises

Promises can be vaguely defined as "a proxy for a value that will eventually become available." While we can write synchronous code inside promises, promise-based code flows in a strictly asynchronous manner. Promises can make asynchronous flows easier to reason about—once you've mastered promises, that is.

4.1.1 Getting Started with Promises

As an example, let's take a look at the new `fetch` API for the browser. This API is a simplification of `XMLHttpRequest`. It aims to be super simple to use for the most basic use cases: making a `GET` request against an HTTP resource. It provides an extensive API that caters to advanced use cases, but that's not our focus for now. In its most basic incarnation, you can make a GET /items HTTP request using a piece of code like the following.

```
fetch('/items')
```

The fetch('/items') statement doesn't seem all that exciting. It makes a "fire and forget" GET request against /items, meaning you ignore the response and whether the request succeeded. The fetch method returns a Promise. You can chain a callback using the .then method on that promise, and that callback will be executed once the /items resource finishes loading, receiving a response object parameter.

```
fetch('/items').then(response => {
  // do something
})
```

The following bit of code displays the promise-based API with which fetch is actually implemented in browsers. Calls to fetch return a Promise object. Much like with events, you can bind as many reactions as you'd like, using the .then and .catch methods.

```
const p = fetch('/items')
p.then(res => {
  // handle response
})
p.catch(err => {
  // handle error
})
```

Reactions passed to .then can be used to handle the fulfillment of a promise, which is accompanied by a fulfillment value; and reactions passed to .catch are executed with a rejection reason that can be used when handling rejections. You can also register a reaction to rejections in the second argument passed to .then. The previous piece of code could also be expressed as the following.

```
const p = fetch('/items')
p.then(
  res => {
    // handle response
  },
  err => {
    // handle error
  }
)
```

Another alternative is to omit the fulfillment reaction in `.then(ful fillment, rejection)`, this being similar to the omission of a rejection reaction when calling `.then`. Using `.then(null, rejec tion)` is equivalent to `.catch(rejection)`, as shown in the following snippet of code.

```
const p = fetch('/items')
p.then(res => {
  // handle response
})
p.then(null, err => {
  // handle error
})
```

Promises as an Alternative to Callbacks and Events

Traditionally JavaScript relied on callbacks instead of promises and chaining. If the `fetch` function asked for a callback, you'd have to add one that would then get executed whenever the `fetch` operation ends. Typical asynchronous code flow conventions in Node.js established a best practice of reserving the first parameter in the callback for errors—that may or may not occur—during the fetching process. The rest of the parameters can be used to read the results of the asynchronous operation. Most commonly, a single data parameter is used. The next bit of code shows how `fetch` would look if it had a callback-based API.

```
fetch('/items', (err, res) => {
  if (err) {
    // handle error
  } else {
    // handle response
  }
})
```

The callback wouldn't be invoked until the `/items` resource has been retrieved, or an error arises from the `fetch` operation. Execution remains asynchronous and nonblocking. Note that in this model you could only specify a single callback. That callback would be responsible for all functionality derived from the response, and it'd be up to the consumer to come up with a mechanism to compose different aspects of handling the response into that single callback.

Besides traditional callbacks, another API design choice might have been to use an event-driven model. In this case the object returned by `fetch` would be able to register callbacks for different kinds of events, binding as many event handlers as needed for any events—just like when you attach event listeners to the browser DOM. Typically there's an `error` event that's raised when things go awry, and other events that are raised when something notable happens. In the following piece of code, we show how `fetch` would look if it had an event-based API.

```
fetch('/items')
  .on('error', err => {
    // handle error
  })
  .on('data', res => {
    // handle response
  })
```

Binding several listeners for each type of event would eliminate the concern we had earlier about having to centralize response handling in a single callback. Events, however, make it hard to chain callbacks and have them fire when another asynchronous task is fulfilled, and that's where promises come in. Moreover, events are better suited to handle streams of values, making them somewhat inappropriate in this particular use case. Section 9.7, "Asynchronous Code Flows," on page 304 discusses proper asynchronous code flow design in more detail, expanding on which kinds of constructs are better suited for which kinds of code flows.

When it comes to promises, chaining is a major source of confusion. In an event-based API, chaining is made possible by having the `.on` method attach the event listener and then returning the event emitter itself. Promises are different. The `.then` and `.catch` methods return a new promise every time. That's important because chaining can have wildly different results depending on where you append a `.then` or a `.catch` call.

Visualizing Promise Chains: A Major Source of Confusion

The `.then` and `.catch` methods return a new promise every time, creating a tree-like data structure. If you had a `p1` promise and a `p2` promise returned by `p1.then`, the `p1` and `p2` promises would be nodes connected by the `p1.then` reaction handler. Reactions create new promises that are attached to the tree as children of the promise they're reacting to.

When we chain promises, we need to understand that p1.then(r1).then(r2) creates two new p2 and p3 promises. The second reaction, r2, is going to fire if p2 fulfills, while the r1 reaction will fire when p1 is fulfilled. When we have a statement such as p1.then(r1); p1.then(r2), in contrast, both r1 and r2 will fire if p1 is fulfilled. A discrepancy occurs when p1 fulfills but p2 doesn't.

Figuring out the tree-like nature of promises is the key to unlocking a deep understanding of how promises behave. To this end, I've created an online tool called Promisees (*https://mjavascript.com/out/ promisees*) you can use to play around with promise chains while visualizing the tree structure they leave behind, as shown in Figure 4-1.

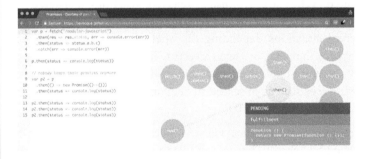

Figure 4-1. Promisees lets you write a piece of code and visualize how the underlying graph evolves as promises are settled in fulfillment or rejection

A promise is created by passing the Promise constructor a resolver that decides how and when the promise is settled, by calling either a resolve method that will settle the promise in fulfillment or a reject method that'd settle the promise as a rejection. Until the promise is settled by calling either function, it'll be in a pending state and any reactions attached to it won't be executed. The following snippet of code creates a promise from scratch where we'll wait for a second before randomly settling the promise with a fulfillment or rejection result.

```
new Promise(function (resolve, reject) {
  setTimeout(function () {
    if (Math.random() > 0.5) {
```

```
        resolve('random success')
      } else {
        reject(new Error('random failure'))
      }
    }, 1000)
  })
```

Promises can also be created using `Promise.resolve` and `Promise.reject`. These methods create promises that will immediately settle with a fulfillment value and a rejection reason, respectively.

```
Promise
  .resolve({ result: 123 })
  .then(data => console.log(data.result))
// <- 123
```

When a p promise is fulfilled, reactions registered with `p.then` are executed. When a p promise is rejected, reactions registered with `p.catch` are executed. Those reactions can, in turn, result in three different situations depending on whether they return a value, a `Promise`, a thenable, or throw an error. *Thenables* are objects considered promise-like that can be cast into a `Promise` using `Promise.resolve` as observed in Section 4.1.3, "Creating a Promise from Scratch," on page 100.

A reaction may return a value, which would cause the promise returned by `.then` to become fulfilled with that value. In this sense, promises can be chained to transform the fulfillment value of the previous promise over and over, as shown in the following snippet of code.

```
Promise
  .resolve(2)
  .then(x => x * 7)
  .then(x => x - 3)
  .then(x => console.log(x))
// <- 11
```

A reaction may return a promise. In contrast with the previous piece of code, the promise returned by the first `.then` call in the following snippet will be blocked until the one returned by its reaction is fulfilled, which will take two seconds to settle because of the `setTime out` call.

```
Promise
  .resolve(2)
  .then(x => new Promise(function (resolve) {
```

```
    setTimeout(() => resolve(x * 1000), x * 1000)
  }))
  .then(x => console.log(x))
// <- 2000
```

A reaction may also throw an error, which would cause the promise returned by .then to become rejected and thus follow the .catch branch, using said error as the rejection reason. The following example shows how we attach a fulfillment reaction to the fetch operation. Once the fetch is fulfilled the reaction will throw an error and cause the rejection reaction attached to the promise returned by .then to be executed.

```
const p = fetch('/items')
  .then(res => { throw new Error('unexpectedly') })
  .catch(err => console.error(err))
```

Let's take a step back and pace ourselves, walking over more examples in each particular use case.

4.1.2 Promise Continuation and Chaining

In the previous section we've established that you can chain any number of .then calls, each returning its own new promise, but how exactly does this work? What is a good mental model of promises, and what happens when an error is raised?

When an error happens in a promise resolver, you can catch that error using p.catch as shown next.

```
new Promise((resolve, reject) => reject(new Error('oops')))
  .catch(err => console.error(err))
```

A promise will settle as a rejection when the resolver calls reject, but also if an exception is thrown inside the resolver as well, as demonstrated by the next snippet.

```
new Promise((resolve, reject) => { throw new Error('oops') })
  .catch(err => console.error(err))
```

Errors that occur while executing a fulfillment or rejection reaction behave in the same way: they result in a promise being rejected, the one returned by the .then or .catch call that was passed the reaction where the error originated. It's easier to explain this with code, such as the following piece.

```
Promise
  .resolve(2)
  .then(x => { throw new Error('failed') })
  .catch(err => console.error(err))
```

It might be easier to decompose that series of chained method calls into variables, as shown next. The following piece of code might help you visualize the fact that, if you attached the .catch reaction to p1, you wouldn't be able to catch the error originated in the .then reaction. While p1 is fulfilled, p2—a different promise than p1, resulting from calling p1.then—is rejected due to the error being thrown. That error could be caught, instead, if we attached the rejection reaction to p2.

```
const p1 = Promise.resolve(2)
const p2 = p1.then(x => { throw new Error('failed') })
const p3 = p2.catch(err => console.error(err))
```

Here is another situation where it might help you to think of promises as a tree-like data structure. In Figure 4-2 it becomes clear that, given the error originates in the p2 node, we couldn't notice it by attaching a rejection reaction to p1.

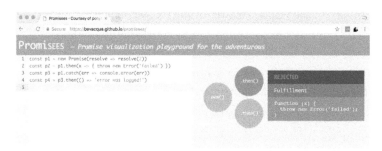

Figure 4-2. Understanding the tree structure of promises reveals that rejection reactions can only catch errors that arise in a given branch of promise-based code.

In order for the reaction to handle the rejection in p2, we'd have to attach the reaction to p2 instead, as shown in Figure 4-3.

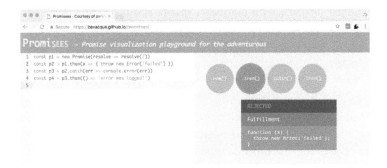

Figure 4-3. By attaching a rejection handler on the branch where an error is produced, we're able to handle the rejection.

We've established that the promise you attach your reactions onto is important, as it determines what errors it can capture and what errors it cannot. It's also worth noting that as long as an error remains uncaught in a promise chain, a rejection handler will be able to capture it. In the following example we've introduced an intermediary .then call in between p2, where the error originated, and p4, where we attach the rejection reaction. When p2 settles with a rejection, p3 becomes settled with a rejection, as it depends on p2 directly. When p3 settles with a rejection, the rejection handler in p4 fires.

```
const p1 = Promise.resolve(2)
const p2 = p1.then(x => { throw new Error('failed') })
const p3 = p2.then(x => x * 2)
const p4 = p3.catch(err => console.error(err))
```

Typically, promises like p4 fulfill because the rejection handler in .catch doesn't raise any errors. That means a fulfillment handler attached with p4.then would be executed afterwards. The following example shows how you could print a statement to the browser console by creating a p4 fulfillment handler that depends on p3 to settle successfully with fulfillment.

```
const p1 = Promise.resolve(2)
const p2 = p1.then(x => { throw new Error('failed') })
const p3 = p2.catch(err => console.error(err))
const p4 = p3.then(() => console.log('crisis averted'))
```

Similarly, if an error occurred in the p3 rejection handler, we could capture that one as well using .catch. The next piece of code shows how an exception being thrown in p3 could be captured using p3.catch just like with any other errors arising in previous examples.

```
const p1 = Promise.resolve(2)
const p2 = p1.then(x => { throw new Error('failed') })
const p3 = p2.catch(err => { throw new Error('oops') })
const p4 = p3.catch(err => console.error(err))
```

The following example prints err.message once instead of twice. That's because no errors happened in the first .catch, so the rejection branch for that promise wasn't executed.

```
fetch('/items')
  .then(res => res.a.prop.that.does.not.exist)
  .catch(err => console.error(err.message))
  .catch(err => console.error(err.message))
// <- 'Cannot read property "prop" of undefined'
```

In contrast, the next snippet will print err.message twice. It works by saving a reference to the promise returned by .then, and then tacking two .catch reactions onto it. The second .catch in the previous example was capturing errors produced in the promise returned from the first .catch, while in this case both rejection handlers branch off of p.

```
const p = fetch('/items').then(res =>
  res.a.prop.that.does.not.exist
)
p.catch(err => console.error(err.message))
p.catch(err => console.error(err.message))
// <- 'Cannot read property "prop" of undefined'
// <- 'Cannot read property "prop" of undefined'
```

We should observe, then, that promises can be chained arbitrarily. As we just saw, you can save a reference to any point in the promise chain and then append more promises on top of it. This is one of the fundamental points to understanding promises.

Let's use the following snippet as a crutch to enumerate the sequence of events that arise from creating and chaining a few promises. Take a moment to inspect the following bit of code.

```
const p1 = fetch('/items')
const p2 = p1.then(res => res.a.prop.that.does.not.exist)
const p3 = p2.catch(err => {})
const p4 = p3.catch(err => console.error(err.message))
```

Here is an enumeration of what is going on as that piece of code is executed:

1. fetch returns a brand new p1 promise.

2. p1.then returns a brand new p2 promise, which will react if p1 is fulfilled.

3. p2.catch returns a brand new p3 promise, which will react if p2 is rejected.

4. p3.catch returns a brand new p4 promise, which will react if p3 is rejected.

5. When p1 is fulfilled, the p1.then reaction is executed.

6. Afterwards, p2 is rejected because of an error in the p1.then reaction.

7. Since p2 was rejected, p2.catch reactions are executed, and the p2.then branch is ignored.

8. The p3 promise from p2.catch is fulfilled, because it doesn't produce an error or result in a rejected promise.

9. Because p3 was fulfilled, the p3.catch is never followed. The p3.then branch would've been used instead.

You should think of promises as a tree structure. This bears repetition: you should think of promises as a tree structure.[1] Let's reinforce this concept with Figure 4-4.

```
1 const p1 = fetch('/items')
2 const p2 = p1.then(res => res.a.prop.that.does.not.exist)
3 const p3 = p2.catch(err => {})
4 const p4 = p3.catch(err => console.error(err.message))
5 |
```

Figure 4-4. Given the tree structure, we realize that p3 is fulfilled, as it doesn't produce an exception nor is it rejected. For that reason, p4 can never follow the rejection branch, given its parent was fulfilled.

It all starts with a single promise, which we'll next learn how to construct. Then you add branches with .then or .catch. You can tack

---

1 I wrote an online visualization tool called Promisees where you can see the tree structure underlying a Promise chain (*https://mjavascript.com/out/promisees*).

as many `.then` or `.catch` calls as you want onto each branch, creating new branches and so on.

4.1.3 Creating a Promise from Scratch

We already know that promises can be created using a function such as `fetch`, `Promise.resolve`, `Promise.reject`, or the `Promise` constructor function. We've already used `fetch` extensively to create promises in previous examples. Let's take a more nuanced look at the other three ways we can create a promise.

Promises can be created from scratch by using `new Promise(resolver)`. The `resolver` parameter is a function that will be used to settle the promise. The `resolver` takes two arguments: a `resolve` function and a `reject` function.

The pair of promises shown in the next snippet are settled in fulfillment and rejection, respectively. Here we're settling the first promise with a fulfillment value of `'result'`, and rejecting the second promise with an `Error` object, specifying `'reason'` as its message.

```
new Promise(resolve => resolve('result'))
new Promise((resolve, reject) => reject(new Error('reason')))
```

Resolving and rejecting promises without a value is possible, but not that useful. Usually promises will fulfill with a `result` such as the response from an Ajax call, as we've seen with `fetch`. You'll definitely want to state the `reason` for your rejections—typically wrapping them in an `Error` object so that you can report back a stack trace.

As you may have guessed, there's nothing inherently synchronous about promise resolvers. Settlement can be completely asynchronous for fulfillment and rejection alike. Even if the resolver calls `resolve` right away, the result won't trickle down to reactions until the next tick. That's the whole point of promises! The following example creates a promise that becomes fulfilled after two seconds elapse.

```
new Promise(resolve => setTimeout(resolve, 2000))
```

Note that only the first call made to one of these functions will have an impact—once a promise is settled its outcome can't change. The following code snippet creates a promise that's fulfilled after the provided `delay` or rejected after a three-second timeout. We're taking advantage of the fact that calling either of these functions after a promise has been settled has no effect, in order to create a race condition where the first call to be made will be the one that sticks.

```
function resolveUnderThreeSeconds(delay) {
  return new Promise(function (resolve, reject) {
    setTimeout(resolve, delay)
    setTimeout(reject, 3000)
  })
}
resolveUnderThreeSeconds(2000) // becomes fulfilled after 2s
resolveUnderThreeSeconds(7000) // becomes rejected after 3s
```

When creating a new promise p1, you could call `resolve` with another promise p2—besides calling `resolve` with nonpromise values. In those cases, p1 will be resolved but blocked on the outcome of p2. Once p2 settles, p1 will be settled with its value and outcome. The following bit of code is, thus, effectively the same as simply doing `fetch('/items')`.

```
new Promise(resolve => resolve(fetch('/items')))
```

Note that this behavior is only possible when using `resolve`. If you try to replicate the same behavior with `reject` you'll find that the p1 promise is rejected with the p2 promise as the rejection `reason`. While `resolve` may result in a promise being fulfilled or rejected, `reject` always results in the promise being rejected. If you `resolve` to a rejected promise or a promise that's eventually rejected, then your promise will be rejected as well. The opposite isn't true for rejections. If you `reject` in a resolver, the promise will be rejected no matter what value is passed into `reject`.

In some cases you'll know beforehand about a value you want to settle a promise with. In these cases you could create a promise from scratch, as shown next. This can be convenient when you want to set off the benefits of promise chaining, but don't otherwise have a clear initiator that returns a `Promise`—such as a call to `fetch`.

```
new Promise(resolve => resolve(12))
```

That could prove to be too verbose when you don't need anything other than a pre-settled promise. You could use `Promise.resolve` instead, as a shortcut. The following statement is equivalent to the previous one. The differences between this statement and the previous one are purely semantics: you avoid declaring a `resolver` function and the syntax is more friendly to promise continuation and chaining when it comes to readability.

```
Promise.resolve(12)
```

Like in the `resolve(fetch)` case we saw earlier, you could use `Promise.resolve` as a way of wrapping another promise or casting a thenable into a proper promise. The following piece of code shows how you could use `Promise.resolve` to cast a thenable into a proper promise and then consume it as if it were any other promise.

```
Promise
  .resolve({ then: resolve => resolve(12) })
  .then(x => console.log(x))
// <- 12
```

When you already know the rejection reason for a promise, you can use `Promise.reject`. The following piece of code creates a promise that's going to settle into a rejection along with the specified reason. You can use `Promise.reject` within a reaction as a dynamic alternative to `throw` statements. Another use for `Promise.reject` is as an implicit return value for an arrow function, something that can't be done with a `throw` statements.

```
Promise.reject(reason)
fetch('/items').then(() =>
  Promise.reject(new Error('arbitrarily'))
)
fetch('/items').then(() => { throw new Error('arbitrarily')}})
```

Presumably, you won't be calling `new Promise` directly very often. The promise constructor is often invoked internally by libraries that support promises or native functions like `fetch`. Given that `.then` and `.catch` provide tree structures that unfold beyond the original promise, a single call to `new Promise` in the entry point to an API is often sufficient. Regardless, understanding promise creation is essential when leveraging promise-based control flows.

4.1.4 Promise States and Fates

Promises can be in three distinct states: pending, fulfilled, and rejected. Pending is the default state. A promise can then transition into either fulfillment or rejection.

A promise can be resolved or rejected exactly once. Attempting to resolve or reject a promise for a second time won't have any effect.

When a promise is resolved with a nonpromise, nonthenable value, it settles in fulfillment. When a promise is rejected, it's also considered to be settled.

A promise p1 that's resolved to another promise or thenable p2 stays in the pending state, but is nevertheless resolved: it can't be resolved again nor rejected. When p2 settles, its outcome is forwarded to p1, which becomes settled as well.

Once a promise is fulfilled, reactions that were attached with p.then will be executed as soon as possible. The same goes for rejected promises and p.catch reactions. Reactions attached after a promise is settled are also executed as soon as possible.

The contrived example shown next could be used to explain how you can make a fetch request, and create a second fetch promise in a .then reaction to the first request. The second request will only begin when and if the first promise settles in fulfillment. The con sole.log statement will only begin when and if the second promise settles in fulfillment, printing done to the console.

```
fetch('/items')
  .then(() => fetch('/item/first'))
  .then(() => console.log('done'))
```

A less contrived example would involve other steps. In the following piece of code we use the outcome of the first fetch request in order to construct the second request. To do that, we use the res.json method, which returns a promise that resolves to the object from parsing a JSON response. Then we use that object to construct the endpoint we want to request in our second call to fetch, and finally we print the item object from the second response to the console.

```
fetch('/items')
  .then(res => res.json())
  .then(items => fetch(`/item/${ items[0].slug }`))
  .then(res => res.json())
  .then(item => console.log(item))
```

We're not limited to returning promises or thenables. We could also return values from .then and .catch reactions. Those values would be passed to the next reaction in the chain. In this sense, a reaction can be regarded as the transformation of input from the previous reaction in the chain into the input for the next reaction in the chain. The following example starts by creating a promise fulfilled with [1, 2, 3]. Then there's a reaction that maps those values into

[2, 4, 6]. Those values are then printed to the console in the following reaction in the chain.

```
Promise
  .resolve([1, 2, 3])
  .then(values => values.map(value => value * 2))
  .then(values => console.log(values))
  // <- [2, 4, 6]
```

Note that you can transform data in rejection branches as well. Keep in mind that, as we first learned in Section 4.1.3, "Creating a Promise from Scratch," on page 100, when a .catch reaction executes without errors and doesn't return a rejected promise either, it will fulfill, following .then reactions.

4.1.5 Promise#finally Proposal

There's a TC39 proposal[2] for a Promise#finally method, which would invoke a reaction when a promise settles, regardless of whether it was fulfilled or rejected.

We can think of the following bit of code as a rough ponyfill for Promise#finally. We pass the reaction callback to p.then as both a fulfillment reaction and a rejection reaction.

```
function finally(p, fn) {
  return p.then(
    fn,
    fn
  )
}
```

There are a few semantic differences involved. For one, reactions passed to Promise#finally don't receive any arguments, since the promise could've settled as either a fulfillment value or a rejection reason. Typically, Promise#finally variants in user-land are used for use cases such as hiding a loading spinner that was shown before a fetch request and other cleanup, where we don't need access to the promise's settlement value. The following snippet has an updated ponyfill which doesn't pass any arguments to either reaction.

```
function finally(p, fn) {
  return p.then(
```

---

2 This proposal is in stage 2 at the time of this writing. You can find the proposal draft at GitHub (*https://mjavascript.com/out/proposal-promise-finally*).

```
      () => fn(),
      () => fn()
  )
}
```

Reactions passed to `Promise#finally` resolve to the result of the parent promise.

```
const p1 = Promise.resolve('value')
const p2 = p1.finally(() => {})
const p3 = p2.then(data => console.log(data))
// <- 'value'
```

This is unlike `p.then(fn, fn)`, which would produce a new fulfillment value unless it's explicitly forwarded in the reaction, as shown next.

```
const p1 = Promise.resolve('value')
const p2 = p1.then(() => {}, () => {})
const p3 = p2.then(data => console.log(data))
// <- undefined
```

The following code listing has a complete ponyfill for `Promise#finally`.

```
function finally(p, fn) {
  return p.then(
    result => resolve(fn()).then(() => result),
    err => resolve(fn()).then(() => Promise.reject(err))
  )
}
```

Note that if the reaction passed to `Promise#finally` is rejected or throws, then the promise returned by `Promise#finally` will settle with that rejection reason, as shown next.

```
const p1 = Promise.resolve('value')
const p2 = p1.finally(() => Promise.reject('oops'))
const p3 = p2.catch(err => console.log(err))
// <- 'oops'
```

As we can observe after carefully reading the code for our ponyfill, if either reaction results in an exception being thrown then the promise would be rejected. At the same time, returning a rejected promise via `Promise.reject` or some other means would imply `resolve(fn())` results in a rejected promise, which won't follow the `.then` reactions used to return the original settlement value of the promise we're calling `.finally` on.

4.1.6 Leveraging Promise.all and Promise.race

When writing asynchronous code flows, there are pairs of tasks where one of them depends on the outcome of another, so they must run in series. There are also pairs of tasks that don't need to know the outcome of each other in order to run, so they can be executed concurrently. Promises already excel at asynchronous series flows, as a single promise can trigger a chain of events that happen one after another. Promises also offer a couple of solutions for concurrent tasks, in the form of two API methods: `Promise.all` and `Promise.race`.

In most cases you'll want code that can be executed concurrently to take advantage of that, as it could make your code run much faster. Suppose you wanted to pull the description of two products in your catalog, using two distinct API calls, and then print out both of them to the console. The following piece of code would run both operations concurrently, but it would need separate print statements. In the case of printing to the console, that wouldn't make much of a difference, but if we needed to make single function call passing in both products, we couldn't do that with two separate `fetch` requests.

```
fetch('/products/chair')
  .then(r => r.json())
  .then(p => console.log(p))
fetch('/products/table')
  .then(r => r.json())
  .then(p => console.log(p))
```

The `Promise.all` method takes an array of promises and returns a single promise p. When all promises passed to `Promise.all` are fulfilled, p becomes fulfilled as well with an array of results sorted according to the provided promises. If a single promise becomes rejected, p settles with its rejection reason immediately. The following example uses `Promise.all` to fetch both products and print them to the console using a single `console.log` statement.

```
Promise
  .all([
    fetch('/products/chair'),
    fetch('/products/table')
  ])
  .then(products => console.log(products[0], products[1]))
```

Given that the results are provided as an array, its indices have no semantic meaning to our code. Using parameter destructuring to pull out variable names for each product might make more sense when reading the code. The following example uses destructuring to clean that up. Keep in mind that even though there's a single argument, destructuring forces us to use parentheses in the arrow function parameter declaration.

```
Promise
  .all([
    fetch('/products/chair'),
    fetch('/products/table')
  ])
  .then(([chair, table]) => console.log(chair, table))
```

The following example shows how if a single promise is rejected, p will be rejected as well. It's important to understand that, as a single rejected promise might prevent an otherwise fulfilled array of promises from fulfilling p. In the example, rather than wait until p2 and p3 settle, p becomes immediately rejected.

```
const p1 = Promise.reject('failed')
const p2 = fetch('/products/chair')
const p3 = fetch('/products/table')
const p = Promise
  .all([p1, p2, p3])
  .catch(err => console.log(err))
  // <- 'failed'
```

In summary, Promise.all has three possible outcomes:

- Settle with all fulfillment results as soon as all of its dependencies are fulfilled
- Settle with a single rejection reason as soon as one of its dependencies is rejected
- Stay in a pending state because at least one dependency stays in pending state and no dependencies are rejected

The Promise.race method is similar to Promise.all, except the first dependency to settle will "win" the race, and its result will be passed along to the promise returned by Promise.race.

```
Promise
  .race([
    new Promise(resolve => setTimeout(() => resolve(1), 1000)),
    new Promise(resolve => setTimeout(() => resolve(2), 2000))
  ])
```

```
  .then(result => console.log(result))
  // <- 1
```

Rejections will also finish the race, and the resulting promise will be rejected. Using `Promise.race` could be useful in scenarios where we want to time out a promise we otherwise have no control over. For instance, in the following piece of code there's a race between a `fetch` request and a promise that becomes rejected after a five-second timeout. If the request takes more than five seconds, the race will be rejected.

```
function timeout(delay) {
  return new Promise(function (resolve, reject) {
    setTimeout(() => reject('timeout'), delay)
  })
}
Promise
  .race([
    fetch('/large-resource-download'),
    timeout(5000)
  ])
  .then(res => console.log(res))
  .catch(err => console.log(err))
```

4.2 Iterator Protocol and Iterable Protocol

JavaScript gets two new protocols in ES6: iterators and iterables. These two protocols are used to define iteration behavior for any object. We'll start by learning about how to turn an object into an iterable sequence. Later, we'll look into laziness and how iterators can define infinite sequences. Lastly, we'll go over practical considerations while defining iterables.

4.2.1 Understanding Iteration Principles

Any object can adhere to the iterable protocol by assigning a function to the `Symbol.iterator` property for that object. Whenever an object needs to be iterated its iterable protocol method, assigned to `Symbol.iterator`, is called once.

The spread operator was first introduced in Chapter 2, and it's one of a few language features in ES6 that leverage iteration protocols. When using the spread operator on a hypothetical `iterable` object, as shown in the following code snippet, `Symbol.iterator` would be asked for an object that adheres to the iterator protocol. The returned iterator will be used to obtain values out of the object.

```
const sequence = [...iterable]
```

As you might remember, symbol properties can't be directly embedded into object literal keys. The following bit of code shows how you'd add a symbol property using pre-ES6 language semantics.

```
const example = {}
example[Symbol.iterator] = fn
```

We could, however, use a computed property name to fit the symbol key in the object literal, avoiding an extra statement like the one in the previous snippet, as demonstrated next.

```
const example = {
  [Symbol.iterator]: fn
}
```

The method assigned to `Symbol.iterator` must return an object that adheres to the iterator protocol. That protocol defines how to get values out of an iterable sequence. The protocol dictates iterators must be objects with a `next` method. The `next` method takes no arguments and should return an object with these two properties found below:

- `value` is the current item in the sequence

- `done` is a Boolean indicating whether the sequence has ended

Let's use the following piece of code as a crutch to understand the concepts behind iteration protocols. We're turning the `sequence` object into an iterable by adding a `Symbol.iterator` property. The iterable returns an iterator object. Each time `next` is asked for the following value in the sequence, an element from the `items` array is provided. When `i` goes beyond the last index on the `items` array, we return `done: true`, indicating the sequence has ended.

```
const items = ['i', 't', 'e', 'r', 'a', 'b', 'l', 'e']
const sequence = {
  [Symbol.iterator]() {
    let i = 0
    return {
      next() {
        const value = items[i]
        i++
        const done = i > items.length
        return { value, done }
```

```
        }
      }
    }
  }
```

JavaScript is a progressive language: new features are additive, and they practically never break existing code. For that reason, iterables can't be taken advantage of in existing constructs such as forEach and for..in. In ES6, there are a few ways to go over iterables: for..of, the ... spread operator, and Array.from.

The for..of iteration method can be used to loop over any iterable. The following example demonstrates how we could use for..of to loop over the sequence object we put together in the previous example, because it is an iterable object.

```
for (const item of sequence) {
  console.log(item)
  // <- 'i'
  // <- 't'
  // <- 'e'
  // <- 'r'
  // <- 'a'
  // <- 'b'
  // <- 'l'
  // <- 'e'
}
```

Regular objects can be made iterable with Symbol.iterator, as we've just learned. Under the ES6 paradigm, constructs like Array, String, NodeList in the DOM, and arguments are all iterable by default, giving for..of increased usability. To get an array out of any iterable sequence of values, you could use the spread operator, spreading every item in the sequence onto an element in the resulting array. We could also use Array.from to the same effect. In addition, Array.from can also cast array-like objects, those with a length property and items in zero-based integer properties, into arrays.

```
console.log([...sequence])
// <- ['i', 't', 'e', 'r', 'a', 'b', 'l', 'e']
console.log(Array.from(sequence))
// <- ['i', 't', 'e', 'r', 'a', 'b', 'l', 'e']
console.log(Array.from({ 0: 'a', 1: 'b', 2: 'c', length: 3 }))
// <- ['a', 'b', 'c']
```

As a recap, the sequence object adheres to the iterable protocol by assigning a method to [Symbol.iterator]. That means that the object is iterable: it can be iterated. Said method returns an object that adheres to the `iterator` protocol. The iterator method is called once whenever we need to start iterating over the object, and the returned iterator is used to pull values out of `sequence`. To iterate over iterables, we can use `for..of`, the spread operator, or `Array.from`.

In essence, the selling point about these protocols is that they provide expressive ways to effortlessly iterate over collections and array-likes. Having the ability to define how any object may be iterated is huge, because it enables libraries to converge under a protocol the language natively understands: iterables. The upside is that implementing the iterator protocol doesn't have a high-effort cost because, due to its additive nature, it won't break existing behavior.

For example, jQuery and `document.querySelectorAll` both return array-likes. If jQuery implemented the iterator protocol on their collection's prototype, then you could iterate over collection elements using the native `for..of` construct.

```
for (const element of $('li')) {
  console.log(element)
  // <- a <li> in the jQuery collection
}
```

Iterable sequences aren't necessarily finite. They may have an uncountable amount of elements. Let's delve into that topic and its implications.

4.2.2 Infinite Sequences

Iterators are lazy in nature. Elements in an iterator sequence are generated one at a time, even when the sequence is finite. Note that infinite sequences couldn't be represented without the laziness property. An infinite sequence can't be represented as an array, meaning that using the spread operator or `Array.from` to cast a sequence into an array would crash JavaScript execution, as we'd go into an infinite loop.

The following example shows an iterator that represents an infinite sequence of random floating numbers between 0 and 1. Note how items returned by `next` don't ever have a `done` property set to `true`, which would signal that the sequence has ended. It uses a pair of arrow functions that implicitly return objects. The first one returns the iterator object used to loop over the infinite sequence of random numbers. The second arrow function is used to pull each individual value in the sequence, using `Math.random`.

```
const random = {
  [Symbol.iterator]: () => ({
    next: () => ({ value: Math.random() })
  })
}
```

Attempting to cast the iterable `random` object into an array using either `Array.from(random)` or `[...random]` would crash our program, since the sequence never ends. We must be very careful with these types of sequences as they can easily crash and burn our browser and Node.js server processes.

There are a few different ways you can access a sequence safely, without risking an infinite loop. The first option is to use destructuring to pull values in specific positions of the sequence, as shown in the following piece of code.

```
const [one, another] = random
console.log(one)
// <- 0.23235511826351285
console.log(another)
// <- 0.28749457537196577
```

Destructuring infinite sequences doesn't scale very well, particularly if we want to apply dynamic conditions, such as pulling the first i values out of the sequence or pulling values until we find one that doesn't match a condition. In those cases we're better off using `for..of`, where we're better able to define conditions that prevent infinite loops while taking as many elements as we need, in a programmatic fashion. The next example loops over our infinite sequence using `for..of`, but it breaks the loop as soon as a value is higher than `0.8`. Given that `Math.random` produces values anywhere between `0` and `1`, the loop will eventually break.

```
for (const value of random) {
  if (value > 0.8) {
    break
  }
  console.log(value)
}
```

It can be hard to understand code like that when reading it later, as a lot of the code is focused on how the sequence is iterated, printing values from `random` until one of those values is large enough.

Abstracting away part of the logic into another method might make the code more readable.

As another example, a common pattern when extracting values from an infinite or very large sequence is to "take" the first few elements in the sequence. While you could accommodate that use case through for..of and break, you'd be better off abstracting it into a take method. The following example shows a potential implementation of take. It receives a sequence parameter and the amount of entries you'd like to take from the sequence. It returns an iterable object, and whenever that object is iterated it constructs an iterator for the provided sequence. The next method defers to the original sequence while the amount is at least 1, and then ends the sequence.

```
function take(sequence, amount) {
  return {
    [Symbol.iterator]() {
      const iterator = sequence[Symbol.iterator]()
      return {
        next() {
          if (amount-- < 1) {
            return { done: true }
          }
          return iterator.next()
        }
      }
    }
  }
}
```

Our implementation works great on infinite sequences because it provides them with a constant exit condition: whenever the amount counter is depleted, the sequence returned by take ends. Instead of looping to pull values out of random, you can now write a piece of code like the following.

```
[...take(random, 2)]
// <- [0.304253100650385, 0.5851333604659885]
```

This pattern allows you to reduce any infinite sequence into a finite one. If your desired finite sequence wasn't just "the first N values," but rather our original "all values before the first one larger than 0.8," you could easily adapt take by changing its exit condition. The range function shown next has a low parameter that defaults to 0, and a high parameter defaulting to 1. Whenever a value in the sequence is out of bounds, we stop pulling values from it.

```
function range(sequence, low = 0, high = 1) {
  return {
    [Symbol.iterator]() {
      const iterator = sequence[Symbol.iterator]()
      return {
        next() {
          const item = iterator.next()
          if (item.value < low || item.value > high) {
            return { done: true }
          }
          return item
        }
      }
    }
  }
}
```

Now, instead of breaking in the `for..of` loop because we fear that the infinite sequence will never end, we guaranteed that the loop will eventually break outside of our desired range. This way, your code becomes less concerned with how the sequence is generated, and more concerned with what the sequence will be used for. As shown in the following example, you won't even need a `for..of` loop here either, because the escape condition now resides in the intermediary range function.

```
const low = [...range(random, 0, 0.8)]
// <- [0.68912092433311, 0.059788614744320, 0.09396195202134]
```

This sort of abstraction of complexity into another function often helps keep code focused on its intent, while striving to avoid a `for..of` loop when all we wanted was to produce a derivated sequence. It also shows how sequences can be composed and piped into one another. In this case, we first created a multipurpose and infinite random sequence, and then piped it through a range function that returns a derivated sequence that ends when it meets values that are below or above a desired range. An important aspect of iterators is that despite having been composed, the iterators produced by the range function can be lazily iterated as well, effectively meaning you can compose as many iterators you need into mapping, filtering, and exit condition helpers.

Identifying Infinite Sequences

Iterators don't have any knowledge that the sequences they produce are infinite. In a similar situation to the famous halting problem (Figure 4-5), there is no way of knowing whether the sequence is infinite or not in code.

```
DEFINE DOES IT HALT (PROGRAM):
{
    RETURN TRUE;
}
```

THE BIG PICTURE SOLUTION
TO THE HALTING PROBLEM

Figure 4-5. The halting problem depicted in an XKCD comic (https://mjavascript.com/out/xkcd-1266)

You typically have a good idea of whether a sequence is infinite or not. Whenever you have an infinite sequence it's up to you to add an escape condition that ensures the program won't crash in an attempt to loop over every single value in the sequence. While for..of won't run into the problem unless there's no escape condition, using mechanisms such as spread or Array.from would immediately result in the program crashing into an infinite loop in the case of infinite sequences.

Besides the technical implications of creating iterable objects, let's go over a couple of practical examples on how we can benefit from iterators.

4.2.3 Iterating Object Maps as Key/Value Pairs

There's an abundance of practical situations that benefit from turning an object into an iterable. Object maps, pseudoarrays that are meant to be iterated, the random number generator we came up with in Section 4.2.2, "Infinite Sequences," on page 111, and classes or plain objects with properties that are often iterated could all turn a profit from following the iterable protocol.

Oftentimes, JavaScript objects are used to represent a map between string keys and arbitrary values. In the next snippet, as an example, we have a map of color names and hexadecimal RGB representations of that color. There are cases when you'd welcome the ability to effortlessly loop over the different color names, hexadecimal representations, or key/value pairs.

```
const colors = {
  green: '#0e0',
  orange: '#f50',
  pink: '#e07'
}
```

The following code snippet implements an iterable that produces a [key, value] sequence for each color in the colors map. Given that that's assigned to the Symbol.iterator property, we'd be able to go over the list with minimal effort.

```
const colors = {
  green: '#0e0',
  orange: '#f50',
  pink: '#e07',
  [Symbol.iterator]() {
    const keys = Object.keys(colors)
    return {
      next() {
        const done = keys.length === 0
        const key = keys.shift()
        return {
          done,
          value: [key, colors[key]]
        }
      }
    }
  }
}
```

When we wanted to pull out all the key/value pairs, we could use the ... spread operator as shown in the following bit of code.

```
console.log([...colors])
// <- [['green', '#0e0'], ['orange', '#f50'], ['pink', '#e07']]
```

The fact that we're polluting our previously tiny colors map with a large iterable definition could represent a problem, as the iterable behavior has little to do with the concern of storing pairs of color names and codes. A good way of decoupling the two aspects of col ors would be to extract the logic that attaches a key/value pair iterator into a reusable function. This way, we could eventually move keyValueIterable somewhere else in our codebase and leverage it for other use cases as well.

```
function keyValueIterable(target) {
  target[Symbol.iterator] = function () {
    const keys = Object.keys(target)
    return {
      next() {
        const done = keys.length === 0
        const key = keys.shift()
        return {
          done,
          value: [key, target[key]]
        }
      }
    }
  }
  return target
}
```

We could then call keyValueIterable passing in the colors object, turning colors into an iterable object. You could in fact use keyVa lueIterable on any objects where you want to iterate over key/value pairs, as the iteration behavior doesn't make assumptions about the object. Once we've attached a Symbol.iterator behavior, we'll be able to treat the object as an iterable. In the next code snippet, we iterate over the key/value pairs and print only the color codes.

```
const colors = keyValueIterable({
  green: '#0e0',
  orange: '#f50',
  pink: '#e07'
})
for (const [ , color] of colors) {
  console.log(color)
  // <- '#0e0'
  // <- '#f50'
  // <- '#e07'
}
```

A song player might be another interesting use case.

4.2.4 Building Versatility Into Iterating a Playlist

Imagine you were developing a song player where a playlist could be reproduced once and then stopped, or be put on repeat and reproduced indefinitely. Whenever you have a use case of looping

---

through a list indefinitely, you could leverage the iterable protocol as well.

Suppose a human adds a few songs to her library, and they are stored in an array as shown in the next bit of code.

```
const songs = [
  'Bad moon rising - Creedence',
  'Don't stop me now - Queen',
  'The Scientist - Coldplay',
  'Somewhere only we know - Keane'
]
```

We could create a `playlist` function that returns a sequence, representing all the songs that will be played by our application. This function would take the `songs` provided by the human as well as the `repeat` value, which indicates how many times she wants the songs to be reproduced in a loop—once, twice, or `Infinity` times—before coming to an end.

The following piece of code shows how we could implement `play list`. We start with an empty playlist and use an `index` number to track where in the song list we are positioned. We return the next song in the list by incrementing the `index`, until there aren't any songs left in the current loop. At this point we decrement the `repeat` counter and reset the `index`. The sequence ends when there aren't any songs left and `repeat` reaches zero.

```
function playlist(songs, repeat) {
  return {
    [Symbol.iterator]() {
      let index = 0
      return {
        next() {
          if (index >= songs.length) {
            repeat--
            index = 0
          }
          if (repeat < 1) {
            return { done: true }
          }
          const song = songs[index]
          index++
          return { done: false, value: song }
        }
      }
    }
  }
}
```

```
    }
  }
```

The following bit of code shows how the `playlist` function can take an array and produce a sequence that goes over the provided array for the specified amount of times. If we specified `Infinity`, the resulting sequence would be infinite, and otherwise it'd be finite.

```
console.log([...playlist(['a', 'b'], 3)])
// <- ['a', 'b', 'a', 'b', 'a', 'b']
```

To iterate over the playlist we'd probably come up with a `player` function. Assuming a `playSong` function that reproduces a song and invokes a callback when the song ends, our `player` implementation could look like the following function, where we asynchronously loop the iterator coming from a sequence, requesting new songs as previous ones finish playback. Given that there's always a considerable waiting period in between `g.next` calls—while the songs are actually playing inside `playSong`—there's little risk of being stuck in an infinite loop that'd crash the runtime, even when the sequence produced by `playlist` is infinite.

```
function player(sequence) {
  const g = sequence()
  more()
  function more() {
    const item = g.next()
    if (item.done) {
      return
    }
    playSong(item.value, more)
  }
}
```

Putting everything together, the music library would play a song list on repeat with a few lines of code, as presented in the next code snippet.

```
const songs = [
  'Bad moon rising - Creedence',
  'Don't stop me now - Queen',
  'The Scientist - Coldplay',
  'Somewhere only we know - Keane'
]
const sequence = playlist(songs, Infinity)
player(sequence)
```

A change allowing the human to shuffle her playlist wouldn't be complicated to introduce. We'd have to tweak the `playlist` function to include a `shuffle` flag, and if that flag is present we'd sort the song list at random.

```
function playlist(inputSongs, repeat, shuffle) {
  const songs = shuffle ? shuffleSongs(inputSongs) : inputSongs
  return {
    [Symbol.iterator]() {
      let index = 0
      return {
        next() {
          if (index >= songs.length) {
            repeat--
            index = 0
          }
          if (repeat < 1) {
            return { done: true }
          }
          const song = songs[index]
          index++
          return { done: false, value: song }
        }
      }
    }
  }
}
function shuffleSongs(songs) {
  return songs.slice().sort(() => Math.random() > 0.5 ? 1 : -1)
}
```

Lastly, we'd have to pass in the `shuffle` flag as `true` if we wanted to shuffle songs in the playlist. Otherwise, songs would be reproduced in the original order provided by the user. Here again we've abstracted away something that usually would involve many lines of code used to decide what song comes next into a neatly decoupled function that's only concerned with producing a sequence of songs to be reproduced by a song player.

```
console.log([...playlist(['a', 'b'], 3, true)])
// <- ['a', 'b', 'b', 'a', 'a', 'b']
```

You may have noticed how the `playlist` function doesn't necessarily need to concern itself with the sort order of the songs passed to it. A better design choice may well be to extract shuffling into the calling code. If we kept the original `playlist` function without a `shuffle` parameter, we could still use a snippet like the following to obtain a shuffled song collection.

```
function shuffleSongs(songs) {
  return songs.slice().sort(() => Math.random() > 0.5 ? 1 : -1)
}
```

```
}
console.log([...playlist(shuffleSongs(['a', 'b']), 3)])
// <- ['a', 'b', 'b', 'a', 'a', 'b']
```

Iterators are an important tool in ES6 that help us not only to decouple code, but also to come up with constructs that were previously harder to implement, such as the ability of dealing with a sequence of songs indistinctly—regardless of whether the sequence is finite or infinite. This indifference is, in part, what makes writing code leveraging the iterator protocol more elegant. It also makes it risky to cast an unknown iterable into an array (with, say, the ... spread operator), as you're risking crashing your program due to an infinite loop.

Generators are an alternative way of creating functions that return an iterable object, without explicitly declaring an object literal with a Symbol.iterator method. They make it easier to implement functions, such as the range or take functions in Section 4.2.2, "Infinite Sequences," on page 111, while also allowing for a few more interesting use cases.

4.3 Generator Functions and Generator Objects

Generators are a new feature in ES6. The way they work is that you declare a generator function that returns generator objects g. Those g objects can then be iterated using any of Array.from(g), [...g], or for..of loops. Generator functions allow you to declare a special kind of iterator. These iterators can suspend execution while retaining their context.

4.3.1 Generator Fundamentals

We already examined iterators in the previous section, learning how their .next() method is called one at a time to pull values from a sequence. Instead of a next method whenever you return a value, generators use the yield keyword to add values into the sequence.

Here is an example generator function. Note the * after function. That's not a typo, that's how you mark a generator function as a generator.

```
function* abc() {
  yield 'a'
```

```
    yield 'b'
    yield 'c'
}
```

Generator objects conform to both the iterable protocol and the iterator protocol:

- A generator object chars is built using the abc function
- Object chars is an iterable because it has a Symbol.iterator method
- Object chars is also an iterator because it has a .next method
- The iterator for chars is itself

The same statements can also be demonstrated using JavaScript code.

```
const chars = abc()
typeof chars[Symbol.iterator] === 'function'
typeof chars.next === 'function'
chars[Symbol.iterator]() === chars
console.log(Array.from(chars))
// <- ['a', 'b', 'c']
console.log([...chars])
// <- ['a', 'b', 'c']
```

When you create a generator object, you'll get an iterator that uses the generator function to produce an iterable sequence. Whenever a yield expression is reached, its value is emitted by the iterator and generator function execution becomes suspended.

The following example shows how iteration can trigger side effects within the generator function. The console.log statements after each yield statement will be executed when generator function execution becomes unsuspended and asked for the next element in the sequence.

```
function* numbers() {
  yield 1
  console.log('a')
  yield 2
  console.log('b')
  yield 3
  console.log('c')
}
```

Suppose you created a generator object for numbers, spread its contents onto an array, and printed it to the console. Taking into

---

account the side effects in numbers, can you guess what the console output would look like for the following piece of code? Given that the spread operator iterates over the sequence to completion in order to give you an array, all side effects would be executed while constructing the array via destructuring, before the console.log statement printing the array is ever reached.

```
console.log([...numbers()])
// <- 'a'
// <- 'b'
// <- 'c'
// <- [1, 2, 3]
```

If we now used a for..of loop instead, we'd be able to preserve the order declared in the numbers generator function. In the next example, elements in the numbers sequence are printed one at a time in a for..of loop. The first time the generator function is asked for a number, it yields 1 and execution becomes suspended. The second time, execution is unsuspended where the generator left off, 'a' is printed to the console as a side effect, and 2 is yielded. The third time, 'b' is the side effect, and 3 is yielded. The fourth time, 'c' is a side effect and the generator signals that the sequence has ended.

```
for (const number of numbers()) {
  console.log(number)
  // <- 1
  // <- 'a'
  // <- 2
  // <- 'b'
  // <- 3
  // <- 'c'
}
```

Using yield* to Delegate Sequence Generation

Generator functions can use yield* to delegate to a generator object or any other iterable object.

Given that strings in ES6 adhere to the iterable protocol, you could write a piece of code like the following to split hello into individual characters.

```
function* salute() {
  yield* 'hello'
}
```

```
console.log([...salute()])
// <- ['h', 'e', 'l', 'l', 'o']
```

Naturally, you could use [...'hello'] as a simpler alternative. However, it's when combining multiple yield statements that we'll start to see the value in delegating to another iterable. The next example shows a salute generator modified into taking a name parameter and producing array that contains the characters for the 'hello you' string.

```
function* salute(name) {
  yield* 'hello '
  yield* name
}
console.log([...salute('you')])
// <- ['h', 'e', 'l', 'l', 'o', ' ', 'y', 'o', 'u']
```

To reiterate, you can yield* anything that adheres to the iterable protocol, not merely strings. That includes generator objects, arrays, arguments, NodeList in the browser, and just about anything, provided it implements System.iterator. The following example demonstrates how you could mix yield and yield* statements to describe a sequence of values using generator functions, an iterable object, and the spread operator. Can you deduce what the console.log statement would print?

```
const salute = {
  [Symbol.iterator]() {
    const items = ['h', 'e', 'l', 'l', 'o']
    return {
      next: () => ({
        done: items.length === 0,
        value: items.shift()
      })
    }
  }
}
function* multiplied(base, multiplier) {
  yield base + 1 * multiplier
  yield base + 2 * multiplier
}
function* trailmix() {
  yield* salute
  yield 0
  yield* [1, 2]
  yield* [...multiplied(3, 2)]
  yield [...multiplied(6, 3)]
  yield* multiplied(15, 5)
```

```
}
console.log([...trailmix()])
```

Here's the sequence produced by the `trailmix` generator function.

```
['h', 'e', 'l', 'l', 'o', 0, 1, 2, 5, 7, [9, 12], 20, 25]
```

Besides iterating over a generator object using spread, `for..of`, and `Array.from`, we could use the generator object directly, and iterate over that. Let's investigate how that'd work.

4.3.2 Iterating over Generators by Hand

Generator iteration isn't limited to `for..of`, `Array.from`, or the spread operator. Just like with any iterable object, you can use its `Symbol.iterator` to pull values on demand using `.next`, rather than in a strictly synchronous `for..of` loop or all at once with `Array.from` or spread. Given that a generator object is both iterable and iterator, you won't need to call `g[Symbol.iterator]()` to get an iterator: you can use `g` directly because it's the same object as the one returned by the `Symbol.iterator` method.

Assuming the `numbers` iterator we created earlier, the following example shows how you could iterate it by hand using the generator object and a `while` loop. Remember that any items returned by an iterator need a `done` property that indicates whether the sequence has ended, and a `value` property indicating the current value in the sequence.

```
const g = numbers()
while (true) {
  const item = g.next()
  if (item.done) {
    break
  }
  console.log(item.value)
}
```

Using iterators to loop over a generator might look like a complicated way of implementing a `for..of` loop, but it also allows for some interesting use cases. Particularly: `for..of` is always a synchronous loop, whereas with iterators we're in charge of deciding when to invoke `g.next`. In turn, that translates into additional opportunities such as running an asynchronous operation and then calling g.next once we have a result.

Whenever .next() is called on a generator, there are four different kinds of "events" that can suspend execution in the generator while returning a result to the caller of .next(). We'll promptly explore each of these scenarios:

- A yield expression returning the next value in the sequence
- A return statement returning the last value in the sequence
- A throw statement halts execution in the generator entirely
- Reaching the end of the generator function signals { done: true }, as the function implicitly returns undefined

Once the g generator finishes iterating over a sequence, subsequent calls to g.next() will have no effect and just return { done: true }. The following code snippet demonstrates the idempotence we can observe when calling g.next repeatedly once a sequence has ended.

```
function* generator() {
  yield 'only'
}
const g = generator()
console.log(g.next())
// <- { done: false, value: 'only' }
console.log(g.next())
// <- { done: true }
console.log(g.next())
// <- { done: true }
```

4.3.3 Mixing Generators into Iterables

Let's do a quick recap of generators. Generator functions return generator objects when invoked. A generator object has a next method, which returns the next element in the sequence. The next method returns objects with a { value, done } shape.

The following example shows an infinite Fibonacci number generator. We then instantiate a generator object and read the first eight values in the sequence.

```
function* fibonacci() {
  let previous = 0
  let current = 1
```

```
    while (true) {
      yield current
      const next = current + previous
      previous = current
      current = next
    }
  }
}
const g = fibonacci()
console.log(g.next()) // <- { value: 1, done: false }
console.log(g.next()) // <- { value: 1, done: false }
console.log(g.next()) // <- { value: 2, done: false }
console.log(g.next()) // <- { value: 3, done: false }
console.log(g.next()) // <- { value: 5, done: false }
console.log(g.next()) // <- { value: 8, done: false }
console.log(g.next()) // <- { value: 13, done: false }
console.log(g.next()) // <- { value: 21, done: false }
```

Iterables follow a similar pattern. They enforce a contract that dictates we should return an object with a next method. That method should return sequence elements following a { value, done } shape. The following example shows a fibonacci iterable that's a rough equivalent of the generator we were just looking at.

```
const fibonacci = {
  [Symbol.iterator]() {
    let previous = 0
    let current = 1
    return {
      next() {
        const value = current
        const next = current + previous
        previous = current
        current = next
        return { value, done: false }
      }
    }
  }
}
const sequence = fibonacci[Symbol.iterator]()
console.log(sequence.next()) // <- { value: 1, done: false }
console.log(sequence.next()) // <- { value: 1, done: false }
console.log(sequence.next()) // <- { value: 2, done: false }
console.log(sequence.next()) // <- { value: 3, done: false }
console.log(sequence.next()) // <- { value: 5, done: false }
console.log(sequence.next()) // <- { value: 8, done: false }
console.log(sequence.next()) // <- { value: 13, done: false }
console.log(sequence.next()) // <- { value: 21, done: false }
```

Let's reiterate. An iterable should return an object with a next method: generator functions do just that. The next method should return objects with a { value, done } shape: generator functions do that too. What happens if we change the fibonacci iterable to use a generator function for its Symbol.iterator property? As it turns out, it just works.

The following example shows the iterable fibonacci object using a generator function to define how it will be iterated. Note how that iterable has the exact same contents as the fibonacci generator function we saw earlier. We can use yield, yield*, and all of the semantics found in generator functions hold.

```
const fibonacci = {
  * [Symbol.iterator]() {
    let previous = 0
    let current = 1
    while (true) {
      yield current
      const next = current + previous
      previous = current
      current = next
    }
  }
}
const g = fibonacci[Symbol.iterator]()
console.log(g.next()) // <- { value: 1, done: false }
console.log(g.next()) // <- { value: 1, done: false }
console.log(g.next()) // <- { value: 2, done: false }
console.log(g.next()) // <- { value: 3, done: false }
console.log(g.next()) // <- { value: 5, done: false }
console.log(g.next()) // <- { value: 8, done: false }
console.log(g.next()) // <- { value: 13, done: false }
console.log(g.next()) // <- { value: 21, done: false }
```

Meanwhile, the iterable protocol also holds up. To verify that, you might use a construct like for..of, instead of manually creating the generator object. The following example uses for..of and introduces a circuit breaker to prevent an infinite loop from crashing the program.

```
for (const value of fibonacci) {
  console.log(value)
  if (value > 20) {
    break
  }
}
// <- 1
// <- 1
// <- 2
// <- 3
```

```
// <- 5
// <- 8
// <- 13
// <- 21
```

Moving onto more practical examples, let's see how generators can help us iterate tree data structures concisely.

4.3.4 Tree Traversal Using Generators

Algorithms to work with tree structures can be tricky to understand, often involving recursion. Consider the following bit of code, where we define a `Node` class that can hold a `value` and an arbitrary amount of child nodes.

```
class Node {
  constructor(value, ...children) {
    this.value = value
    this.children = children
  }
}
```

Trees can be traversed using depth-first search, where we always try to go deeper into the tree structure, and when we can't we move to the next children on the list. In the following tree structure, a depth-first search algorithm would traverse the tree visiting the nodes following the `1, 2, 3, 4, 5, 6, 7, 8, 9, 10` order.

```
const root = new Node(1,
  new Node(2),
  new Node(3,
    new Node(4,
      new Node(5,
        new Node(6)
      ),
      new Node(7)
    )
  ),
  new Node(8,
    new Node(9),
    new Node(10)
  )
)
```

One way of implementing depth-first traversal for our tree would be using a generator function that yields the current node's value, and then iterates over its children yielding every item in their sequences using the yield* operator as a way of composing the recursive component of the iterator.

```
function* depthFirst(node) {
  yield node.value
  for (const child of node.children) {
    yield* depthFirst(child)
  }
}
console.log([...depthFirst(root)])
// <- [1, 2, 3, 4, 5, 6, 7, 8, 9, 10]
```

A slightly different way of declaring the traversal algorithm would be to make the Node class iterable using the depthFirst generator. The following piece of code also takes advantage that child is a Node class—and thus an iterable—using yield* in order to yield the iterable sequence for that child as part of the sequence for its parent node.

```
class Node {
  constructor(value, ...children) {
    this.value = value
    this.children = children
  }
  * [Symbol.iterator]() {
    yield this.value
    for (const child of this.children) {
      yield* child
    }
  }
}
console.log([...root])
// <- [1, 2, 3, 4, 5, 6, 7, 8, 9, 10]
```

If we wanted to change traversal to a breadth-first algorithm, we could change the iterator into an algorithm like the one in the following piece of code. Here, we use a first-in first-out queue to keep a buffer of nodes we haven't visited yet. In each step of the iteration, starting with the root node, we print the current node's value and push its children onto the queue. Children are always added to the end of the queue, but we pull items from the beginning of the queue. That means we'll always go through all the nodes at any given depth before going deeper into the tree structure.

```
class Node {
  constructor(value, ...children) {
    this.value = value
    this.children = children
  }
```

```
  * [Symbol.iterator]() {
    const queue = [this]
    while (queue.length) {
      const node = queue.shift()
      yield node.value
      queue.push(...node.children)
    }
  }
}
console.log([...root])
// <- [1, 2, 3, 8, 4, 9, 10, 5, 7, 6]
```

Generators are useful due to their expressiveness, while the iterator
protocol allows us to define a sequence we can iterate at our own
pace, which comes in handy when a tree has thousands of nodes and
we need to throttle iteration for performance reasons.

4.3.5 Consuming Generator Functions for Flexibility

Thus far in the chapter we've talked about generators in terms of
constructing a consumable sequence. Generators can also be presented as an interface to a piece of code that decides how the generator
function is to be iterated over.

In this section, we'll be writing a generator function that gets passed
to a method, which loops over the generator consuming elements of
its sequence. Even though you might think that writing code like
this is unconventional at first, most libraries built around generators
have their users write the generators while the library retains control
over the iteration.

The following bit of code could be used as an example of how we'd
like modelProvider to work. The consumer provides a generator
function that yields crumbs to different parts of a model, getting
back the relevant part of the model each time. A generator object
can pass results back to the generator function by way of
g.next(result). When we do this, a yield expression evaluates to
the result produced by the generator object.

```
modelProvider(function* () {
  const items = yield 'cart.items'
  const item = items.reduce(
    (left, right) => left.price > right.price ? left : right
  )
  const details = yield `products.${ item.id }`
```

```
    console.log(details)
  })
```

Whenever a resource is yielded by the user-provided generator, execution in the generator function is suspended until the iterator calls g.next again, which may even happen asynchronously behind the scenes. The next code snippet implements a modelProvider function that iterates over paths yielded by the generator. Note also how we're passing data to g.next().

```
const model = {
  cart: {
    items: [item1, …, itemN]
  },
  products: {
    product1: { … },
    productN: { … }
  }
}
function modelProvider(paths) {
  const g = paths()
  pull()
  function pull(data) {
    const { value, done } = g.next(data)
    if (done) {
      return
    }
    const crumbs = value.split('.')
    const data = crumbs.reduce(followCrumbs, model)
    pull(data)
  }
}
function followCrumbs(data, crumb) {
  if (!data || !data.hasOwnProperty(crumb)) {
    return null
  }
  return data[crumb]
}
```

The largest benefit of asking consumers to provide a generator function is that providing them with the yield keyword opens up a world of possibilities where execution in their code may be suspended while the iterator performs an asynchronous operation in between g.next calls. Let's explore more asynchronous uses of generators in the next section.

4.3.6 Dealing with Asynchronous Flows

Going back to the example where we call modelProvider with a user-provided generator, let's consider what would change about our code if the model parts were to be provided asynchronously. The beauty of generators is that if the way we iterate over the sequence of paths were to become asynchronous, the user-provided function wouldn't have to change at all. We already have the ability to suspend execution in the generator while we fetch a piece of the model, and all it'd take would be to ask a service for the answer to the current path, return that value via an intermediary yield statement or in some other way, and then call g.next on the generator object.

Let's assume we're back at the following usage of modelProvider.

```
modelProvider(function* () {
  const items = yield 'cart.items'
  const item = items.reduce(
    (left, right) => left.price > right.price ? left : right
  )
  const details = yield `products.${ item.id }`
  console.log(details)
})
```

We'll be using fetch to make requests for each HTTP resource— which, as you may recall, returns a Promise. Note that given an asynchronous scenario we can't use for..of to go over the sequence, which is limited to synchronous loops.

The next code snippet sends an HTTP request for each query to the model, and the server is now in charge of producing the relevant bits of the model, without the client having to keep any state other than the relevant user authentication bits, such as cookies.

```
function modelProvider(paths) {
  const g = paths()
  pull()
  function pull(data) {
    const { value, done } = g.next(data)
    if (done) {
      return
    }
    fetch(`/model?query=${ encodeURIComponent(value) }`)
      .then(response => response.json())
      .then(data => pull(data))
  }
}
```

Always keep in mind that, while a `yield` expression is being evaluated, execution of the generator function is paused until the next item in the sequence—the next query for the model, in our example —is requested to the iterator. In this sense, code in a generator function looks and feels as if it were synchronous, even though `yield` pauses execution in the generator until `g.next` resumes execution.

While generators let us write asynchronous code that appears synchronous, this introduces an inconvenience. How do we handle errors that arise in the iteration? If an HTTP request fails, for instance, how do we notify the generator and then handle the error notification in the generator function?

4.3.7 Throwing Errors at a Generator

Before shifting our thinking into user-provided generators, where they retain control of seemingly synchronous functions thanks to `yield` and suspension, we would've been hard pressed to find a use case for `g.throw`, a method that can be used to report errors that take place while the generator is suspended. Its applications become apparent when we think in terms of the flow control code driving the moments spent in between `yield` expressions, where things could go wrong. When something goes wrong processing an item in the sequence, the code that's consuming the generator needs to be able to `throw` that error into the generator.

In the case of `modelProvider`, the iterator may experience network issues—or a malformed HTTP response—and fail to provide a piece of the model. In the following snippet of code, the `fetch` step was modified by adding an error callback that will be executed if parsing fails in `response.json()`, in which case we'll throw the exception at the generator function.

```
fetch(`/model?query=${ encodeURIComponent(value) }`)
  .then(response => response.json())
  .then(data => pull(data))
  .catch(err => g.throw(err))
```

When `g.next` is called, execution in generator code is unsuspended. The `g.throw` method also unsuspends the generator, but it causes an exception to be thrown at the location of the `yield` expression. An unhandled exception in a generator would stop iteration by preventing other `yield` expressions from being reachable. Generator code could wrap `yield` expressions in `try/catch` blocks to gracefully manage exceptions forwarded by iteration code—as shown in the following code snippet. This would allow subsequent `yield` expressions to be reached, suspending the generator and putting the iterator in charge once again.

```
modelProvider(function* () {
  try {
    console.log('items in the cart:', yield 'cart.items')
  } catch (e) {
    console.error('uh oh, failed to fetch model.cart.items!', e)
  }
  try {
    console.log(`these are our products: ${ yield 'products' }`)
  } catch (e) {
    console.error('uh oh, failed to fetch model.products!', e)
  }
})
```

Even though generator functions allow us to suspend execution and then resume asynchronously, we can use the same error handling semantics—try, `catch`, and throw—as with regular functions. Having the ability to use `try`/`catch` blocks in generator code lets us treat the code as if it were synchronous, even when there are HTTP requests sitting behind `yield` expressions, in iterator code.

4.3.8 Returning on Behalf of a Generator

Besides `g.next` and `g.throw`, generator objects have one more method at their disposal to determine how a generator sequence is iterated: `g.return(value)`. This method unsuspends the generator function and executes return value at the location of `yield`, typically ending the sequence being iterated by the generator object. This is no different to what would occur if the generator function actually had a return statement in it.

```
function* numbers() {
  yield 1
  yield 2
  yield 3
}
const g = numbers()
console.log(g.next())
// <- { done: false, value: 1 }
console.log(g.return())
// <- { done: true }
```

```
console.log(g.next())
// <- { done: true }
```

Given that g.return(value) performs return value at the location of yield where the generator function was last suspended, a try/finally block could avoid immediate termination of the generated sequence, as statements in the finally block would be executed right before exiting. As shown in the following piece of code, that means yield expressions within the finally block can continue producing items for the sequence.

```
function* numbers() {
  try {
    yield 1
  } finally {
    yield 2
    yield 3
  }
  yield 4
  yield 5
}
const g = numbers()
console.log(g.next())
// <- { done: false, value: 1 }
console.log(g.return(-1))
// <- { done: false, value: 2 }
console.log(g.next())
// <- { done: false, value: 3 }
console.log(g.next())
// <- { done: true, value -1 }
```

Let's now look at a simple generator function, where a few values are yielded and then a return statement is encountered.

```
function* numbers() {
  yield 1
  yield 2
  return 3
  yield 4
}
```

While you may place return value statements anywhere in a generator function, the returned value won't show up when iterating the generator using the spread operator or Array.from to build an array, nor when using for..of, as shown next.

```
console.log([...numbers()])
// <- [1, 2]
console.log(Array.from(numbers()))
// <- [1, 2]
```

```
for (const number of numbers()) {
  console.log(number)
  // <- 1
  // <- 2
}
```

This happens because the iterator result provided by executing g.return or a return statement contains the done: true signal, indicating that the sequence has ended. Even though that same iterator result also contains a sequence value, none of the previously shown methods take it into account when pulling a sequence from the generator. In this sense, return statements in generators should mostly be used as circuit-breakers and not as a way of providing the last value in a sequence.

The only way of actually accessing the value returned from a generator is to iterate over it using a generator object, and capturing the iterator result value even though done: true is present, as displayed in the following snippet.

```
const g = numbers()
console.log(g.next())
// <- { done: false, value: 1 }
console.log(g.next())
// <- { done: false, value: 2 }
console.log(g.next())
// <- { done: true, value: 3 }
console.log(g.next())
// <- { done: true }
```

Due to the confusing nature of the differences between yield expressions and return statements, return in generators would be best avoided except in cases where a specific method wants to treat yield and return differently, the end goal always being to provide an abstraction in exchange for a simplified development experience.

In the following section, we'll build an iterator that leverages differences in yield versus return to perform both input and output based on the same generator function.

4.3.9 Asynchronous I/O Using Generators

The following piece of code shows a self-describing generator function where we indicate input sources and an output destination. This hypothetical method could be used to pull product information from the yielded endpoints, which could then be saved to the returned endpoint. An interesting aspect of this interface is that as a user you don't have to spend any time figuring out how to read and write information. You merely determine the sources and destination, and the underlying implementation figures out the rest.

```
saveProducts(function* () {
  yield '/products/modern-javascript'
  yield '/products/mastering-modular-javascript'
  return '/wishlists/books'
})
```

As a bonus, we'll have `saveProducts` return a promise that's fulfilled after the order is pushed to the returned endpoint, meaning the consumer will be able to execute callbacks after the order is filed. The generator function should also receive product data via the `yield` expressions, which can be passed into it by calling `g.next` with the associated product data.

```
saveProducts(function* () {
  const p2 = yield '/products/modern-javascript'
  const p2 = yield '/products/mastering-modular-javascript'
  return '/wishlists/books'
}).then(response => {
  // continue after storing the product list
})
```

Conditional logic could be used to allow `saveProducts` to target a user's shopping cart instead of one of their wish lists.

```
saveProducts(function* () {
  yield '/products/modern-javascript'
  yield '/products/mastering-modular-javascript'
  if (addToCart) {
    return '/cart'
  }
  return '/wishlists/books'
})
```

One of the benefits of taking this blanket "inputs and output" approach is that the implementation could be changed in a variety of ways, while keeping the API largely unchanged. The input resources could be pulled via HTTP requests or from a temporary cache, they could be pulled one by one or concurrently, or there could be a mechanism that combines all yielded resources into a single HTTP request. Other than semantic differences of pulling one value at a time versus pulling them all at the same time to combine them into a single request, the API would barely change in the face of significant changes to the implementation.

We'll go over an implementation of saveProducts bit by bit. First off, the following piece of code shows how we could combine fetch and its promise-based API to make an HTTP request for a JSON document about the first yielded product.

```
function saveProducts(productList) {
  const g = productList()
  const item = g.next()
  fetch(item.value)
    .then(res => res.json())
    .then(product => {})
}
```

In order to pull product data in a concurrent series—asynchronously, but one at a time—we'll wrap the fetch call in a recursive function that gets invoked as we get responses about each product. Each step of the way we'll be fetching a product, calling g.next to unsuspend the generator function asking for the next yielded item in the sequence, and then calling more to fetch that item.

```
function saveProducts(productList) {
  const g = productList()
  more(g.next())
  function more(item) {
    if (item.done) {
      return
    }
    fetch(item.value)
      .then(res => res.json())
      .then(product => {
        more(g.next(product))
      })
  }
}
```

Thus far we're pulling all inputs and passing their details back to the generator via g.next(product)—an item at a time. In order to leverage the return statement, we'll save the products in a temporary array and then POST the list onto the output endpoint present on the iterator item when the sequence is marked as having ended.

```
function saveProducts(productList) {
  const products = []
  const g = productList()
  more(g.next())
  function more(item) {
```

```
      if (item.done) {
        save(item.value)
      } else {
        details(item.value)
      }
    }
    function details(endpoint) {
      fetch(endpoint)
        .then(res => res.json())
        .then(product => {
          products.push(product)
          more(g.next(product))
        })
    }
    function save(endpoint) {
      fetch(endpoint, {
        method: 'POST',
        body: JSON.stringify({ products })
      })
    }
  }
```

At this point product descriptions are being pulled down, cached in the products array, forwarded to the generator body, and eventually saved in one fell swoop using the endpoint provided by the return statement.

In our original API design we suggested we'd return a promise from saveProducts so that callbacks could be chained and executed after the save operation. As we mentioned earlier, fetch returns a promise. By adding return statements all the way through our function calls, you can observe how saveProducts returns the output of more, which returns the output of save or details, both of which return the promise created by a fetch call. In addition, each details call returns the result of calling more from inside the details promise, meaning the original fetch won't be fulfilled until the second fetch is fulfilled, allowing us to chain these promises, which will ultimately resolve when the save call is executed and resolved.

```
  function saveProducts(productList) {
    const products = []
    const g = productList()
    return more(g.next())
    function more(item) {
      if (item.done) {
        return save(item.value)
      }
```

```
      return details(item.value)
    }
    function details(endpoint) {
      return fetch(endpoint)
        .then(res => res.json())
        .then(product => {
          products.push(product)
          return more(g.next(product))
        })
    }
    function save(endpoint) {
      return fetch(endpoint, {
          method: 'POST',
          body: JSON.stringify({ products })
        })
        .then(res => res.json())
    }
  }
```

As you may have noticed, the implementation doesn't hardcode any important aspects of the operation, which means you could use the inputs and output pattern in a generic way as long as you have zero or more inputs you want to pipe into one output. The consumer ends up with an elegant-looking method that's easy to understand— they yield input stores and return an output store. Furthermore, our use of promises makes it easy to concatenate this operation with others. This way, we're keeping a potential tangle of conditional statements and flow control mechanisms in check, by abstracting away flow control into the iteration mechanism under the saveProd ucts method.

We've looked into flow control mechanisms such as callbacks, events, promises, iterators, and generators. The following two sections delve into async/await, async iterators, and async generators, all of which build upon a mixture of the flow control mechanisms we've uncovered thus far in this chapter.

4.4 Async Functions

Languages like Python and C# have had async/await for a while. In ES2017, JavaScript gained native syntax that can be used to describe asynchronous operations.

Let's go over a quick recap comparing promises, callbacks, and generators. Afterwards we'll look into async functions in JavaScript, and how this new feature can help make our code more readable.

4.4.1 Flavors of Async Code

Let's suppose we had code like the following. Here I'm wrapping a fetch request in a getRandomArticle function. The promise fulfills with the JSON body when successful, and follows standard fetch rejection mechanics otherwise.

```
function getRandomArticle() {
  return fetch('/articles/random', {
    headers: new Headers({
      Accept: 'application/json'
    })
  })
  .then(res => res.json())
}
```

The next piece of code shows how typical usage for getRandomArti cle might look like. We build a promise chain that takes the JSON object for the article and passes it through an asynchronous render View view rendering function, which fulfills as an HTML page. We then replace the contents of our page with that HTML. In order to avoid silent errors, we'll also print any rejection reasons using con sole.error.

```
getRandomArticle()
  .then(model => renderView(model))
  .then(html => setPageContents(html))
  .then(() => console.log('Successfully changed page!'))
  .catch(err => console.error(err))
```

Chained promises can become hard to debug: the root cause of a flow control error can be challenging to track down, and writing promise-based code flows is typically much easier than reading them, which leads to code that becomes difficult to maintain over time.

If we were to use plain JavaScript callbacks, our code would become repetitive, as demonstrated in the next code listing. At the same time, we're running into callback hell: we're adding a level of indentation for each step in our asynchronous code flow, making our code increasingly harder to read with each step we add.

```
getRandomArticle((err, model) => {
  if (err) {
    return console.error(err)
  }
  renderView(model, (err, html) => {
    if (err) {
      return console.error(err)
    }
    setPageContents(html, err => {
      if (err) {
        return console.error(err)
      }
      console.log('Successfully changed page!')
    })
  })
})
```

Libraries can, of course, help with callback hell and repetitive error handling. Libraries like async take advantage of normalized callbacks where the first argument is reserved for errors. Using their waterfall method, our code becomes terse again.

```
async.waterfall([
  getRandomArticle,
  renderView,
  setPageContents
], (err, html) => {
  if (err) {
    return console.error(err)
  }
  console.log('Successfully changed page!')
})
```

Let's look at a similar example, but this time we'll be using generators. The following is a rewrite of getRandomArticle where we consume a generator for the sole purpose of changing the way in which getRandomArticle is consumed.

```
function getRandomArticle(gen) {
  const g = gen()
  fetch('/articles/random', {
    headers: new Headers({
      Accept: 'application/json'
    })
  })
  .then(res => res.json())
  .then(json => g.next(json))
  .catch(err => g.throw(err))
}
```

The following piece of code shows how you can pull the json from getRandomArticle by way of a yield expression. Even though that looks somewhat synchronous, there's now a generator function wrapper involved. As soon as we want to add more steps, we need to heavily modify getRandomArticle so that it yields the results we want, and make the necessary changes to the generator function in order to consume the updated sequence of results.

```
getRandomArticle(function* printRandomArticle() {
  const json = yield
  // render view
})
```

Generators may not be the most straightforward way of accomplishing the results that we want in this case: you're only moving the complexity somewhere else. We might as well stick with promises.

Besides involving an unintuitive syntax into the mix, your iterator code will be highly coupled to the generator function that's being consumed. That means you'll have to change it often as you add new yield expressions to the generator code.

A better alternative would be to use an async function.

4.4.2 Using async/await

Async functions let us take a promise-based implementation and take advantage of the synchronous-looking generator style. A huge benefit in this approach is that you won't have to change the original getRandomArticle at all: as long as it returns a promise it can be awaited.

Note that await may only be used inside async functions, marked with the async keyword. Async functions work similarly to generators, by suspending execution in the local context until a promise settles. If the awaited expression isn't originally a promise, it gets casted into a promise.

The following piece of code consumes our original getRandomArticle, which relied on promises. Then it runs that model through an asynchronous renderView function, which returns a bit of HTML, and updates the page. Note how we can use try/catch to handle errors in awaited promises from within the async function, treating completely asynchronous code as if it were synchronous.

```
async function read() {
  try {
    const model = await getRandomArticle()
    const html = await renderView(model)
    await setPageContents(html)
    console.log('Successfully changed page!')
  } catch (err) {
    console.error(err)
  }
}

read()
```

An async function always returns a `Promise`. In the case of uncaught exceptions, the returned promise settles in rejection. Otherwise, the returned promise resolves to the return value. This aspect of async functions allows us to mix them with regular promise-based continuation as well. The following example shows how the two may be combined.

```
async function read() {
  const model = await getRandomArticle()
  const html = await renderView(model)
  await setPageContents(html)
  return 'Successfully changed page!'
}

read()
  .then(message => console.log(message))
  .catch(err => console.error(err))
```

Making the `read` function a bit more reusable, we could return the resulting `html`, and allow consumers to do continuation using promises or yet another async function. That way, your `read` function becomes only concerned with pulling down the HTML for a view.

```
async function read() {
  const model = await getRandomArticle()
  const html = await renderView(model)
  return html
}
```

Following the example, we can use plain promises to print the HTML.

```
read().then(html => console.log(html))
```

Using async functions wouldn't be all that difficult for continuation, either. In the next snippet, we create a `write` function used for continuation.

```
async function write() {
  const html = await read()
  console.log(html)
}
```

What about concurrent asynchronous flows?

4.4.3 Concurrent Async Flows

In asynchronous code flows, it is commonplace to execute two or more tasks concurrently. While async functions make it easier to write asynchronous code, they also lend themselves to code that executes one asynchronous operation at a time. A function with multiple `await` expressions in it will be suspended one at a time on each `await` expression until that `Promise` is settled, before unsuspending execution and moving onto the next `await` expression—this is a similar case to what we observe with generators and `yield`.

```
async function concurrent() {
  const p1 = new Promise(resolve =>
    setTimeout(resolve, 500, 'fast')
  )
  const p2 = new Promise(resolve =>
    setTimeout(resolve, 200, 'faster')
  )
  const p3 = new Promise(resolve =>
    setTimeout(resolve, 100, 'fastest')
  )
  const r1 = await p1 // execution is blocked until p1 settles
  const r2 = await p2
  const r3 = await p3
}
```

We can use `Promise.all` to work around that issue, creating a single promise that we can `await` on. This way, our code blocks until every promise in a list is settled, and they can be resolved concurrently.

The following example shows how you could `await` on three different promises that could be resolved concurrently. Given that `await` suspends your async function and the `await Promise.all` expression ultimately resolves into a `results` array, you can take advantage of destructuring to pull individual results out of that array.

```
async function concurrent() {
  const p1 = new Promise(resolve =>
  setTimeout(resolve, 500, 'fast')
)
  const p2 = new Promise(resolve =>
  setTimeout(resolve, 200, 'faster')
)
  const p3 = new Promise(resolve =>
  setTimeout(resolve, 100, 'fastest')
)
  const [r1, r2, r3] = await Promise.all([p1, p2, p3])
  console.log(r1, r2, r3)
  // 'fast', 'faster', 'fastest'
}
```

We could use `Promise.race` to get the result from the promise that fulfills quicker.

```
async function race() {
  const p1 = new Promise(resolve => setTimeout(resolve, 500, 'fast'))
  const p2 = new Promise(resolve => setTimeout(resolve, 200, 'faster'))
  const p3 = new Promise(resolve => setTimeout(resolve, 100, 'fastest'))
  const result = await Promise.race([p1, p2, p3])
  console.log(result)
  // 'fastest'
}
```

4.4.4 Error Handling

Errors are swallowed silently within an `async` function, just like inside normal Promises, due to async functions being wrapped in a `Promise`. Uncaught exceptions raised in the body of your async function or during suspended execution while evaluating an `await` expression will reject the promise returned by the `async` function.

That is, unless we add `try/catch` blocks around `await` expressions. For the portion of the async function code that's wrapped, errors are treated under typical `try/catch` semantics.

Naturally, this can be seen as a strength: you can leverage `try/catch` conventions, something you were unable to do with asynchronous callbacks, and somewhat able to when using promises. In this sense, async functions are akin to generators, where we can take advantage of `try/catch` thanks to function execution suspension turning asynchronous flows into seemingly synchronous code.

Furthermore, you're able to catch these exceptions from outside the `async` function, by adding a `.catch` clause to the promise they return. While this is a flexible way of combining the try/catch error handling flavor with .catch clauses in promises, it can also lead to confusion and ultimately cause to errors going unhandled, unless everyone reading the code is comfortable with async function semantics in terms of the promise wrapper and how try/catch works under this context.

```
read()
  .then(html => console.log(html))
  .catch(err => console.error(err))
```

As you can see, there are quite a few ways in which we can notice exceptions and then handle, log, or offload them.

4.4.5 Understanding Async Function Internals

Async functions leverage both generators and promises internally. Let's suppose we have the following async function.

```
async function example(a, b, c) {
  // example function body
}
```

The next bit shows how the example declaration could be converted into a plain old function that returns the result of feeding a generator function to a spawn helper.

```
function example(a, b, c) {
  return spawn(function* () {
    // example function body
  })
}
```

Inside the generator function, we'll assume yield to be the syntactic equivalent of await.

In spawn, a promise is wrapped around code that will step through the generator function—made out of user code—in series, forwarding values to the generator code (the async function's body).

The following listing should aid you in understanding how the async/await algorithm iterates over a sequence of await expressions using a generator. Each item in the sequence is wrapped in a promise and then gets chained with the next step in the sequence. The promise returned by the underlying generator function becomes settled when the sequence ends or one of the promises is rejected.

```
function spawn(generator) {
  // wrap everything in a promise
  return new Promise((resolve, reject) => {
    const g = generator()

    // run the first step
    step(() => g.next())

    function step(nextFn) {
      const next = runNext(nextFn)
      if (next.done) {
        // finished with success, resolve the promise
        resolve(next.value)
        return
      }
      // not finished, chain off the yielded promise
      // and run next step
      Promise
        .resolve(next.value)
        .then(
          value => step(() => g.next(value)),
          err => step(() => g.throw(err))
        )
    }

    function runNext(nextFn) {
      try {
        // resume the generator
        return nextFn()
      } catch (err) {
        // finished with failure, reject the promise
        reject(err)
      }
    }
  })
}
```

Consider the following async function. In order to print the result, we're also using promise-based continuation. Let's follow the code as a thought exercise.

```
async function exercise() {
  const r1 = await new Promise(resolve =>
  setTimeout(resolve, 500, 'slowest')
)
  const r2 = await new Promise(resolve =>
  setTimeout(resolve, 200, 'slow')
)
```

```
    return [r1, r2]
  }

exercise().then(result => console.log(result))
// <- ['slowest', 'slow']
```

First, we could translate the function to our spawn-based logic. We wrap the body of our async function in a generator passed to spawn, and replace any await expressions with yield.

```
function exercise() {
  return spawn(function* () {
    const r1 = yield new Promise(resolve =>
    setTimeout(resolve, 500, 'slowest')
  )
    const r2 = yield new Promise(resolve =>
    setTimeout(resolve, 200, 'slow')
  )
    return [r1, r2]
  })
}

exercise().then(result => console.log(result))
// <- ['slowest', 'slow']
```

When spawn is called with the generator function, it immediately creates a generator object and executes step a first time, as seen in the next code snippet. The step function will also be used whenever we reach a yield expression; those are equivalent to the await expressions in our async function.

```
function spawn(generator) {
  // wrap everything in a promise
  return new Promise((resolve, reject) => {
    const g = generator()

    // run the first step
    step(() => g.next())
    // …
  })
}
```

The first thing that happens in the step function is calling the nextFn function inside a try/catch block. This resumes execution in the generator function. If the generator function were to produce an error, we'd fall into the catch clause, and the underlying promise for our async function would be rejected without any further steps, as shown next.

```
function step(nextFn) {
  const next = runNext(nextFx)
  // …
}

function runNext(nextFn) {
  try {
    // resume the generator
    return nextFn()
  } catch (err) {
    // finished with failure, reject the promise
    reject(err)
  }
}
```

Back to the async function, code up until the following expression is evaluated. No errors are incurred, and execution in the async function is suspended once again.

```
yield new Promise(resolve =>
  setTimeout(resolve, 500, 'slowest')
)
```

The yielded expression is received by step as next.value, while next.done indicates whether the generator sequence has ended. In this case, we receive the Promise in the function controlling exactly how iteration should occur. At this time, next.done is false, meaning we won't be resolving the async function's wrapper Promise. We wrap next.value in a fulfilled Promise, just in case we haven't received a Promise.

We then wait on the Promise to be fulfilled or rejected. If the promise is fulfilled, we push the fulfillment value to the generator function by advancing the generator sequence with value. If the promise is rejected, we would've used g.throw, which would've resulted in an error being raised in the generator function, causing the async function's wrapper promise to be rejected at runNext.

```
function step(nextFn) {
  const next = runNext(nextFn)
  if (next.done) {
    // finished with success, resolve the promise
    resolve(next.value)
    return
  }
  // not finished
  // chain off the yielded promise and run next step
  Promise
    .resolve(next.value)
```

```
    .then(
      value => step(() => g.next(value)),
      err => step(() => g.throw(err))
    )
}
```

Using g.next() on its own means that the generator function resumes execution. By passing a value to g.next(value), we've made it so that the yield expression evaluates to that value. The value in question is, in this case, the fulfillment value of the originally yielded Promise, which is 'slowest'.

Back in the generator function, we assign 'slowest' to r1.

```
const r1 = yield new Promise(resolve =>
  setTimeout(resolve, 500, 'slowest')
)
```

Then, execution runs up until the second yield statement. The yield expression once again causes execution in the async function to be suspended, and sends the new Promise to the spawn iterator.

```
yield new Promise(resolve => setTimeout(resolve, 200, 'slow'))
```

The same process is repeated this time: next.done is false because we haven't reached the end of the generator function. We wrap the Promise in another promise just in case, and once the promise settles with 'slow', we resume execution in the generator function.

Then we reach the return statement in the generator function. Once again, execution is suspended in the generator function, and returned to the iterator.

```
return [r1, r2]
```

At this point, next evaluates to the following object.

```
{
  value: ['slowest', 'slow'],
  done: true
}
```

Immediately, the iterator checks that next.done is indeed true, and resolves the async function to ['slowest', 'slow'].

```
if (next.done) {
  // finished with success, resolve the promise
  resolve(next.value)
```

```
    return
  }
```

Now that the promise returned by exercise is settled in fulfillment, the log statement is finally printed.

```
exercise().then(result => console.log(result))
// <- ['slowest', 'slow']
```

Async functions, then, are little more than a sensible default when it comes to iterating generator functions in such a way that makes passing values back and forth as frictionless as possible. Some syntactic sugar hides away the generator function, the spawn function used to iterate over the sequence of yielded expressions, and yield becomes await.

Another way of thinking of async functions is in terms of promises. Consider the following example, where we have an async function that awaits for a promise that's the result of a function call, and then awaits on mapping every user through a function. How would you translate it, in terms of promises?

```
async function getUserProfiles() {
  const users = await findAllUsers()
  const models = await Promise.all(users.map(toUserModel))
  const profiles = models.map(model => model.profile)
  return profiles
}
```

The following snippet has a rough equivalent of the getUserPro files async function. Note how, for the most part, we can change await statements into chained promises while moving variable declarations in the async function into reactions on each of those promises, as needed. Given async functions always return a Promise, we leave that unchanged in this case, but we'd have to remember to mentally assign a return value of Promise.resolve(result) to any async function we want to translate into promises in our heads.

```
function getUserProfiles() {
  const userPromise = findAllUsers()
  const modelPromise = userPromise.then(users =>
    Promise.all(users.map(toUserModel))
  )
  const profilePromise = modelPromise.then(models =>
    models.map(model => model.profile)
  )
```

```
    return profilePromise
  }
```

Noting that async functions are syntactic sugar on top of generators and promises, we can also make a point about the importance of learning how each of these constructs work in order to get better insight into how you can mix, match, and combine all the different flavors of asynchronous code flows together.

4.5 Asynchronous Iteration

As explained in Section 4.2, "Iterator Protocol and Iterable Protocol," on page 108, you may recall how iterators leverage Symbol.iterator as an interface to define how an object is to be iterated.

```
const sequence = {
  [Symbol.iterator]() {
    const items = ['i', 't', 'e', 'r', 'a', 'b', 'l', 'e']
    return {
      next: () => ({
        done: items.length === 0,
        value: items.shift()
      })
    }
  }
}
```

You may also recall that the sequence object can be iterated in a number of different ways, such as the spread operator, Array.from, and for..of, among others.

```
[...sequence]
// <- ['i', 't', 'e', 'r', 'a', 'b', 'l', 'e']
Array.from(sequence)
// <- ['i', 't', 'e', 'r', 'a', 'b', 'l', 'e']

for (const item of sequence) {
  console.log(item)
  // <- 'i'
  // <- 't'
  // <- 'e'
  // <- 'r'
  // <- 'a'
  // <- 'b'
  // <- 'l'
```

```
    // <- 'e'
}
```

The contract for an iterator mandates that the next method of Sym
bol.iterator instances returns an object with value and done
properties. The value property indicates the current value in the
sequence, while done is a Boolean indicating whether the sequence
has ended.

4.5.1 Async Iterators

In async iterators, the contract has a subtle difference: next is supposed to return a Promise that resolves to an object containing
value and done properties. The promise enables the sequence to
define asynchronous tasks before the next item in the series is
resolved. A new Symbol.asyncIterator is introduced to declare
asynchronous iterators, in order to avoid confusion that would
result from reusing Symbol.iterator.

The sequence iterable could be made compatible with the async
iterator interface with two small changes: we replace Symbol.itera
tor with Symbol.asyncIterator, and we wrap the return value for
the next method in Promise.resolve, thus returning a Promise.

```
const sequence = {
  [Symbol.asyncIterator]() {
    const items = ['i', 't', 'e', 'r', 'a', 'b', 'l', 'e']
    return {
      next: () => Promise.resolve({
        done: items.length === 0,
        value: items.shift()
      })
    }
  }
}
```

A case could be made for an infinite sequence that increases its
value at a certain time interval. The following example has an inter
val function that returns an infinite async sequence. Each step
resolves to the next value in the sequence after duration.

```
const interval = duration => ({
  [Symbol.asyncIterator]: () => ({
    i: 0,
    next() {
      return new Promise(resolve =>
        setTimeout(() => resolve({
```

```
        value: this.i++,
        done: false
      }), duration)
    )
  }
 })
})
```

In order to consume an async iterator, we can leverage the new `for await..of` construct introduced alongside async iterators. This is yet another way of writing code that behaves asynchronously yet looks synchronous. Note that `for await..of` statements are only allowed inside async functions.

```
async function print() {
  for await (const i of interval(1000)) {
    console.log(`${ i } seconds elapsed.`)
  }
}
print()
```

Note that async iterators—as well as async generators—are in stage 3 of the ECMAScript process as of the time of this writing.

4.5.2 Async Generators

Like with regular iterators, there are async generators to complement async iterators. An async generator function is like a generator function, except that it also supports `await` and `for await..of` declarations. The following example shows a `fetchInterval` generator that fetches a resource periodically at an interval.

```
async function* fetchInterval(duration, ...params) {
  for await (const i of interval(duration)) {
    yield await fetch(...params)
  }
}
```

When stepped over, async generators return objects with a `{ next, return, throw }` signature, whose methods return promises for `{ value, done }`. This is in contrast with regular generators, which return `{ value, done }` directly.

You can consume the `fetchInterval` async generator in exactly the same way you could consume the object-based `interval` async iterator. The following example consumes the `fetchInterval` generator to poll an `/api/status` HTTP resource and leverage its JSON response. After each step ends, we wait for a second and repeat the process.

```
async function process() {
  for await (const response of fetchInterval(
  1000,
  '/api/status'
)) {
    const data = await response.json()
    // use updated data
  }
}
process()
```

As highlighted in Section 4.2.2, "Infinite Sequences," on page 111, it's important to break out of these kinds of sequences, in order to avoid infinite loops.

CHAPTER 5

Leveraging ECMAScript Collections

JavaScript data structures are flexible enough that we're able to turn any object into a hash-map, where we map string keys to arbitrary values. For example, one might use an object to map npm package names to their metadata, as shown next.

```
const registry = {}
function set(name, meta) {
  registry[name] = meta
}
function get(name) {
  return registry[name]
}
set('contra', { description: 'Asynchronous flow control' })
set('dragula', { description: 'Drag and drop' })
set('woofmark', { description: 'Markdown and WYSIWYG editor' })
```

There are several problems with this approach, outlined here:

- Security issues where user-provided keys like __proto__, toString, or anything in Object.prototype break expectations and make interaction with this kind of hash-map data structures more cumbersome

- When iterating using for..in we need to rely on Object#hasOwnProperty to make sure properties aren't inherited

- Iteration over list items with Object.keys(registry).forEach is also verbose

- Keys are limited to strings, making it hard to create hash-maps where you'd like to index values by DOM elements or other nonstring references

The first problem could be fixed using a prefix, and being careful to always get or set values in the hash-map through functions that add those prefixes, to avoid mistakes.

```
const registry = {}
function set(name, meta) {
  registry['pkg:' + name] = meta
}
function get(name) {
  return registry['pkg:' + name]
}
```

An alternative could also be using `Object.create(null)` instead of an empty object literal. In this case, the created object won't inherit from `Object.prototype`, meaning it won't be harmed by __proto__ and friends.

```
const registry = Object.create(null)
function set(name, meta) {
  registry[name] = meta
}
function get(name) {
  return registry[name]
}
```

For iteration we could create a `list` function that returns key/value tuples.

```
const registry = Object.create(null)
function list() {
  return Object.keys(registry).map(key => [key, registry[key]])
}
```

Or we could implement the iterator protocol on our hash-map. Here we are trading complexity in favor of convenience: the iterator code is more complicated to read than the former case where we had a `list` function with familiar `Object.keys` and `Array#map` methods. In the following example, however, accessing the list is even easier and more convenient than through `list`: following the iterator protocol means there's no need for a custom `list` function.

```
const registry = Object.create(null)
registry[Symbol.iterator] = () => {
  const keys = Object.keys(registry)
  return {
```

```
    next() {
      const done = keys.length === 0
      const key = keys.shift()
      const value = [key, registry[key]]
      return { done, value }
    }
  }
}
console.log([...registry])
```

When it comes to using nonstring keys, though, we hit a hard limit in ES5 code. Luckily for us, though, ES6 collections provide us with an even better solution. ES6 collections don't have key-naming issues, and they facilitate collection behaviors, like the iterator we've implemented on our custom hash-map, out the box. At the same time, ES6 collections allow arbitrary keys, and aren't limited to string keys like regular JavaScript objects.

Let's plunge into their practical usage and inner workings.

5.1 Using ES6 Maps

ES6 introduces built-in collections, such as Map, meant to alleviate implementation of patterns such as those we outlined earlier when building our own hash-map from scratch. Map is a key/value data structure in ES6 that more naturally and efficiently lends itself to creating maps in JavaScript without the need for object literals.

5.1.1 First Look into ES6 Maps

Here's how what we had earlier would have looked when using ES6 maps. As you can see, the implementation details we've had to come up with for our custom ES5 hash-map are already built into Map, vastly simplifying our use case.

```
const map = new Map()
map.set('contra', { description: 'Asynchronous flow control' })
map.set('dragula', { description: 'Drag and drop' })
map.set('woofmark', {
  description: 'Markdown and WYSIWYG editor'
})
console.log([...map])
```

Once you have a map, you can query whether it contains an entry by a key provided via the map.has method.

```
map.has('contra')
// <- true
map.has('jquery')
// <- false
```

Earlier, we pointed out that maps don't cast keys the way traditional objects do. This is typically an advantage, but you need to keep in mind that they won't be treated the same when querying the map, either. The following example uses the Map constructor, which takes an iterable of key/value pairs and then illustrates how maps don't cast their keys to strings.

```
const map = new Map([[1, 'the number one']])
map.has(1)
// <- true
map.has('1')
// <- false
```

The map.get method takes a map entry key and returns the value if an entry by the provided key is found.

```
map.get('contra')
// <- { description: 'Asynchronous flow control' }
```

Deleting values from the map is possible through the map.delete method, providing the key for the entry you want to remove.

```
map.delete('contra')
map.get('contra')
// <- undefined
```

You can clear the entries for a Map entirely, without losing the reference to the map itself. This can be handy in cases where you want to reset state for an object.

```
const map = new Map([[1, 2], [3, 4], [5, 6]])
map.has(1)
// <- true
map.clear()
map.has(1)
// <- false
[...map]
// <- []
```

Maps come with a read-only .size property that behaves similarly to Array#length—at any point in time it gives you the current amount of entries in the map.

```
const map = new Map([[1, 2], [3, 4], [5, 6]])
map.size
// <- 3
```

```
map.delete(3)
map.size
// <- 2
map.clear()
map.size
// <- 0
```

You're able to use arbitrary objects when choosing map keys: you're not limited to using primitive values like symbols, numbers, or strings. Instead, you can use functions, objects, dates—and even DOM elements, too. Keys won't be cast to strings as we observe with plain JavaScript objects, but instead their references are preserved.

```
const map = new Map()
map.set(new Date(), function today() {})
map.set(() => 'key', { key: 'door' })
map.set(Symbol('items'), [1, 2])
```

As an example, if we chose to use a symbol as the key for a map entry, we'd have to use a reference to that same symbol to get the item back, as demonstrated in the following snippet of code.

```
const map = new Map()
const key = Symbol('items')
map.set(key, [1, 2])
map.get(Symbol('items')) // not the same reference as "key"
// <- undefined
map.get(key)
// <- [1, 2]
```

Assuming an array of key/value pair items you want to include on a map, we could use a for..of loop to iterate over those items and add each pair to the map using map.set, as shown in the following code snippet. Note how we're using destructuring during the for..of loop in order to effortlessly pull the key and value out of each two-dimensional item in items.

```
const items = [
  [new Date(), function today() {}],
  [() => 'key', { key: 'door' }],
  [Symbol('items'), [1, 2]]
]
const map = new Map()
for (const [key, value] of items) {
  map.set(key, value)
}
```

Maps are iterable objects as well, because they implement a Symbol.iterator method. Thus, a copy of the map can be created using a for..of loop using similar code to what we've just used to create a map out of the items array.

```
const copy = new Map()
for (const [key, value] of map) {
  copy.set(key, value)
}
```

In order to keep things simple, you can initialize maps directly using any object that follows the iterable protocol and produces a collection of [key, value] items. The following code snippet uses an array to seed a newly created Map. In this case, iteration occurs entirely in the Map constructor.

```
const items = [
  [new Date(), function today() {}],
  [() => 'key', { key: 'door' }],
  [Symbol('items'), [1, 2]]
]
const map = new Map(items)
```

Creating a copy of a map is even easier: you feed the map you want to copy into a new map's constructor, and get a copy back. There isn't a special new Map(Map) overload. Instead, we take advantage that map implements the iterable protocol and also consumes iterables when constructing a new map. The following code snippet demonstrates how simple that is.

```
const copy = new Map(map)
```

Just like maps are easily fed into other maps because they're iterable objects, they're also easy to consume. The following piece of code demonstrates how we can use the spread operator to this effect.

```
const map = new Map()
map.set(1, 'one')
map.set(2, 'two')
map.set(3, 'three')
console.log([...map])
// <- [[1, 'one'], [2, 'two'], [3, 'three']]
```

In the following piece of code we've combined several new features in ES6: Map, the for..of loop, let variables, and a template literal.

```
const map = new Map()
map.set(1, 'one')
map.set(2, 'two')
map.set(3, 'three')
for (const [key, value] of map) {
  console.log(`${ key }: ${ value }`)
```

```
// <- '1: one'
// <- '2: two'
// <- '3: three'
}
```

Even though map items are accessed through a programmatic API, their keys are unique, just like with hash-maps. Setting a key over and over again will only overwrite its value. The following code snippet demonstrates how writing the `'a'` item over and over again results in a map containing only a single item.

```
const map = new Map()
map.set('a', 1)
map.set('a', 2)
map.set('a', 3)
console.log([...map])
// <- [['a', 3]]
```

ES6 maps compare keys using an algorithm called `SameValueZero` in the specification, where `NaN` equals `NaN` but `-0` equals `+0`. The following piece of code shows how even though `NaN` is typically evaluated to be different than itself, `Map` considers `NaN` to be a constant value that's always the same.

```
console.log(NaN === NaN)
// <- false
console.log(-0 === +0)
// <- true
const map = new Map()
map.set(NaN, 'one')
map.set(NaN, 'two')
map.set(-0, 'three')
map.set(+0, 'four')
console.log([...map])
// <- [[NaN, 'two'], [0, 'four']]
```

When you iterate over a `Map`, you are actually looping over its `.entries()`. That means that you don't need to explicitly iterate over `.entries()`. It'll be done on your behalf anyway: `map[Symbol.iterator]` points to `map.entries`. The `.entries()` method returns an iterator for the key/value pairs in the map.

```
console.log(map[Symbol.iterator] === map.entries)
// <- true
```

There are two other `Map` iterators you can leverage: `.keys()` and `.values()`. The first enumerates keys in a map while the second enumerates values, as opposed to `.entries()`, which enumerates key/value pairs. The following snippet illustrates the differences between all three methods.

```
const map = new Map([[1, 2], [3, 4], [5, 6]])
console.log([...map.keys()])
// <- [1, 3, 5]
console.log([...map.values()])
// <- [2, 4, 6]
console.log([...map.entries()])
// <- [[1, 2], [3, 4], [5, 6]]
```

Map entries are always iterated in insertion order. This contrasts with `Object.keys`, which is specified to follow an arbitrary order. Although in practice, insertion order is typically preserved by Java-Script engines regardless of the specification.

Maps have a `.forEach` method that's equivalent in behavior to that in ES5 `Array` objects. The signature is (`value`, `key`, `map`), where `value` and `key` correspond to the current item in the iteration, while `map` is the map being iterated. Once again, keys do not get cast into strings in the case of `Map`, as demonstrated here.

```
const map = new Map([
  [NaN, 1],
  [Symbol(), 2],
  ['key', 'value'],
  [{ name: 'Kent' }, 'is a person']
])
map.forEach((value, key) => console.log(key, value))
// <- NaN 1
// <- Symbol() 2
// <- 'key' 'value'
// <- { name: 'Kent' } 'is a person'
```

Earlier, we brought up the ability of providing arbitrary object references as the key to a `Map` entry. Let's go into a concrete use case for that API.

5.1.2 Hash-Maps and the DOM

In ES5, whenever we wanted to associate a DOM element with an API object connecting that element with some library, we had to implement a verbose and slow pattern such as the one in the following code listing. That code returns an API object with a few methods associated to a given DOM element, allowing us to put DOM ele-

ments on a map from which we can later retrieve the API object for
a DOM element.

```
const map = []
function customThing(el) {
  const mapped = findByElement(el)
  if (mapped) {
    return mapped
  }
  const api = {
    // custom thing api methods
  }
  const entry = storeInMap(el, api)
  api.destroy = destroy.bind(null, entry)
  return api
}
function storeInMap(el, api) {
  const entry = { el, api }
  map.push(entry)
  return entry
}
function findByElement(query) {
  for (const { el, api } of map) {
    if (el === query) {
      return api
    }
  }
}
function destroy(entry) {
  const index = map.indexOf(entry)
  map.splice(index, 1)
}
```

One of the most valuable aspects of Map is the ability to index by any
object, such as DOM elements. That, combined with the fact that
Map also has collection manipulation abilities greatly simplifies
things. This is crucial for DOM manipulation in jQuery and other
DOM-heavy libraries, which often need to map DOM elements to
their internal state.

The following example shows how Map would reduce the burden of
maintenance in user code.

```
const map = new Map()
function customThing(el) {
  const mapped = findByElement(el)
  if (mapped) {
    return mapped
  }
  const api = {
```

```
  // custom thing api methods
    destroy: destroy.bind(null, el)
  }
  storeInMap(el, api)
  return api
}
function storeInMap(el, api) {
  map.set(el, api)
}
function findByElement(el) {
  return map.get(el)
}
function destroy(el) {
  map.delete(el)
}
```

The fact that mapping functions have become one-liners thanks to native `Map` methods means we could inline those functions instead, as readability is no longer an issue. The following piece of code is a vastly simplified alternative to the ES5 piece of code we started with. Here we're not concerned with implementation details anymore, but have instead boiled the DOM-to-API mapping to its bare essentials.

```
const map = new Map()
function customThing(el) {
  const mapped = map.get(el)
  if (mapped) {
    return mapped
  }
  const api = {
    // custom thing api methods
    destroy: () => map.delete(el)
  }
  map.set(el, api)
  return api
}
```

Maps aren't the only kind of built-in collection in ES6; there's also `WeakMap`, `Set`, and `WeakSet`. Let's proceed by digging into `WeakMap`.

5.2 Understanding and Using WeakMap

For the most part, you can think of `WeakMap` as a subset of `Map`. The `WeakMap` collection has a reduced API surface with fewer affordances than what we could find in `Map`. Collections created using `WeakMap` are not iterable like `Map`, meaning there is no iterable protocol in

WeakMap, no WeakMap#entries, no WeakMap#keys, no WeakMap#values, no WeakMap#forEach, and no WeakMap#clear methods.

Another distinction found in WeakMap is that every key must be an object. This is in contrast with Map, where, while object references were allowed as keys, they weren't enforced. Remember that Symbol is a value type, and as such, isn't allowed either.

```
const map = new WeakMap()
map.set(Date.now, 'now')
map.set(1, 1)
// <- TypeError
map.set(Symbol(), 2)
// <- TypeError
```

In exchange for having a more limited feature set, WeakMap key references are weakly held, meaning that the objects referenced by WeakMap keys are subject to garbage collection if there are no references to them—other than weak references. This kind of behavior is useful when you have metadata about a person, for example, but you want the person to be garbage-collected when and if the only reference back to person is their associated metadata. You can now keep that metadata in a WeakMap using person as the key.

In that sense, a WeakMap is most useful when the component maintaining it doesn't own the mapped objects, but wants to assign its own information to them without modifying the original objects or their lifecycle; letting memory be reclaimed when, for example, a DOM node is removed from the document.

To initialize a WeakMap, you are able to provide an iterable through the constructor. This should be a list of key/value pairs, just like with Map.

```
const map = new WeakMap([
  [new Date(), 'foo'],
  [() => 'bar', 'baz']
])
```

While WeakMap has a smaller API surface in order to effectively allow for weak references, it still carries .has, .get, and .delete methods like Map does. The brief snippet of code shown next demonstrates these methods.

```
const date = new Date()
const map = new WeakMap([[date, 'foo'], [() => 'bar', 'baz']])
map.has(date)
```

```
// <- true
map.get(date)
// <- 'foo'
map.delete(date)
map.has(date)
// <- false
```

5.2.1 Is WeakMap a Worse Map?

The distinction that makes WeakMap worth the trouble is in its name. Given that WeakMap holds references to its keys weakly, those objects are subject to garbage collection if there are no other references to them other than as WeakMap keys. This is in contrast with Map, which holds strong object references, preventing Map keys and values from being garbage-collected.

Correspondingly, use cases for WeakMap revolve around the need to specify metadata or extend an object while still being able to garbage-collect that object if there are no other references to it. A perfect example might be the underlying implementation for pro cess.on('unhandledRejection') in Node.js, which uses a WeakMap to keep track of rejected promises that weren't dealt with yet. By using WeakMap, the implementation prevents memory leaks because the WeakMap won't be grabbing onto the state related to those promises strongly. In this case, we have a simple map that weakly holds onto state, but is flexible enough to handle entries being removed from the map when promises are no longer referenced anywhere else.

Keeping data about DOM elements that should be released from memory when they're no longer of interest is another important use case, and in this regard using WeakMap is an even better solution to the DOM-related API caching solution we implemented earlier using Map.

In so many words, then: no, WeakMap is definitely not worse than Map —they just cater to different use cases.

5.3 Sets in ES6

The Set built-in is a new collection type in ES6 used to represent a grouping of values. In several aspects, Set is similar to Map:

- `Set` is also iterable

- `Set` constructor also accepts an iterable

- `Set` also has a `.size` property

- `Set` values can be arbitrary values or object references, like `Map` keys

- `Set` values must be unique, like `Map` keys

- `NaN` equals `NaN` when it comes to `Set` too

- All of `.keys`, `.values`, `.entries`, `.forEach`, `.has`, `.delete`, and `.clear`

At the same time, sets are different from `Map` in a few key ways. Sets don't hold key/value pairs; there's only one dimension. You can think of sets as being similar to arrays where every element is distinct from each other.

There isn't a `.get` method in `Set`. A `set.get(value)` method would be redundant: if you already have the `value` then there isn't anything else to get, as that's the only dimension. If we wanted to check for whether the `value` is in the set, there's `set.has(value)` to fulfill that role.

Similarly, a `set.set(value)` method wouldn't be aptly named, as you aren't setting a key to a `value`, but merely adding a value to the set instead. Thus, the method to add values to a set is `set.add`, as demonstrated in the next snippet.

```
const set = new Set()
set.add({ an: 'example' })
```

Sets are iterable, but unlike maps you only iterate over values, not key/value pairs. The following example demonstrates how sets can be spread over an array using the spread operator and creating a single dimensional list.

```
const set = new Set(['a', 'b', 'c'])
console.log([...set])
// <- ['a', 'b', 'c']
```

In the following example you can note how a set won't contain duplicate entries: every element in a `Set` must be unique.

```
const set = new Set(['a', 'b', 'b', 'c', 'c'])
console.log([...set])
// <- ['a', 'b', 'c']
```

The following piece of code creates a Set with all of the <div> elements on a page and then prints how many were found. Then, we query the DOM again and call set.add again for every DOM element. Given that they're all already in the set, the .size property won't change, meaning the set remains the same.

```
function divs() {
  return document.querySelectorAll('div')
}
const set = new Set(divs())
console.log(set.size)
// <- 56
divs().forEach(div => set.add(div))
console.log(set.size)
// <- 56
```

Given that a Set has no keys, the Set#entries method returns an iterator of [value, value] for each element in the set.

```
const set = new Set(['a', 'b', 'c'])
console.log([...set.entries()])
// <- [['a', 'a'], ['b', 'b'], ['c', 'c']]
```

The Set#entries method is consistent with Map#entries, which returns an iterator of [key, value] pairs. Using Set#entries as the default iterator for Set collections wouldn't be valuable, since it's used in for..of, when spreading a set, and in Array.from. In all of those cases, you probably want to iterate over a sequence of values in the set, but not a sequence of [value, value] pairs.

As demonstrated next, the default Set iterator uses Set#values, as opposed to Map, which defined its iterator as Map#entries.

```
const map = new Map()
console.log(map[Symbol.iterator] === map.entries)
// <- true
const set = new Set()
console.log(set[Symbol.iterator] === set.entries)
// <- false
console.log(set[Symbol.iterator] === set.values)
// <- true
```

The Set#keys method also returns an iterator for values, again for consistency, and it's in fact a reference to the Set#values iterator.

```
const set = new Set()
console.log(set.keys === set.values)
// <- true
```

5.4 ES6 WeakSets

In a similar fashion to Map and WeakMap, WeakSet is the weak version of Set that can't be iterated over. The values in a WeakSet must be unique object references. If nothing else is referencing a value found in a WeakSet, it'll be subject to garbage collection.

You can only .set, .delete, and check if the WeakSet .has a given value. Just like in Set, there's no .get because sets are one-dimensional.

Like with WeakMap, we aren't allowed to add primitive values such as strings or symbols to a WeakSet.

```
const set = new WeakSet()
set.add('a')
// <- TypeError
set.add(Symbol())
// <- TypeError
```

Passing iterators to the constructor is allowed, even though a Weak Set instance is not iterable itself. That iterable will be iterated when the set is constructed, adding each entry in the iterable sequence to the set. The following snippet of code serves as an example.

```
const set = new WeakSet([
  new Date(),
  {},
  () => {},
  [1]
])
```

As a use case for WeakSet, you may consider the following piece of code where we have a Car class that ensures its methods are only called upon car objects that are instances of the Car class by using a WeakSet.

```
const cars = new WeakSet()
class Car {
  constructor() {
    cars.add(this)
  }
  fuelUp() {
    if (!cars.has(this)) {
```

```
      throw new TypeError('Car#fuelUp called on a non-Car!')
    }
  }
}
```

For a better use case, consider the following `listOwnProperties` interface, where the provided object is recursively iterated in order to print every property of a tree. The `listOwnProperties` function should also know how to handle circular references, instead of becoming stuck in an infinite loop. How would you implement such an API?

```
const circle = { cx: 20, cy: 5, r: 15 }
circle.self = circle
listOwnProperties({
  circle,
  numbers: [1, 5, 7],
  sum: (a, b) => a + b
})
// <- circle.cx: 20
// <- circle.cy: 5
// <- circle.r: 15
// <- circle.self: [circular]
// <- numbers.0: 1
// <- numbers.1: 5
// <- numbers.2: 7
// <- sum: (a, b) => a + b
```

One way to do it would be by keeping a list of seen references in a WeakSet, so that we don't need to worry about nonlinear lookups. We use a WeakSet instead of a Set because we don't need any of the extra features that can be found in a Set.

```
function listOwnProperties(input) {
  recurse(input)

  function recurse(source, lastPrefix, seen = new WeakSet()) {
    Object.keys(source).forEach(printOrRecurse)

    function printOrRecurse(key) {
      const value = source[key]
      const prefix = lastPrefix
        ? `${ lastPrefix }.${ key }`
        : key
      const shouldRecur = (
        isObject(value) ||
        Array.isArray(value)
      )
      if (shouldRecur) {
        if (!seen.has(value)) {
```

```
      seen.add(value)
      recurse(value, prefix, seen)
    } else {
      console.log(`${ prefix }: [circular]`)
    }
  } else {
    console.log(`${ prefix }: ${ value }`)
  }
 }
 }
}
function isObject(value) {
  return Object.prototype.toString.call(value) ===
    '[object Object]'
}
```

A far more common use case would be to keep a list of DOM elements. Consider the case of a DOM library that needs to manipulate DOM elements in some way the first time it interacts with them, but which also can't leave any traces behind. Perhaps the library wants to add children onto the target element but it has no surefire way of identifying those children, and it doesn't want to meddle with the target either. Or maybe it wants to do something contextual, but only the first time it's called.

```
const elements = new WeakSet()
function dommy(target) {
  if (elements.has(target)) {
    return
  }
  elements.add(target)
  // do work ..
})
```

Whatever the reason, whenever we want to keep flags associated with a DOM element without visibly altering that DOM element, WeakSet is probably the way to go. If instead you wanted to associate arbitrary data instead of a simple flag, then maybe you should use WeakMap. When it comes to deciding whether to use Map, WeakMap, Set, or WeakSet, there's a series of questions you should ask yourself. For instance, if you need to keep object-related data, then you should know to look at weak collections. If your only concern is whether something is present, then you probably need a Set. If you are looking to create a cache, you should probably use a Map.

Collections in ES6 provide built-in solutions for common use cases that were previously cumbersome to implement by users, such as the case of Map, or hard to execute correctly, as in the case of Weak Map, where we allow references to be released if they're no longer interesting, avoiding memory leaks.

CHAPTER 6

Managing Property Access with Proxies

Proxies are an interesting and powerful feature in ES6 that act as intermediaries between API consumers and objects. In a nutshell, you can use a Proxy to determine the desired behavior whenever the properties of an underlying target object are accessed. A handler object can be used to configure traps for your Proxy, which define and restrict how the underlying object is accessed, as we'll see in a bit.

6.1 Getting Started with Proxy

By default, proxies don't do much—in fact they don't do anything. If you don't provide any configuration, your proxy will just work as a pass-through to the target object, also known as a "no-op forwarding proxy," meaning that all operations on the proxy object defer to the underlying object.

In the following piece of code, we create a no-op forwarding Proxy. You can observe how by assigning a value to proxy.exposed, that value is passed onto target.exposed. You could think of proxies as the gatekeepers of their underlying objects: they may allow certain operations to go through and prevent others from passing, but they carefully inspect every single interaction with their underlying objects.

```
const target = {}
const handler = {}
const proxy = new Proxy(target, handler)
proxy.exposed = true
console.log(target.exposed)
// <- true
console.log(proxy.somethingElse)
// <- undefined
```

We can make the proxy object a bit more interesting by adding traps. Traps allow you to intercept interactions with target in several different ways, as long as those interactions happen through the proxy object. For instance, we could use a get trap to log every attempt to pull a value out of a property in target, or a set trap to prevent certain properties from being written to. Let's kick things off by learning more about get traps.

6.1.1 Trapping get Accessors

The proxy in the following code listing is able to track any and every property access event because it has a handler.get trap. It can also be used to transform the value returned by accessing any given property before returning a value to the accessor.

```
const handler = {
  get(target, key) {
    console.log(`Get on property "${ key }"`)
    return target[key]
  }
}
const target = {}
const proxy = new Proxy(target, handler)
proxy.numbers = [1, 1, 2, 3, 5, 8, 13]
proxy.numbers
// 'Get on property "numbers"'
// <- [1, 1, 2, 3, 5, 8, 13]
proxy['something-else']
// 'Get on property "something-else"'
// <- undefined
```

As a complement to proxies, ES6 introduces a Reflect built-in object. The traps in ES6 proxies are mapped one-to-one to the Reflect API: for every trap, there's a matching reflection method in Reflect. These methods can be particularly useful when we want the default behavior of proxy traps, but we don't want to concern ourselves with the implementation of that behavior.

In the following code snippet we use `Reflect.get` to provide the default behavior for `get` operations, while not worrying about accessing the `key` property in `target` by hand. While in this case the operation may seem trivial, the default behavior for other traps may be harder to remember and implement correctly. We can forward every parameter in the trap to the reflection API and return its result.

```
const handler = {
  get(target, key) {
    console.log(`Get on property "${ key }"`)
    return Reflect.get(target, key)
  }
}
const target = {}
const proxy = new Proxy(target, handler)
```

The `get` trap doesn't necessarily have to return the original `tar get[key]` value. Imagine the case where you wanted properties prefixed by an underscore to be inaccessible. In this case, you could throw an error, letting the consumer know that the property is inaccessible through the proxy.

```
const handler = {
  get(target, key) {
    if (key.startsWith('_')) {
      throw new Error(`Property "${ key }" is inaccessible.`)
    }
    return Reflect.get(target, key)
  }
}
const target = {}
const proxy = new Proxy(target, handler)
proxy._secret
// <- Uncaught Error: Property "_secret" is inaccessible.
```

To the keen observer, it may be apparent that disallowing access to certain properties through the proxy becomes most useful when creating a proxy with clearly defined access rules for the underlying `tar get` object, and exposing that proxy instead of the `target` object. That way you can still access the underlying object freely, but consumers are forced to go through the proxy and play by its rules, putting you in control of exactly how they can interact with the object. This wasn't possible before proxies were introduced in in ES6.

6.1.2 Trapping set Accessors

As the in counterpart of `get` traps, `set` traps can intercept property assignment. Suppose we wanted to prevent assignment on properties starting with an underscore. We could replicate the `get` trap we implemented earlier to block assignment as well.

The `Proxy` in the next example prevents underscored property access for both `get` and `set` when accessing `target` through proxy. Note how the `set` trap returns `true` here? Returning `true` in a `set` trap means that setting the property `key` to the provided `value` should succeed. If the return value for the `set` trap is `false`, setting the property value will throw a `TypeError` under strict mode, and otherwise fail silently. If we were using `Reflect.set` instead, as brought up earlier, we wouldn't need to concern ourselves with these implementation details: we could just `return Reflect.set(target, key, value)`. That way, when somebody reads our code later, they'll be able to understand that we're using `Reflect.set`, which is equivalent to the default operation, equivalent to the case where a `Proxy` object isn't part of the equation.

```
const handler = {
  get(target, key) {
    invariant(key, 'get')
    return Reflect.get(target, key)
  },
  set(target, key, value) {
    invariant(key, 'set')
    return Reflect.set(target, key, value)
  }
}
function invariant(key, action) {
  if (key.startsWith('_')) {
    throw new Error(`Can't ${ action } private "${ key }"
    property`)
  }
}
const target = {}
const proxy = new Proxy(target, handler)
```

The following piece of code demonstrates how the proxy responds to consumer interaction.

```
proxy.text = 'the great black pony ate your lunch'
console.log(target.text)
// <- 'the great black pony ate your lunch'
proxy._secret
```

```
// <- Error: Can't get private "_secret" property
proxy._secret = 'invalidate'
// <- Error: Can't set private "_secret" property
```

The object being proxied, `target` in our latest example, should be completely hidden from consumers, so that they are forced to access it exclusively through `proxy`. Preventing direct access to the `target` object means that they will have to obey the access rules defined on the `proxy` object—such as *"properties prefixed with an underscore are off-limits."*

To that end, you could wrap the proxied object in a function and then return the `proxy`.

```
function proxied() {
  const target = {}
  const handler = {
    get(target, key) {
      invariant(key, 'get')
      return Reflect.get(target, key)
    },
    set(target, key, value) {
      invariant(key, 'set')
      return Reflect.set(target, key, value)
    }
  }
  return new Proxy(target, handler)
}
function invariant(key, action) {
  if (key.startsWith('_')) {
    throw new Error(`Can't ${ action } private "${ key }"
    property`)
  }
}
```

Usage stays the same, except that now access to `target` is completely governed by `proxy` and its mischievous traps. At this point, any `_secret` properties in `target` are completely inaccessible through the proxy, and since `target` can't be accessed directly from outside the `proxied` function, they're sealed off from consumers for good.

A general-purpose approach would be to offer a proxying function that takes an `original` object and returns a proxy. You can then call that function whenever you're about to expose a public API, as shown in the following code block. The `concealWithPrefix` function wraps the `original` object in a `Proxy` where properties prefixed with a `prefix` value (or _ if none is provided) can't be accessed.

```
function concealWithPrefix(original, prefix='_') {
  const handler = {
    get(original, key) {
      invariant(key, 'get')
      return Reflect.get(original, key)
    },
    set(original, key, value) {
      invariant(key, 'set')
      return Reflect.set(original, key, value)
    }
  }
  return new Proxy(original, handler)
  function invariant(key, action) {
    if (key.startsWith(prefix)) {
      throw new Error(`Can't ${ action } private "${ key }"
      property`)
    }
  }
}
const target = {
  _secret: 'secret',
  text: 'everyone-can-read-this'
}
const proxy = concealWithPrefix(target)
// expose proxy to consumers
```

You might be tempted to argue that you could achieve the same
behavior in ES5 simply by using variables privately scoped to the
concealWithPrefix function, without the need for the Proxy itself.
The difference is that proxies allow you to "privatize" property
access dynamically. Without relying on Proxy, you couldn't mark
every property that starts with an underscore as private. You could
use Object.freeze[1] on the object, but then you wouldn't be able to
modify the property references yourself, either. Or you could define
get and set accessors for every property, but then again you wouldn't
be able to block access on every single property, only the ones you
explicitly configured getters and in setters for.

---

1 The Object.freeze method prevents adding new properties, removing existing ones,
and modifying property value references. Note that it doesn't make the values themselves immutable: their properties can still change, provided Object.freeze isn't called
on those objects as well.

6.1.3 Schema Validation with Proxies

Sometimes we have an object with user input that we want to validate against a schema, a model of how that input is supposed to be structured, what properties it should have, what types those properties should be, and how those properties should be filled. We'd like to verify that a customer email field contains an email address, a numeric cost field contains a number, and a required name field isn't missing.

There are a number of ways in which you could do schema validation. You could use a validation function that throws errors if an invalid value is found on the object, but you'd have to ensure the object is off limits once you've deemed it valid. You could validate each property individually, but you'd have to remember to validate them whenever they're changed. You could also use a Proxy. By providing consumers with a Proxy to the actual model object, you'd ensure that the object never enters an invalid state, as an exception would be thrown otherwise.

Another aspect of schema validation via Proxy is that it helps you separate validation concerns from the target object, where validation occurs sometimes in the wild. The target object would stay as a plain JavaScript object, meaning that while you give consumers a validating proxy, you keep an untainted version of the data that's always valid, as guaranteed by the proxy.

Just like a validation function, the handler settings can be reutilized across several Proxy instances, without having to rely on prototypal inheritance or ES6 classes.

In the following example, we have a simple validator object, with a set trap that looks up properties in a map. When a property gets set through the proxy, its key is looked up on the map. If the map contains a rule for that property, it'll run that function to assert whether the assignment is deemed valid. As long as the person properties are set through a proxy using the validator, the model invariants will be satisfied according to our predefined validation rules.

```
const validations = new Map()
const validator = {
  set(target, key, value) {
    if (validations.has(key)) {
      return validations[key](value)
    }
```

```
    return Reflect.set(target, key, value)
  }
}
validations.set('age', validateAge)

function validateAge(value) {
  if (typeof value !== 'number' || Number.isNaN(value)) {
    throw new TypeError('Age must be a number')
  }
  if (value <= 0) {
    throw new TypeError('Age must be a positive number')
  }
  return true
}
```

The following piece of code shows how we could consume the validator handler. This general-purpose proxy handler is passed into a Proxy for the person object. The handler then enforces our schema by ensuring that values set through the proxy pass the schema validation rules for any given property. In this case, we've added a validation rule that says age must be a positive numeric value.

```
const person = {}
const proxy = new Proxy(person, validator)
proxy.age = 'twenty three'
// <- TypeError: Age must be a number
proxy.age = NaN
// <- TypeError: Age must be a number
proxy.age = 0
// <- TypeError: Age must be a positive number
proxy.age = 28
console.log(person.age)
// <- 28
```

While proxies offer previously unavailable granular control over what a consumer can and cannot do with an object, as defined by access rules defined by the implementor, there's also a harsher variant of proxies that allows us to completely shut off access to target whenever we deem it necessary: revocable proxies.

6.2 Revocable Proxies

Revocable proxies offer more fine-grained control than plain Proxy objects. The API is a bit different in that there is no new keyword involved, as opposed to new Proxy(target, handler); and a { proxy, revoke } object is returned, instead of just the proxy object being returned. Once `revoke()` is called, the `proxy` will throw an error on any operation.

Let's go back to our pass-through `Proxy` example and make it revocable. Note how we're no longer using `new`, how calling `revoke()` over and over has no effect, and how an error is thrown if we attempt to interact with the underlying object in any way.

```
const target = {}
const handler = {}
const { proxy, revoke } = Proxy.revocable(target, handler)
proxy.isUsable = true
console.log(proxy.isUsable)
// <- true
revoke()
revoke()
revoke()
console.log(proxy.isUsable)
// <- TypeError: illegal operation attempted on a revoked proxy
```

This type of `Proxy` is particularly useful because you can completely cut off access to the `proxy` granted to a consumer. You could expose a revocable `Proxy` and keep around the `revoke` method, perhaps in a `WeakMap` collection. When it becomes clear that the consumer shouldn't have access to `target` anymore—not even through `proxy` —you `.revoke()` their access rights.

The following example shows two functions. The `getStorage` function can be used to get proxied access into `storage`, and it keeps a reference to the `revoke` function for the returned `proxy` object. Whenever we want to cut off access to `storage` for a given `proxy`, `revokeStorage` will call its associated `revoke` function and remove the entry from the `WeakMap`. Note that making both functions accessible to the same set of consumers won't pose security concerns: once access through a proxy has been revoked, it can't be restored.

```
const proxies = new WeakMap()
const storage = {}

function getStorage() {
  const handler = {}
  const { proxy, revoke } = Proxy.revocable(storage, handler)
  proxies.set(proxy, { revoke })
  return proxy
}

function revokeStorage(proxy) {
```

```
    proxies.get(proxy).revoke()
    proxies.delete(proxy)
  }
```

Given that revoke is available on the same scope where your han
dler traps are defined, you could set up unforgiving access rules
such that if a consumer attempts to access a private property more
than once, you revoke their proxy access entirely.

6.3 Proxy Trap Handlers

Perhaps the most interesting aspect of proxies is how you can use
them to intercept just about any interaction with the target object
—not only plain get or set operations.

We've already covered get, which traps property access; and set,
which traps property assignment. Next up we'll discuss the different
kinds of traps you can set up.

6.3.1 has Trap

We can use handler.has to conceal any property you want when it
comes to the in operator. In the set trap code samples we prevented
changes and even access to properties with a certain prefix, but
unwanted accessors could still probe the proxy to figure out whether
these properties exist. There are three alternatives here:

- Do nothing, in which case key in proxy falls through to
  Reflect.has(target, key), the equivalent of key in target

- Return true or false regardless of whether key is or is not
  present in target

- Throw an error signaling that the in operation is illegal

Throwing an error is quite final, and it certainly doesn't help in
those cases where you want to conceal the fact that the property
even exists. You would be acknowledging that the property is, in
fact, protected. Throwing is, however, valid in those cases where you
want the consumer to understand why the operation is failing, as
you can explain the failure reason in an error message.

It's often best to indicate that the property is not in the object, by
returning false instead of throwing. A fall-through case where you

return the result of the key in target expression is a good default case to have.

Going back to the getter/setter example in Section 6.1.2, "Trapping set Accessors," on page 180, we'll want to return false for properties in the prefixed property space and use the default for all other properties. This will keep our inaccessible properties well hidden from unwanted visitors.

```
const handler = {
  get(target, key) {
    invariant(key, 'get')
    return Reflect.get(target, key)
  },
  set(target, key, value) {
    invariant(key, 'set')
    return Reflect.set(target, key, value)
  },
  has(target, key) {
    if (key.startsWith('_')) {
      return false
    }
    return Reflect.has(target, key)
  }
}
function invariant(key, action) {
  if (key.startsWith('_')) {
    throw new Error(`Can't ${ action } private "${ key }"
    property`)
  }
}
```

Note how accessing properties through the proxy will now return false when querying one of the private properties, with the consumer being none the wiser—completely unaware that we've intentionally hid the property from them. Note how _secret in target returns true because we're bypassing the proxy. That means we can still use the underlying object unchallenged by tight access control rules while consumers have no choice but to stick to the proxy's rules.

```
const target = {
  _secret: 'securely-stored-value',
  wellKnown: 'publicly-known-value'
}
const proxy = new Proxy(target, handler)
console.log('wellKnown' in proxy)
// <- true
console.log('_secret' in proxy)
```

```
// <- false
console.log('_secret' in target)
// <- true
```

We could've thrown an exception instead. That would be useful in situations where attempts to access properties in the private space is seen as a mistake that would've resulted in an invalid state, rather than as a security concern in code that aims to be embedded into third-party websites.

Note that if we wanted to prevent Object#hasOwnProperty from finding properties in the private space, the has trap won't help.

```
console.log(proxy.hasOwnProperty('_secret'))
// <- true
```

The getOwnPropertyDescriptor trap in Section 6.4.1, "getOwnPropertyDescriptor Trap," on page 195 offers a solution that's able to intercept Object#hasOwnProperty as well.

6.3.2 deleteProperty Trap

Setting a property to undefined clears its value, but the property is still part of the object. Using the delete operator on a property with code like delete cat.furBall means that the furBall property will be completely gone from the cat object.

```
const cat = { furBall: true }
cat.furBall = undefined
console.log('furBall' in cat)
// <- true
delete cat.furBall
console.log('furBall' in cat)
// <- false
```

The code in the last example where we prevented access to prefixed properties has a problem: you can't change the value of a _secret property, nor even use in to learn about its existence, but you still can remove the property entirely using the delete operator through the proxy object. The following code sample shows that shortcoming in action.

```
const target = { _secret: 'foo' }
const proxy = new Proxy(target, handler)
console.log('_secret' in proxy)
// <- false
console.log('_secret' in target)
// <- true
```

```
delete proxy._secret
console.log('_secret' in target)
// <- false
```

We can use `handler.deleteProperty` to prevent a `delete` operation from working. Just like with the `get` and `set` traps, throwing in the `deleteProperty` trap will be enough to prevent the deletion of a property. In this case, throwing is okay because we want the consumer to know that external operations on prefixed properties are forbidden.

```
const handler = {
  get(target, key) {
    invariant(key, 'get')
    return Reflect.get(target, key)
  },
  set(target, key, value) {
    invariant(key, 'set')
    return Reflect.set(target, key, value)
  },
  deleteProperty(target, key) {
    invariant(key, 'delete')
    return Reflect.deleteProperty(target, key)
  }
}
function invariant(key, action) {
  if (key.startsWith('_')) {
    throw new Error(`Can't ${ action } private "${ key }"
    property`)
  }
}
```

If we ran the exact same piece of code we tried earlier, we'd run into the exception while trying to delete _secret from the proxy. The following example shows the mechanics of the updated `handler`.

```
const target = { _secret: 'foo' }
const proxy = new Proxy(target, handler)
console.log('_secret' in proxy)
// <- true
delete proxy._secret
// <- Error: Can't delete private "_secret" property
```

Consumers interacting with `target` through the `proxy` can no longer delete properties in the _secret property space. That's one less thing to worry about!

6.3.3 defineProperty Trap

The Object.defineProperty function—introduced in ES5—can be used to add new properties to a target object, using a property key and a property descriptor. For the most part, Object.defineProp erty(target, key, descriptor) is used in two kinds of situations:

1. When we need to ensure cross-browser support of getters and setters
2. When we want to define a custom property accessor

Properties added by hand are read-write, they are deletable, and they are enumerable.

Properties added through Object.defineProperty, in contrast, default to being read-only, nondeletable, and nonenumerable. By default, the property is akin to bindings declared using the const statement in that it's read-only, but that doesn't make it immutable.

When creating properties through defineProperty, you can customize the following aspects of the property descriptor:

- configurable = false disables most changes to the property descriptor and makes the property undeletable
- enumerable = false hides the property from for..in loops and Object.keys
- writable = false makes the property value read-only
- value = undefined is the initial value for the property
- get = undefined is a method that acts as the getter for the property
- set = undefined is a method that receives the new value and updates the property's value

Note that you'll have to choose between configuring the value and writable pair or get and set pair. When choosing the former you're configuring a data descriptor. You get a data descriptor when creating plain properties, such as in pizza.topping = 'ham', too. In that case, topping has a value and it may or may not be writa ble. If you pick the second pair of options, you're creating an accessor descriptor that is entirely defined by the methods you can use to get() or set(value) for the property.

The following code sample shows how property descriptors can be completely different depending on whether we use the declarative option or go through the programmatic API. We use `Object.getOwnPropertyDescriptor`, which receives a `target` object and a property key, to pull the object descriptor for properties we create.

```
const pizza = {}
pizza.topping = 'ham'
Object.defineProperty(pizza, 'extraCheese', { value: true })
console.log(Object.getOwnPropertyDescriptor(pizza, 'topping'))
// {
//   value: 'ham',
//   writable: true,
//   enumerable: true,
//   configurable: true
// }
console.log(
  Object.getOwnPropertyDescriptor(pizza, 'extraCheese')
)
// {
//   value: true,
//   writable: false,
//   enumerable: false,
//   configurable: false
// }
```

The `handler.defineProperty` trap can be used to intercept properties being defined. Note that this trap intercepts the declarative `pizza.extraCheese = false` property declaration flavor as well as `Object.defineProperty` calls. As arguments for the trap, you get the `target` object, the property key, and the `descriptor`.

The next example prevents the addition of any properties added through the `proxy`. When the handler returns false, the property declaration fails loudly with an exception under strict mode, and silently without an exception when we're in sloppy mode. Strict mode is superior to sloppy mode due to its performance gains and hardened semantics. It is also the default mode in ES6 modules, as we'll see in Chapter 8. For those reasons, we'll assume strict mode in all the code examples.

```
const handler = {
  defineProperty(target, key, descriptor) {
    return false
  }
}
const target = {}
```

```
const proxy = new Proxy(target, handler)
proxy.extraCheese = false
// <- TypeError: 'defineProperty' on proxy: trap returned false
```

If we go back to the prefixed properties use case, we could add a
defineProperty trap to prevent the creation of private properties
through the proxy. In the following example we will throw on
attempts to define a property in the private prefixed space by reusing the invariant function.

```
const handler = {
  defineProperty(target, key, descriptor) {
    invariant(key, 'define')
    return Reflect.defineProperty(target, key, descriptor)
  }
}
function invariant(key, action) {
  if (key.startsWith('_')) {
    throw new Error(`Can't ${ action } private "${ key }"
    property`)
  }
}
```

Let's try it out on a target object. We'll attempt to declare a property with and without the prefix. Setting a property in the private
property space at the proxy level will now throw an error.

```
const target = {}
const proxy = new Proxy(target, handler)
proxy.topping = 'cheese'
proxy._secretIngredient = 'salsa'
// <- Error: Can't define private "_secretIngredient" property
```

The proxy object is safely hiding _secret properties behind a trap
that guards them from definition through either proxy[key] =
value or Object.defineProperty(proxy, key, { value }). If we
factor in the previous traps we saw, we could prevent _secret properties from being read, written, queried, and created.

There's one more trap that can help conceal _secret properties.

6.3.4 ownKeys Trap

The handler.ownKeys method may be used to return an Array of
properties that will be used as a result for Reflect.ownKeys(). It
should include all properties of target: enumerable, nonenumerable, and symbols as well. A default implementation, as

always, could pass through to the reflection method on the proxied target object.

```
const handler = {
  ownKeys(target) {
    return Reflect.ownKeys(target)
  }
}
```

Interception wouldn't affect the output of Object.keys in this case, since we're simply passing through to the default implementation.

```
const target = {
  [Symbol('id')]: 'ba3dfcc0',
  _secret: 'sauce',
  _toppingCount: 3,
  toppings: ['cheese', 'tomato', 'bacon']
}
const proxy = new Proxy(target, handler)
for (const key of Object.keys(proxy)) {
  console.log(key)
  // <- '_secret'
  // <- '_toppingCount'
  // <- 'toppings'
}
```

Do note that the ownKeys interceptor is used during all of the following operations:

- Reflect.ownKeys() returns every own key on the object
- Object.getOwnPropertyNames() returns only nonsymbol properties
- Object.getOwnPropertySymbols() returns only symbol properties
- Object.keys() returns only nonsymbol enumerable properties
- for..in returns only nonsymbol enumerable properties

In the use case where we want to shut off access to a prefixed property space, we could take the output of Reflect.ownKeys(target) and filter off of that. That'd be the same approach that methods such as Object.getOwnPropertySymbols follow internally.

In the next example, we're careful to ensure that any keys that aren't strings, namely Symbol property keys, always return true. Then, we filter out string keys that begin with '_'.

```
const handler = {
  ownKeys(target) {
    return Reflect.ownKeys(target).filter(key => {
      const isStringKey = typeof key === 'string'
      if (isStringKey) {
        return !key.startsWith('_')
      }
      return true
    })
  }
}
```

If we now used the `handler` in the preceding snippet to pull the object keys, we'll only find the properties in the public, nonprefixed space. Note how the `Symbol` isn't being returned either. That's because `Object.keys` filters out `Symbol` property keys before returning its result.

```
const target = {
  [Symbol('id')]: 'ba3dfcc0',
  _secret: 'sauce',
  _toppingCount: 3,
  toppings: ['cheese', 'tomato', 'bacon']
}
const proxy = new Proxy(target, handler)
for (const key of Object.keys(proxy)) {
  console.log(key)
  // <- 'toppings'
}
```

Symbol iteration wouldn't be affected by our `handler` because `Symbol` keys have a type of `'symbol'`, which would cause our `.filter` function to return true.

```
const target = {
  [Symbol('id')]: 'ba3dfcc0',
  _secret: 'sauce',
  _toppingCount: 3,
  toppings: ['cheese', 'tomato', 'bacon']
}
const proxy = new Proxy(target, handler)
for (const key of Object.getOwnPropertySymbols(proxy)) {
  console.log(key)
  // <- Symbol(id)
}
```

We were able to hide properties prefixed with _ from key enumeration while leaving symbols and other properties unaffected. What's more, there's no need to repeat ourselves in several trap handlers: a single `ownKeys` trap took care of all different enumeration methods.

The only caveat is that we need to be careful about handling Symbol property keys.

6.4 Advanced Proxy Traps

For the most part, the traps that we discussed so far have to do with property access and manipulation. Up next is the last trap we'll cover that's related to property access. Every other trap in this section has to do with the object we are proxying itself, instead of its properties.

6.4.1 getOwnPropertyDescriptor Trap

The getOwnPropertyDescriptor trap is triggered when querying an object for the property descriptor for some key. It should return a property descriptor or undefined when the property doesn't exist. There is also the option of throwing an exception, aborting the operation entirely.

If we go back to the canonical private property space example, we could implement a trap, such as the one in the next code snippet, to prevent consumers from learning about property descriptors of private properties.

```
const handler = {
  getOwnPropertyDescriptor(target, key) {
    invariant(key, 'get property descriptor for')
    return Reflect.getOwnPropertyDescriptor(target, key)
  }
}
function invariant(key, action) {
  if (key.startsWith('_')) {
    throw new Error(`Can't ${ action } private "${ key }" property`)
  }
}
const target = {}
const proxy = new Proxy(target, handler)
Reflect.getOwnPropertyDescriptor(proxy, '_secret')
// <- Error: Can't get property descriptor for private
// "_secret" property
```

One problem with this approach might be that you're effectively telling external consumers that they're unauthorized to access prefixed properties. It might be best to conceal them entirely by returning undefined. That way, private properties will behave no differently than properties that are truly absent from the target object. The following example shows how `Object.getOwnPropertyDescriptor` returns `undefined` for an nonexistent `dressing` property, and how it does the same for a `_secret` property. Existing properties that aren't in the private property space produce their property descriptors as usual.

```
const handler = {
  getOwnPropertyDescriptor(target, key) {
    if (key.startsWith('_')) {
      return
    }
    return Reflect.getOwnPropertyDescriptor(target, key)
  }
}
const target = {
  _secret: 'sauce',
  topping: 'mozzarella'
}
const proxy = new Proxy(target, handler)
console.log(Object.getOwnPropertyDescriptor(proxy, 'dressing'))
// <- undefined
console.log(Object.getOwnPropertyDescriptor(proxy, '_secret'))
// <- undefined
console.log(Object.getOwnPropertyDescriptor(proxy, 'topping'))
// {
//   value: 'mozzarella',
//   writable: true,
//   enumerable: true,
//   configurable: true
// }
```

The `getOwnPropertyDescriptor` trap is able to intercept the implementation of `Object#hasOwnProperty`, which relies on property descriptors to check whether a property exists.

```
console.log(proxy.hasOwnProperty('topping'))
// <- true
console.log(proxy.hasOwnProperty('_secret'))
// <- false
```

When you're trying to hide things, it's best to have them try and behave as if they fell in some other category than the category they're actually in, thus concealing their behavior and passing it off for something else. Throwing, however, sends the wrong message when we want to conceal something: why does a property throw instead of return `undefined`? It must exist but be inaccessible. This is not unlike situations in HTTP API design where we might prefer to return "404 Not Found" responses for sensitive resources, such as an administration backend, when the user is unauthorized to access them, instead of the technically correct "401 Unauthorized" status code.

When debugging concerns outweigh security concerns, you should at least consider the throw statement. In any case, it's important to understand your use case in order to figure out the optimal and least surprising behavior for a given component.

6.4.2 apply Trap

The apply trap is quite interesting; it's specifically tailored to work with functions. When the proxied target function is invoked, the apply trap is triggered. All of the statements in the following code sample would go through the apply trap in your proxy handler object.

```
proxy('cats', 'dogs')
proxy(...['cats', 'dogs'])
proxy.call(null, 'cats', 'dogs')
proxy.apply(null, ['cats', 'dogs'])
Reflect.apply(proxy, null, ['cat', 'dogs'])
```

The apply trap receives three arguments:

- target is the function being proxied
- ctx is the context passed as this to target when applying a call
- args is an array of arguments passed to target when applying the call

The default implementation that doesn't alter the outcome would return the results of calling Reflect.apply.

```
const handler = {
  apply(target, ctx, args) {
    return Reflect.apply(target, ctx, args)
  }
}
```

Besides being able to log all parameters of every function call for proxy, this trap could also be used to add extra parameters or to modify the results of a function call. All of these examples would work without changing the underlying target function, which makes the trap reusable across any functions that need the extra functionality.

The following example proxies a sum function through a twice trap handler that doubles the results of sum without affecting the code around it other than using the proxy instead of the sum function directly.

```
const twice = {
  apply(target, ctx, args) {
    return Reflect.apply(target, ctx, args) * 2
  }
}
function sum(a, b) {
  return a + b
}
const proxy = new Proxy(sum, twice)
console.log(proxy(1, 2))
// <- 6
```

Moving onto another use case, suppose we want to preserve the context for this across function calls. In the following example we have a logger object with a .get method that returns the logger object itself.

```
const logger = {
  test() {
    return this
  }
}
```

If we want to ensure that get always returns logger, we could bind that method to logger, as shown next.

```
logger.test = logger.test.bind(logger)
```

The problem with that approach is that we'd have to do it for every single function on logger that relies on this being a reference to the logger object itself. An alternative could involve using a proxy with a get trap handler, where we modify returned functions by binding them to the target object.

```
const selfish = {
  get(target, key) {
    const value = Reflect.get(target, key)
    if (typeof value !== 'function') {
      return value
    }
    return value.bind(target)
  }
}
const proxy = new Proxy(logger, selfish)
```

This would work for any kind of object, even class instances, without any further modification. The following snippet demonstrates how the original logger is vulnerable to .call and similar operations that can change the this context, while the proxy object ignores those kinds of changes.

```
const something = {}
console.log(logger.test() === logger)
// <- true
console.log(logger.test.call(something) === something)
// <- true
console.log(proxy.test() === logger)
// <- true
console.log(proxy.test.call(something) === logger)
// <- true
```

There's a subtle problem that arises from using selfish in its current incarnation, though. Whenever we get a reference to a method through the proxy, we get a freshly created bound function that's the result of value.bind(target). Consequently, methods no longer appear to be equal to themselves. As shown next, this can result in confusing behavior.

```
console.log(proxy.test !== proxy.test)
// <- true
```

This could be resolved using a WeakMap. We'll go back to our self ish trap handler options, and move that into a factory function. Within that function we'll keep a cache of bound methods, so that we create the bound version of each function only once. While we're at it, we'll make our selfish function receive the target object we want to be proxying, so that the details of how we are binding every method become an implementation concern.

```
function selfish(target) {
  const cache = new WeakMap()
  const handler = {
    get(target, key) {
      const value = Reflect.get(target, key)
      if (typeof value !== 'function') {
        return value
      }
      if (!cache.has(value)) {
        cache.set(value, value.bind(target))
      }
      return cache.get(value)
    }
  }
```

```
    const proxy = new Proxy(target, handler)
    return proxy
}
```

Now that we are caching bound functions and tracking them by the original value, the same object is always returned and simple comparisons don't surprise consumers of selfish anymore.

```
const selfishLogger = selfish(logger)
console.log(selfishLogger.test === selfishLogger.test)
// <- true
console.log(selfishLogger.test() === selfishLogger)
// <- true
console.log(selfishLogger.test.call(something) ===
    selfishLogger)
// <- true
```

The selfish function can now be reused whenever we want all methods on an object to be bound to the host object itself. This is particularly convenient when dealing with classes that heavily rely on this being the instance object.

There are dozens of ways of binding methods to their parent object, all with their own sets of advantages and drawbacks. The proxy-based solution might be the most convenient and hassle-free, but browser support isn't great yet, and Proxy implementations are known to be pretty slow.

We haven't used an apply trap for the selfish examples, which illustrates that not everything is one-size-fits-all. Using an apply trap for this use case would involve the current selfish proxy returning proxies for value functions, and then returning a bound function in the apply trap for the value proxy. While this may sound more correct, in the sense that we're not using .bind but instead relying on Reflect.apply, we'd still need the WeakMap cache and selfish proxy. That is to say we'd be adding an extra layer of abstraction, a second proxy, and getting little value in terms of separation of concerns or maintainability, since both proxy layers would remain coupled to some degree, it'd be best to keep everything in a single layer. While abstractions are a great thing, too many abstractions can become more insurmountable than the problem they attempt to fix.

Up to what point is the abstraction justifiable over a few .bind statements in the constructor of a class object? These are hard questions that always depend on context, but they must be considered

---

when designing a component system so that, in the process of adding abstraction layers meant to help you avoid repeating yourself, you don't add complexity for complexity's sake.

6.4.3 construct Trap

The construct trap intercepts uses of the new operator. In the following code sample, we implement a custom construct trap that behaves identically to the construct trap. We use the spread operator, in combination with the new keyword, so that we can pass any arguments to the Target constructor.

```
const handler = {
  construct(Target, args) {
    return new Target(...args)
  }
}
```

The previous example is identical to using Reflect.construct, shown next. Note that in this case we're not spreading the args over the parameters to the method call. Reflection methods mirror the method signature of proxy traps, and as such Reflect.construct has a signature of Target, args, just like the construct trap method.

```
const handler = {
  construct(Target, args) {
    return Reflect.construct(Target, args)
  }
}
```

Traps like construct allow us to modify or extend the behavior of an object without using a factory function or changing the implementation. It should be noted, however, that proxies should always have a clearly defined goal, and that goal shouldn't meddle too much with the implementation of the underlying target. That is to say, a proxy trap for construct that acts as a switch for several different underlying classes is probably the wrong kind of abstraction: a simple function would do.

Use cases for construct traps should mostly revolve around rebalancing constructor parameters or doing things that should always be done around the constructor, such as logging and tracking object creation.

The following example shows how a proxy could be used to offer a slightly different experience to a portion of the consumers, without changing the implementation of the class. When using the Proxied Target, we can leverage the constructor parameters to declare a name property on the target instance.

```
const handler = {
  construct(Target, args) {
    const [ name ] = args
    const target = Reflect.construct(Target, args)
    target.name = name
    return target
  }
}
class Target {
  hello() {
    console.log(`Hello, ${ this.name }!`)
  }
}
```

In this case, we could've changed Target directly so that it receives a name parameter in its constructor and stores that as an instance property. That is not always the case. You could be unable to modify a class directly, either because you don't own that code or because other code relies on a particular structure already. The following code snippet shows the Target class in action, with its regular API and the modified ProxiedTarget API resulting from using proxy traps for construct.

```
const target = new Target()
target.name = 'Nicolás'
target.hello()
// <- 'Hello, Nicolás'

const ProxiedTarget = new Proxy(Target, handler)
const proxy = new ProxiedTarget('Nicolás')
proxy.hello()
// <- 'Hello, Nicolás'
```

Note that arrow functions can't be used as constructors, and thus we can't use the construct trap on them. Let's move onto the last few traps.

6.4.4 getPrototypeOf Trap

We can use the handler.getPrototypeOf method as a trap for all of the following operations:

- Object#__proto__ property

- Object#isPrototypeOf method

- Object.getPrototypeOf method

- Reflect.getPrototypeOf method

- instanceof operator

This trap is quite powerful, as it allows us to dynamically determine the reported underlying prototype for an object.

You could, for instance, use this trap to make an object pretend it's an Array when accessed through the proxy. The following example does exactly that, by returning Array.prototype as the prototype of proxied objects. Note that instanceof indeed returns true when asked if our plain object is an Array.

```
const handler = {
  getPrototypeOf: target => Array.prototype
}
const target = {}
const proxy = new Proxy(target, handler)
console.log(proxy instanceof Array)
// <- true
```

On its own, this isn't sufficient for the proxy to be a true Array. The following code snippet shows how the Array#push method isn't available on our proxy even though we're reporting a prototype of Array.

```
console.log(proxy.push)
// <- undefined
```

Naturally, we can keep patching the proxy until we get the behavior we want. In this case, we may want to use a get trap to mix the Array.prototype with the actual backend target. Whenever a property isn't found on the target, we'll use reflection again to look the property up on Array.prototype as well. As it turns out, this behavior is good enough to be able to leverage Array's methods.

```
const handler = {
  getPrototypeOf: target => Array.prototype,
  get(target, key) {
    return (
      Reflect.get(target, key) ||
      Reflect.get(Array.prototype, key)
    )
```

```
    }
  }
  const target = {}
  const proxy = new Proxy(target, handler)
```

Note now how `proxy.push` points to the `Array#push` method, how
we can use it unobtrusively as if we were working with an array
object, and also how printing the object logs it as the object it is
rather than as an array of `['first', 'second']`.

```
console.log(proxy.push)
// <- function push() { [native code] }
proxy.push('first', 'second')
console.log(proxy)
// <- { 0: 'first', 1: 'second', length: 2 }
```

Conversely to the `getPrototypeOf` trap, there's `setPrototypeOf`.

6.4.5 setPrototypeOf Trap

There is an `Object.setPrototypeOf` method in ES6 that can be
used to change the prototype of an object into a reference to another
object. It's considered the proper way of setting the prototype, as
opposed to setting the special __proto__ property, which is a feature
that's supported in most browsers but was deprecated in ES6.

Deprecation means that browser vendors are discouraging the use of
__proto__. In other contexts, deprecation also means that the feature might be removed in the future. The web platform, however,
doesn't break backward compatibility, and __proto__ is unlikely to
ever be removed. That being said, deprecation also means you're
discouraged from using the feature. Thus, using the `Object.setPro`
`totypeOf` method is preferable to changing __proto__ when we
want to modify the underlying prototype for an object.

You can use `handler.setPrototypeOf` to set up a trap for
`Object.setPrototypeOf`. The following snippet of code doesn't alter
the default behavior of changing a prototype into `base`. Note that,
for completeness, there is a `Reflect.setPrototypeOf` method that's
equivalent to `Object.setPrototypeOf`.

```
const handler = {
  setPrototypeOf(target, proto) {
    Object.setPrototypeOf(target, proto)
  }
}
const base = {}
```

```
function Target() {}
const proxy = new Proxy(Target, handler)
proxy.setPrototypeOf(proxy, base)
console.log(proxy.prototype === base)
// <- true
```

There are several use cases for `setPrototypeOf` traps. You could have an empty method body, in which case the trap would sink calls to `Object.setPrototypeOf` into a no-op: an operation where nothing occurs. You could `throw` an exception making the failure explicit, if you deem the new prototype to be invalid or you want to prevent consumers from changing the prototype of the proxied object.

You could implement a trap like the following, which mitigates security concerns in a proxy that might be passed away to third-party code, as a way of limiting access to the underlying `Target`. That way, consumers of `proxy` would be unable to modify the prototype of the underlying object.

```
const handler = {
  setPrototypeOf(target, proto) {
    throw new Error('Changing the prototype is forbidden')
  }
}
const base = {}
function Target() {}
const proxy = new Proxy(Target, handler)
proxy.setPrototypeOf(proxy, base)
// <- Error: Changing the prototype is forbidden
```

In these cases, it's best to fail with an exception so that consumers can understand what is going on. By explicitly disallowing prototype changes, the consumer can start looking elsewhere. If we didn't throw an exception, the consumer could still eventually learn that the prototype isn't changing through debugging. You might as well save them from that pain!

6.4.6 preventExtensions Trap

You can use `handler.preventExtensions` to trap the `Object.pre ventExtensions` method introduced in ES5. When extensions are prevented on an object, new properties can't be added any longer: the object can't be extended.

Imagine a scenario where you want to be able to selectively `preven tExtensions` on some objects, but not all of them. In that scenario, you could use a WeakSet to keep track of the objects that should be extensible. If an object is in the set, then the preventExtensions trap should be able to capture those requests and discard them.

The following snippet does exactly that: it keeps objects that can be extended in a WeakSet and prevents the rest from being extended.

```
const canExtend = new WeakSet()
const handler = {
  preventExtensions(target) {
    const canPrevent = !canExtend.has(target)
    if (canPrevent) {
      Object.preventExtensions(target)
    }
    return Reflect.preventExtensions(target)
  }
}
```

Now that we've set up the handler and WeakSet, we can create a target object and a proxy for that target, adding the target to our set. Then, we could try Object.preventExtensions on the proxy and we'll notice it fails to prevent extensions to target. This is the intended behavior, as the target can be found in the canExtend set. Note that while we're seeing a TypeError exception, because the consumer intended to prevent extensions but failed to do so due to the trap, this would be a silent error under sloppy mode.

```
const target = {}
const proxy = new Proxy(target, handler)
canExtend.add(target)
Object.preventExtensions(proxy)
// <- TypeError: 'preventExtensions' on proxy:
// trap returned falsy
```

If we removed the target from the canExtend set before calling Object.preventExtensions, then target would be made non-extensible as originally intended. The following code snippet shows that behavior in action.

```
const target = {}
const proxy = new Proxy(target, handler)
canExtend.add(target)
canExtend.delete(target)
Object.preventExtensions(proxy)
console.log(Object.isExtensible(proxy))
// <- false
```

6.4.7 isExtensible Trap

An extensible object is an object that you can add new properties to, an object you can extend.

The `handler.isExtensible` method can be used for logging or auditing calls to `Object.isExtensible`, but not to decide whether an object is extensible. That's because this trap is subject to a harsh invariant that puts a hard limit to what you can do with it: a `TypeError` is thrown if `Object.isExtensible(proxy) !== Object.isExtensible(target)`.

While this trap is nearly useless other than for auditing purposes, you could also throw an error within the handler if you don't want consumers to know whether the underlying object is extensible or not.

As we've learned over the last few pages, there are myriad use cases for proxies. We can use `Proxy` for all of the following, and that's just the tip of the iceberg:

- Add validation rules on plain old JavaScript objects, and enforce them
- Keep track of every interaction that goes through a proxy
- Implement your own observable objects
- Decorate and extend objects without changing their implementation
- Make certain properties on an object completely invisible to consumers
- Revoke access at will when the consumer should no longer be able to access an object
- Modify the arguments passed to a proxied method
- Modify the result produced by a proxied method
- Prevent deletion of specific properties through the proxy
- Prevent new definitions from succeeding, according to the desired property descriptor
- Shuffle arguments around in a constructor
- Return a result other than the object created via `new` and a constructor

- Swap out the prototype of an object for something else

Proxies are an extremely powerful feature in ES6, with many potential applications, and they're well equipped for code instrumentation and introspection. However, they also have a significant performance impact in JavaScript engine execution as they're virtually impossible to optimize for. This makes proxies impractical for applications where speed is of the essence.

At the same time it's easy to confuse consumers by providing complicated proxies that attempt to do too much. It may be a good idea to avoid them for most use cases, or at least develop consistent and uncomplicated access rules. Make sure you're not producing many side effects in property access, which can lead to confusion even if properly documented.

CHAPTER 7

Built-in Improvements in ES6

Thus far in the book, we've discussed entirely new language syntax, such as property value shorthands, arrow functions, destructuring, or generators; and entirely new built-ins, such as `WeakMap`, `Proxy`, or `Symbol`. This chapter, on the other hand, is mostly devoted to existing built-ins that were improved in ES6. These improvements consist mostly of new instance methods, properties, and utility methods.

7.1 Numbers

ES6 introduces numeric literal representations for binary and octal numbers.

7.1.1 Binary and Octal Literals

Before ES6, your best bet when it comes to binary representation of integers was to just pass them to `parseInt` with a radix of 2.

```
parseInt('101', 2)
// <- 5
```

You can now use the new `0b` prefix to represent binary integer literals. You could also use the `0B` prefix, with a capital `B`. The two notations are equivalent.

```
console.log(0b000) // <- 0
console.log(0b001) // <- 1
console.log(0b010) // <- 2
console.log(0b011) // <- 3
```

```
console.log(0b100) // <- 4
console.log(0b101) // <- 5
console.log(0b110) // <- 6
console.log(0b111) // <- 7
```

In ES3, parseInt interpreted strings of digits starting with a 0 as an octal value. That meant things got weird quickly when you forgot to specify a radix of 10. As a result, specifying the radix of 10 became a best practice, so that user input like 012 wouldn't unexpectedly be parsed as the integer 10.

```
console.log(parseInt('01'))
// <- 1
console.log(parseInt('012'))
// <- 10
console.log(parseInt('012', 10))
// <- 12
```

When ES5 came around, the default radix in parseInt changed, from 8 to 10. It was still recommended that you specified a radix for backward compatibility purposes. If you wanted to parse strings as octal values, you could explicitly pass in a radix of 8 as the second argument.

```
console.log(parseInt('100', 8))
// <- 64
```

You can now use the 0o prefix for octal literals, which are new in ES6. You could also use 0O, which is equivalent. Having a 0 followed by an uppercase O may be hard to distinguish in some typefaces, which is why it is suggested that you stick with the lowercase 0o notation.

```
console.log(0o001) // <- 1
console.log(0o010) // <- 8
console.log(0o100) // <- 64
```

You might be used to hexadecimal literals present in other languages, commonly prefixed with 0x. Those were already introduced to the JavaScript language in ES5. The prefix for literal hexadecimal notation is either 0x, or 0X, as shown in the following code snippet.

```
console.log(0x0ff) // <- 255
console.log(0xf00) // <- 3840
```

Besides these minor syntax changes where octal and binary literals were introduced, a few methods were added to Number in ES6. The first four Number methods that we'll be discussing—Number.isNaN,

Number.isFinite, Number.parseInt, and Number.parseFloat—already existed as functions in the global namespace. In addition, the methods in Number are slightly different in that they don't coerce nonnumeric values into numbers before producing a result.

7.1.2 Number.isNaN

This method is almost identical to the global isNaN method. Number.isNaN returns whether the provided value is NaN, whereas isNaN returns whether value is not a number. These two questions have slightly different answers.

The next snippet quickly shows that, when passed to Number.isNaN, anything that's not NaN will return false, while NaN will produce true. Note how in the last case we're already passing NaN to Number.isNaN, as that's the result of dividing two strings.

```
Number.isNaN(123)
// <- false, integers are not NaN
Number.isNaN(Infinity)
// <- false, Infinity is not NaN
Number.isNaN('a hundred')
// <- false, 'a hundred' is not NaN
Number.isNaN(NaN)
// <- true, NaN is NaN
Number.isNaN('a hundred' / 'two')
// <- true, 'a hundred' / 'two' is NaN, NaN is NaN
```

The isNaN method, in contrast, casts nonnumeric values passed to it before evaluating them against NaN. This results in significantly different return values. In the following example, each alternative produces different results because isNaN, unlike Number.isNaN, casts the value passed to it through Number first.

```
isNaN('a hundred')
// <- true, because Number('a hundred') is NaN
isNaN(new Date())
// <- false, because Number(new Date()) uses Date#valueOf,
//    which returns a unix timestamp
```

Number.isNaN is more precise than its global counterpart, because it doesn't involve casting. There are still a few reasons why Number.isNaN can be a source of confusion.

First off, isNaN casts input through Number(value) before comparison, while Number.isNaN doesn't. Neither Number.isNaN nor isNaN answer the "is this not a number?" question, but instead they answer whether value—or Number(value)—is NaN.

In most cases, what you actually want to know is whether a value identifies as a number—typeof NaN === *number*—and is a number. The isNumber function in the following code snippet does just that. Note that it'd work with both isNaN and Number.isNaN due to type checking. Everything that reports a typeof value of 'number' is a number, except for NaN, so we filter out those out as false positive results.

```
function isNumber(value) {
  return typeof value === 'number' && !Number.isNaN(value)
}
```

You can use that method to figure out whether a value is a number or not. In the next snippet there are a few examples of how isNumber works.

```
isNumber(1)
// <- true
isNumber(Infinity)
// <- true
isNumber(NaN)
// <- false
isNumber('two')
// <- false
isNumber(new Date())
// <- false
```

There is a function, which was already in the language, that somewhat resembles our custom isNumber function: isFinite.

7.1.3 Number.isFinite

The rarely promoted isFinite method has been available since ES3. It returns a Boolean value indicating whether the provided value matches none of Infinity, -Infinity, and NaN.

The isFinite method coerces values through Number(value), while Number.isFinite doesn't. This means that values that can be coerced into non-NaN numbers will be considered finite numbers by isNumber—even though they aren't explicit numbers.

Here are a few examples using the global isFinite function.

```
isFinite(NaN)
// <- false
```

```
isFinite(Infinity)
// <- false
isFinite(-Infinity)
// <- false
isFinite(null)
// <- true, because Number(null) is 0
isFinite(-13)
// <- true, because Number(-13) is -13
isFinite('10')
// <- true, because Number('10') is 10
```

Using Number.isFinite is a safer bet, as it doesn't incur in unexpected casting. You could always use Number.isFinite(Number(value)) if you did want the value to be cast into its numeric representation. Separating the two aspects, casting versus computing, results in more explicit code.

Here are a few examples using the Number.isFinite method.

```
Number.isFinite(NaN)
// <- false
Number.isFinite(Infinity)
// <- false
Number.isFinite(-Infinity)
// <- false
Number.isFinite(null)
// <- false, because null is not a number
Number.isFinite(-13)
// <- true
Number.isFinite('10')
// <- false, because '10' is not a number
```

Creating a ponyfill for Number.isFinite would involve returning false for nonnumeric values, effectively turning off the type-casting feature, and then calling isFinite on the input value.

```
function numberIsFinite(value) {
  return typeof value === 'number' && isFinite(value)
}
```

7.1.4 Number.parseInt

The Number.parseInt method works the same as parseInt. It is, in fact, the same.

```
console.log(Number.parseInt === parseInt)
// <- true
```

The parseInt function has support for hexadecimal literal notation in strings. Specifying the radix is not even necessary: based on the 0x prefix, parseInt infers that the number must be base 16.

```
parseInt('0xf00')
// <- 3840
parseInt('0xf00', 16)
// <- 3840
```

If you provided another radix, parseInt would bail after the first nondigit character.

```
parseInt('0xf00', 10)
// <- 0
parseInt('5xf00', 10)
// <- 5, illustrating there's no special treatment here
```

While parseInt accepts input in hexadecimal literal notation strings, its interface hasn't changed in ES6. Therefore, binary and octal literal notation strings won't be interpreted as such. This introduces a new inconsistency in ES6, where parseInt understands 0x, but not 0b nor 0o.

```
parseInt('0b011')
// <- 0
parseInt('0b011', 2)
// <- 0
parseInt('0o100')
// <- 0
parseInt('0o100', 8)
// <- 0
```

It's up to you to drop the prefix before parseInt, if you wanted to use parseInt to read these literals. You'll also need to specify the corresponding radix of 2 for binary numbers or 8 for octals.

```
parseInt('0b011'.slice(2), 2)
// <- 3
parseInt('0o110'.slice(2), 8)
// <- 72
```

In contrast, the Number function is perfectly able to cast these strings into the correct numbers.

```
Number('0b011')
// <- 3
Number('0o110')
// <- 72
```

7.1.5 Number.parseFloat

Like `parseInt`, `parseFloat` was added to `Number` without any modifications whatsoever.

```
console.log(Number.parseFloat === parseFloat)
// <- true
```

Luckily, `parseFloat` didn't have any special behavior with regard to hexadecimal literal strings, meaning that `Number.parseFloat` is unlikely to introduce any confusion.

The `parseFloat` function was added to `Number` for completeness. In future versions of the language, there will be less global namespace pollution. When a function serves a specific purpose, it'll be added to the relevant built-in, rather than as a global.

7.1.6 Number.isInteger

This is a new method coming in ES6, and it wasn't previously available as a global function. The `isInteger` method returns `true` if the provided `value` is a finite number that doesn't have a decimal part.

```
console.log(Number.isInteger(Infinity)) // <- false
console.log(Number.isInteger(-Infinity)) // <- false
console.log(Number.isInteger(NaN)) // <- false
console.log(Number.isInteger(null)) // <- false
console.log(Number.isInteger(0)) // <- true
console.log(Number.isInteger(-10)) // <- true
console.log(Number.isInteger(10.3)) // <- false
```

You might want to consider the following code snippet as a ponyfill for `Number.isInteger`. The modulus operator returns the remainder of dividing the same operands. If we divide by one, we're effectively getting the decimal part. If that's `0`, then it means the number is an integer.

```
function numberIsInteger(value) {
  return Number.isFinite(value) && value % 1 === 0
}
```

Next up we'll dive into floating-point arithmetic, which is well-documented as having interesting corner cases.

7.1.7 Number.EPSILON

The `EPSILON` property is a new constant value being added to the `Number` built-in. The following snippet shows its value.

```
Number.EPSILON
// <- 2.220446049250313e-16
Number.EPSILON.toFixed(20)
// <- '0.00000000000000022204'
```

Let's take a look at the canonical example of floating-point arithmetic.

```
0.1 + 0.2
// <- 0.30000000000000004
0.1 + 0.2 === 0.3
// <- false
```

What's the margin of error in this operation? Let's move the operands around and find out.

```
0.1 + 0.2 - 0.3
// <- 5.551115123125783e-17
5.551115123125783e-17.toFixed(20)
// <- '0.00000000000000005551'
```

We could use Number.EPSILON to figure out whether the difference is small enough to be negligible; Number.EPSILON denotes a safe margin of error for floating-point arithmetic rounding operations.

```
5.551115123125783e-17 < Number.EPSILON
// <- true
```

The following piece of code can be used to figure out whether the result of a floating-point operation is within the expected margin of error. We use Math.abs, because that way the order of left and right won't matter. In other words, withinMarginOfError(left, right) will produce the same result as withinMarginOfError(right, left).

```
function withinMarginOfError(left, right) {
  return Math.abs(left - right) < Number.EPSILON
}
```

The next snippet shows withinMarginOfError in action.

```
withinMarginOfError(0.1 + 0.2, 0.3)
// <- true
withinMarginOfError(0.2 + 0.2, 0.3)
// <- false
```

Using floating-point representation, not every integer can be represented precisely.

7.1.8 Number.MAX_SAFE_INTEGER and Number.MIN_SAFE_INTEGER

This is the largest integer that can be safely and precisely represented in JavaScript, or any language that represents integers using floating point as specified by the IEEE-754 standard,[1] for that matter. The next bit of code shows exactly how large Number.MAX_SAFE_INTEGER is.

```
Number.MAX_SAFE_INTEGER === Math.pow(2, 53) - 1
// <- true
Number.MAX_SAFE_INTEGER === 9007199254740991
// <- true
```

As you might expect, there's also the opposite constant: the minimum. It's the negative value of Number.MAX_SAFE_INTEGER.

```
Number.MIN_SAFE_INTEGER === -Number.MAX_SAFE_INTEGER
// <- true
Number.MIN_SAFE_INTEGER === -9007199254740991
// <- true
```

Floating point arithmetic becomes unreliable beyond the [MIN_SAFE_INTEGER, MAX_SAFE_INTEGER] range. The 1 === 2 statement evaluates to false, because these are different values. If we add Number.MAX_SAFE_INTEGER to each operand, however, it'd seem 1 === 2 is indeed true.

```
1 === 2
// <- false
Number.MAX_SAFE_INTEGER + 1 === Number.MAX_SAFE_INTEGER + 2
// <- true
Number.MIN_SAFE_INTEGER - 1 === Number.MIN_SAFE_INTEGER - 2
// <- true
```

When it comes to checking whether an integer is safe, a Number.isSafeInteger function has been added to the language.

7.1.9 Number.isSafeInteger

This method returns true for any integer in the [MIN_SAFE_INTEGER, MAX_SAFE_INTEGER] range. Like with other Number methods introduced in ES6, there's no type coercion involved. The input must be numeric, an integer, and within the aforementioned bounds in

---

1 IEEE 754 is the Floating Point Standard (*https://mjavascript.com/out/floating-point*).

order for the method to return `true`. The next snippet shows a comprehensive set of inputs and outputs.

```
Number.isSafeInteger('one') // <- false
Number.isSafeInteger('0') // <- false
Number.isSafeInteger(null) // <- false
Number.isSafeInteger(NaN) // <- false
Number.isSafeInteger(Infinity) // <- false
Number.isSafeInteger(-Infinity) // <- false
Number.isSafeInteger(Number.MIN_SAFE_INTEGER - 1) // <- false
Number.isSafeInteger(Number.MIN_SAFE_INTEGER) // <- true
Number.isSafeInteger(1) // <- true
Number.isSafeInteger(1.2) // <- false
Number.isSafeInteger(Number.MAX_SAFE_INTEGER) // <- true
Number.isSafeInteger(Number.MAX_SAFE_INTEGER + 1) // <- false
```

When we want to verify if the result of an operation is within bounds, we must verify not only the result but also both operands.[2] One—or both—of the operands may be out of bounds, while the result is within bounds but incorrect. Similarly, the result may be out of bounds even if both operands are within bounds. Checking all of `left`, `right`, and the result of `left op right` is, thus, necessary to verify that we can indeed trust the result.

In the following example both operands are within bounds, but the result is incorrect.

```
Number.isSafeInteger(9007199254740000)
// <- true
Number.isSafeInteger(993)
// <- true
Number.isSafeInteger(9007199254740000 + 993)
// <- false
9007199254740000 + 993
// <- 9007199254740992, should be 9007199254740993
```

Certain operations and numbers, such as the following code snippet, may return correct results even when operands are out of bounds. The fact that correct results can't be guaranteed, however, means that these operations can't be trusted.

```
9007199254740000 + 994
// <- 9007199254740994
```

---

2 Dr. Axel Rauschmayer points this out in the article "New number and Math features in ES6" (*https://mjavascript.com/out/math-axel*).

In the next example, one of the operands is out of bounds, and thus we can't trust the result to be accurate.

```
Number.isSafeInteger(9007199254740993)
// <- false
Number.isSafeInteger(990)
// <- true
Number.isSafeInteger(9007199254740993 + 990)
// <- false
9007199254740993 + 990
// <-  9007199254741982, should be 9007199254741983
```

A subtraction in our last example would produce a result that is within bounds, but that result would also be inaccurate.

```
Number.isSafeInteger(9007199254740993)
// <- false
Number.isSafeInteger(990)
// <- true
Number.isSafeInteger(9007199254740993 - 990)
// <- true
9007199254740993 - 990
// <-  9007199254740002, should be 9007199254740003
```

If both operands are out of bounds, the output could end up in the safe space, even though the result is incorrect.

```
Number.isSafeInteger(9007199254740995)
// <- false
Number.isSafeInteger(9007199254740993)
// <- false
Number.isSafeInteger(9007199254740995 - 9007199254740993)
// <- true
9007199254740995 - 9007199254740993
// <- 4, should be 2
```

We can conclude that the only safe way to assert whether an operation produces correct output is with a utility function such as the one shown next. If we can't ascertain that the operation and both operands are within bounds, then the result may be inaccurate, and that's a problem. It's best to throw in those situations and have a way to error-correct, but that's specific to your programs. The important part is to actually catch these kinds of difficult bugs to deal with.

```
function safeOp(result, ...operands) {
  const values = [result, ...operands]
  if (!values.every(Number.isSafeInteger)) {
    throw new RangeError('Operation cannot be trusted!')
  }
  return result
}
```

You could use safeOp to ensure all operands, including the result, are safely within bounds.

```
safeOp(9007199254740000 + 993, 9007199254740000, 993)
// <- RangeError: Operation cannot be trusted!
safeOp(9007199254740993 + 990, 9007199254740993, 990)
// <- RangeError: Operation cannot be trusted!
safeOp(9007199254740993 - 990, 9007199254740993, 990)
// <- RangeError: Operation cannot be trusted!
safeOp(
  9007199254740993 - 9007199254740995,
  9007199254740993,
  9007199254740995
)
// <- RangeError: Operation cannot be trusted!
safeOp(1 + 2, 1, 2)
// <- 3
```

That's all there is when it comes to Number, but we're not done with arithmetics-related improvements quite yet. Let's turn our attention to the Math built-in.

7.2 Math

ES6 introduces heaps of new static methods to the Math built-in. Some of them were specifically engineered toward making it easier to compile C into JavaScript, and you'll seldom need them for day-to-day JavaScript application development. Others are complements to the existing rounding, exponentiation, and trigonometry API surface.

Let's get right to it.

7.2.1 Math.sign

Many languages have a mathematical sign method that returns a vector (-1, 0, or 1) representation for the sign of the provided input. JavaScript's Math.sign method does exactly that. However, the JavaScript flavor of this method has two more possible return values: -0 and NaN. Check out the examples in the following code snippet.

```
Math.sign(1) // <- 1
Math.sign(0) // <- 0
Math.sign(-0) // <- -0
Math.sign(-30) // <- -1
Math.sign(NaN) // <- NaN
Math.sign('one') // <- NaN, because Number('one') is NaN
```

```
Math.sign('0') // <- 0, because Number('0') is 0
Math.sign('7') // <- 1, because Number('7') is 7
```

Note how `Math.sign` casts its input into numeric values? While methods introduced to the `Number` built-in don't cast their input via `Number(value)`, most of the methods added to `Math` share this trait, as we shall see.

7.2.2 Math.trunc

We already had `Math.floor` and `Math.ceil` in JavaScript, with which we can round a number down or up, respectively. Now we also have `Math.trunc` as an alternative, which discards the decimal part without any rounding. Here, too, the input is coerced into a numeric value through `Number(value)`.

```
Math.trunc(12.34567) // <- 12
Math.trunc(-13.58) // <- -13
Math.trunc(-0.1234) // <- -0
Math.trunc(NaN) // <- NaN
Math.trunc('one') // <- NaN, because Number('one') is NaN
Math.trunc('123.456') // <- 123,: Number('123.456') is 123.456
```

Creating a simple ponyfill for `Math.trunc` would involve checking whether the value is greater than zero and applying one of `Math.floor` or `Math.ceil`, as shown in the following code snippet.

```
function mathTrunc(value) {
  return value > 0 ? Math.floor(value) : Math.ceil(value)
}
```

7.2.3 Math.cbrt

The `Math.cbrt` method is short for "cubic root," similarly to how `Math.sqrt` is short for "square root." The following snippet has a few usage examples.

```
Math.cbrt(-1) // <- -1
Math.cbrt(3) // <- 1.4422495703074083
Math.cbrt(8) // <- 2
Math.cbrt(27) // <- 3
```

Note that this method also coerces nonnumerical values into numbers.

```
Math.cbrt('8') // <- 2, because Number('8') is 8
Math.cbrt('one') // <- NaN, because Number('one') is NaN
```

Let's move on.

7.2.4 Math.expm1

This operation is the result of computing e to the value minus 1. In JavaScript, the e constant is defined as Math.E. The function in the following snippet is a rough equivalent of Math.expm1.

```
function expm1(value) {
  return Math.pow(Math.E, value) - 1
}
```

The e^value^ operation can be expressed as Math.exp(value) as well.

```
function expm1(value) {
  return Math.exp(value) - 1
}
```

Note that Math.expm1 has higher precision than merely doing Math.exp(value) - 1, and should be the preferred alternative.

```
expm1(1e-20)
// <- 0
Math.expm1(1e-20)
// <- 1e-20
expm1(1e-10)
// <- 1.000000082740371e-10
Math.expm1(1e-10)
// <- 1.00000000005e-10
```

The inverse function of Math.expm1 is Math.log1p.

7.2.5 Math.log1p

This is the natural logarithm of value plus 1—ln(value + 1)—and the inverse function of Math.expm1. The base e logarithm of a number can be expressed as Math.log in JavaScript.

```
function log1p(value) {
  return Math.log(value + 1)
}
```

Just like with Math.expm1, Math.log1p method is more precise than executing the Math.log(value + 1) operation by hand.

```
log1p(1.00000000005e-10)
// <- 1.000000082690371e-10
Math.log1p(1.00000000005e-10)
// <- 1e-10, exactly the inverse of Math.expm1(1e-10)
```

7.2.6 Math.log10

Base 10 logarithm of a number—$\log_{10}(\texttt{value})$.

```
Math.log10(1000)
// <- 3
```

You could ponyfill `Math.log10` using the `Math.LN10` constant.

```
function mathLog10(value) {
  return Math.log(x) / Math.LN10
}
```

And then there's `Math.log2`.

7.2.7 Math.log2

Base 2 logarithm of a number—$\log_2(\texttt{value})$.

```
Math.log2(1024)
// <- 10
```

You could ponyfill `Math.log2` using the `Math.LN2` constant.

```
function mathLog2(value) {
  return Math.log(x) / Math.LN2
}
```

Note that the ponyfill version won't be as precise as `Math.log2`, as demonstrated in the following example.

```
Math.log2(1 << 29) // native implementation
// <- 29
mathLog2(1 << 29) // ponyfill implementation
// <- 29.000000000000004
```

The `<<` operator performs a "bitwise left shift" (*https://mjava script.com/out/bitwise-shift*). In this operation, the bits on the binary representation of the lefthand-side number are shifted as many places to the left as indicated in the righthand side of the operation. The following couple of examples show how shifting works, using the binary literal notation introduced in Section 7.1.1, "Binary and Octal Literals," on page 209.

```
0b00000001 // 1
0b00000001 << 2 // shift bits two places to the left
0b00000100 // 4

0b00001101 // 1
0b00001101 << 4 // shift bits four places to the left
0b11010000 // 208
```

7.2.8 Trigonometric Functions

The Math object is getting trigonometric functions in ES6:

- Math.sinh(value) returns the hyperbolic sine of value
- Math.cosh(value) returns the hyperbolic cosine of value
- Math.tanh(value) returns the hyperbolic tangent of value
- Math.asinh(value) returns the hyperbolic arc-sine of value
- Math.acosh(value) returns the hyperbolic arc-cosine of value
- Math.atanh(value) returns the hyperbolic arc-tangent of value

7.2.9 Math.hypot

Using Math.hypot returns the square root of the sum of the squares of every provided argument.

```
Math.hypot(1, 2, 3)
// <- 3.741657386773941, the square root of (1*1 + 2*2 + 3*3)
```

We could ponyfill Math.hypot by performing these operations manually. We can use Math.sqrt to compute the square root and Array#reduce, combined with the spread operator, to sum the squares.[3]

```
function mathHypot(...values) {
  const accumulateSquares (total, value) =>
    total + value * value
  const squares = values.reduce(accumulateSquares, 0)
  return Math.sqrt(squares)
}
```

Our handmade function is, surprisingly, more precise than the native one for this particular use case. In the next code sample, we see the hand-rolled hypot function offers precision with one more decimal place.

```
Math.hypot(1, 2, 3) // native implementation
// <- 3.741657386773941
mathHypot(1, 2, 3) // ponyfill implementation
// <- 3.7416573867739413
```

---

3 You can go deeper into functional Array methods by reading the article "Fun with Native Arrays" (*https://mjavascript.com/out/native-arrays*).

7.2.10 Bitwise Computation Helpers

At the beginning of Section 7.2, "Math," on page 220, we talked about how some of the new Math methods are specifically engineered towards making it easier to compile C into JavaScript. Those are the last three methods we'll cover, and they help us deal with 32-bit numbers.

Math.clz32

The name for this method is an acronym for "count leading zero bits in 32-bit binary representations of a number." Keeping in mind that the << operator performs a "bitwise left shift," let's take a look at the next code snippet describing sample input and output for Math.clz32.

```
Math.clz32(0) // <- 32
Math.clz32(1) // <- 31
Math.clz32(1 << 1) // <- 30
Math.clz32(1 << 2) // <- 29
Math.clz32(1 << 29) // <- 2
Math.clz32(1 << 31) // <- 0
```

Math.imul

Returns the result of a C-like 32-bit multiplication.

Math.fround

Rounds value to the nearest 32-bit float representation of a number.

7.3 Strings and Unicode

You may recall template literals from Section 2.5, "Template Literals," on page 42, and how those can be used to mix strings and variables, or any valid JavaScript expression, to produce string output.

```
function greet(name) {
  return `Hello, ${ name }!`
}
greet('Gandalf')
// <- 'Hello, Gandalf!'
```

Besides the template literal syntax, strings got a number of new methods in ES6. These can be categorized as string manipulation methods and Unicode-related methods. Let's start with the former.

7.3.1 String#startsWith

Prior to ES6, whenever we wanted to check if a string begins with a certain other string, we'd use the String#indexOf method, as shown in the following code snippet. A result of 0 means that the string starts with the provided value.

```
'hello gary'.indexOf('gary')
// <- 6
'hello gary'.indexOf('hello')
// <- 0
'hello gary'.indexOf('stephan')
// <- -1
```

If you wanted to check if a string started with another one, then, you'd compare them with String#indexOf and check whether the lookup value is found at the beginning of the string: the 0 index.

```
'hello gary'.indexOf('gary') === 0
// <- false
'hello gary'.indexOf('hello') === 0
// <- true
'hello gary'.indexOf('stephan') === 0
// <- false
```

You can now use the String#startsWith method instead, avoiding the unnecessary complexity of checking whether an index matches 0.

```
'hello gary'.startsWith('gary')
// <- false
'hello gary'.startsWith('hello')
// <- true
'hello gary'.startsWith('stephan')
// <- false
```

In order to figure out whether a string contains a value starting at a specific index, using String#indexOf, we would have to grab a slice of that string first.

```
'hello gary'.slice(6).indexOf('gary') === 0
// <- true
```

We can't simply check whether the index is 6, because that would give you false negatives when the queried value is found before reaching that index of 6. The following example shows how, even when the query 'ell' string is indeed at index 6, merely comparing the String#indexOf result with 6 is insufficient to attain a correct result.

```
'hello ell'.indexOf('ell') === 6
// <- false, because the result was 1
```

We could use the `startIndex` parameter for `indexOf` to get around this problem without relying on `String#slice`. Note that we're still comparing against 6 in this case, because the string wasn't sliced up in a setup operation.

```
'hello ell'.indexOf('ell', 6) === 6
// <- true
```

Instead of keeping all of these string searching implementation details in your head and writing code that's most concerned with how to search, as opposed to what is being searched, we could use `String#startsWith` passing in the optional `startIndex` parameter as well.

```
'hello ell'.startsWith('ell', 6)
// <- true
```

7.3.2 String#endsWith

This method mirrors `String#startsWith` in the same way that `String#lastIndexOf` mirrors `String#indexOf`. It tells us whether a string ends with another string.

```
'hello gary'.endsWith('gary')
// <- true
'hello gary'.endsWith('hello')
// <- false
```

As the opposite of `String#startsWith`, there's a position index that indicates where the lookup should end, instead of where it should start. It defaults to the length of the string.

```
'hello gary'.endsWith('gary', 10)
// <- true
'hello gary'.endsWith('gary', 9)
// <- false, it ends with 'gar' in this case
'hello gary'.endsWith('hell', 4)
// <- true
```

`String#includes` is one last method that can simplify a specific use case for `String#indexOf`.

7.3.3 String#includes

You can use `String#includes` to figure out whether a string contains another one, as shown in the following piece of code.

```
'hello gary'.includes('hell')
// <- true
'hello gary'.includes('ga')
// <- true
'hello gary'.includes('rye')
// <- false
```

This is equivalent to the ES5 use case of `String#indexOf` where we'd test the result against -1, checking to see whether the search string was anywhere to be found, as demonstrated in the next code snippet.

```
'hello gary'.indexOf('ga') !== -1
// <- true
'hello gary'.indexOf('rye') !== -1
// <- false
```

You can also provide `String#includes` with a start index where searching should begin.

```
'hello gary'.includes('ga', 4)
// <- true
'hello gary'.includes('ga', 7)
// <- false
```

Let's move onto something that's not just an `String#indexOf` alternative.

7.3.4 String#repeat

This handy method allows you to repeat a string count times.

```
'ha'.repeat(1)
// <- 'ha'
'ha'.repeat(2)
// <- 'haha'
'ha'.repeat(5)
// <- 'hahahahaha'
'ha'.repeat(0)
// <- ''
```

The provided count should be a non-negative finite number.

```
'ha'.repeat(Infinity)
// <- RangeError
'ha'.repeat(-1)
// <- RangeError
```

Decimal values are floored to the nearest integer.

```
'ha'.repeat(3.9)
// <- 'hahaha', count was floored to 3
```

Using NaN is interpreted as a count of 0.

```
'ha'.repeat(NaN)
// <- ''
```

Non-numeric values are coerced into numbers.

```
'ha'.repeat('ha')
// <- ', because Number('ha') is NaN
'ha'.repeat('3')
// <- 'hahaha', because Number('3') is 3
```

Values in the (-1, 0) range are rounded to -0 because count is passed through ToInteger, as documented by the specification.[4] That step in the specification dictates that count be cast with a formula like the one in the next code snippet.

```
function ToInteger(number) {
  return Math.floor(Math.abs(number)) * Math.sign(number)
}
```

The ToInteger function translates any values in the (-1, 0) range into -0. As a result, when passed to String#repeat, numbers in the (-1, 0) range will be treated as zero, while numbers in the [-1, -Infinity) range will result an exception, as we learned earlier.

```
'na'.repeat(-0.1)
// <- ', because count was rounded to -0
'na'.repeat(-0.9)
// <- ', because count was rounded to -0
'na'.repeat(-0.9999)
// <- ', because count was rounded to -0
'na'.repeat(-1)
// <- Uncaught RangeError: Invalid count value
```

An example use case for String#repeat may be the typical padding function. The indent function in the next code snippet takes a multiline string and indents every line with as many spaces as desired, using a default of two spaces.

```
function indent(text, spaces = 2) {
  return text
    .split('\n')
    .map(line => ' '.repeat(spaces) + line)
    .join('\n')
}
```

---

4 String#repeat in ECMAScript 6 Specification, section 21.1.3.13 (*https://mjava script.com/out/array-repeat*).

```
indent(`a
b
c`, 2)
// <- ' a\n b\n c'
```

7.3.5 String Padding and Trimming

At the time of this writing, there are two new string padding methods slated for publication in ES2017: String#padStart and String#padEnd. Using these methods, we wouldn't have to implement something like indent in the previous code snippet. When performing string manipulation, we often want to pad a string so that it's formatted consistently with a style we have in mind. This can be useful when formatting numbers, currency, HTML, and in a variety of other cases usually involving monospaced text.

Using padStart, we will specify the desired length for the target string and the padding string, which defaults to a single space character. If the original string is at least as long as the specified length, padStart will result in a null operation, returning the original string unchanged.

In the following example, the desired length of a properly padded string is 5, and the original string already has a length of at least 5, so it's returned unchanged.

```
'01.23'.padStart(5)
// <- '01.23'
```

In the next example, the original string has a length of 4, thus padStart adds a single space at the beginning of the string, bringing the length to the desired value of 5.

```
'1.23'.padStart(5)
// <- ' 1.23'
```

The next example is just like the previous one, except it uses '0' for padding instead of the default ' ' value.

```
'1.23'.padStart(5, '0')
// <- '01.23'
```

Note that padStart will keep padding the string until the maximum length is reached.

```
'1.23'.padStart(7, '0')
// <- '0001.23'
```

However, if the padding string is too long, it may be truncated. The provided length is the maximum length of the padded string, except in the case where the original string is already larger than that.

```
'1.23'.padStart(7, 'abcdef')
// <- 'abc1.23'
```

The padEnd method has a similar API, but it adds the padding at the end of the original string, instead of at the beginning. The following snippet illustrates the difference.

```
'01.23'.padEnd(5) // <- '01.23'
'1.23'.padEnd(5) // <- '1.23 '
'1.23'.padEnd(5, '0') // <- '1.230'
'1.23'.padEnd(7, '0') // <- '1.23000'
'1.23'.padEnd(7, 'abcdef') // <- '1.23abc'
```

At the time of this writing, there's a proposal for string trimming in stage 2, containing the String#trimStart and String#trimEnd methods. Using trimStart removes any whitespace from the beginning of a string, while using trimEnd removes any whitespace from the end of a string.

```
'   this should be left-aligned   '.trimStart()
// <- 'this should be left-aligned   '
'   this should be right-aligned   '.trimEnd()
// <- '   this should be right-aligned'
```

Let's switch protocols and learn about Unicode.

7.3.6 Unicode

JavaScript strings are represented using UTF-16 code units.[5] Each code unit can be used to represent a code point in the [U+0000, U+FFFF] range—also known as the BMP, short for Basic Multilingual Plane. You can represent individual code points in the BMP plane using the '\u3456' syntax. You could also represent code units in the [U+0000, U+0255] range using the \x00..\xff notation. For instance, '\xbb' represents '»', the U+00BB code point, as you can also verify by doing String.fromCharCode(0xbb).

For code points beyond U+FFFF, you'd represent them as a surrogate pair. That is to say, two contiguous code units. For instance, the

---

5 Learn more about UCS-2, UCS-4, UTF-16, and UTF-32 (*https://mjavascript.com/out/unicode-encodings*).

horse emoji (🐎) code point is represented with the `'\ud83d\udc0e'` contiguous code units. In ES6 notation you can also represent code points using the `'\u{1f40e}'` notation (that example is also the horse emoji).

Note that the internal representation hasn't changed, so there are still two code units behind that single code point. In fact, `'\u{1f40e}'.length` evaluates to 2, one for each code unit.

The `'\ud83d\udc0e\ud83d\udc71\u2764'` string, found in the next code snippet, evaluates to a few emoji.

```
'\ud83d\udc0e\ud83d\udc71\u2764'
// <- '🐎👱❤'
```

While that string consists of five code units, we know that the length should really be 3—as there are only three emoji.

```
'\ud83d\udc0e\ud83d\udc71\u2764'.length
// <- 5
'🐎👱❤'.length
```

Counting code points before ES6 was tricky, as the language didn't make an effort to help in the Unicode department. Take for instance `Object.keys`, as seen in the following code snippet. It returns five keys for our three-emoji string, because those three code points use five code units in total.

```
Object.keys('🐎👱❤')
// <- ['0', '1', '2', '3', '4']
```

If we now consider a `for` loop, we can observe more clearly how this is a problem. In the following example, we wanted to extract each individual emoji from the `text` string, but we got each code unit instead of the code points they form.

```
const text = '🐎👱❤'
for (let i = 0; i < text.length; i++) {
  console.log(text[i])
  // <- '\ud83d'
  // <- '\udc0e'
  // <- '\ud83d'
  // <- '\udc71'
  // <- '\u2764'
}
```

Luckily for us, in ES6 strings adhere to the iterable protocol. We can use the string iterator to go over code points, even when those code points are made of surrogate pairs.

7.3.7 String.prototype[Symbol.iterator]

Given the problems with looping by code units, the iterables produced by the string iterator yield code points instead.

```
for (const codePoint of '🐴🐌🖤') {
  console.log(codePoint)
  // <- '🐴'
  // <- '🐌'
  // <- '🖤'
}
```

Measuring the length of a string in terms of code points, as we saw earlier, is impossible with String#length, because it counts code units instead. We can, however, use an iterator to split the string into its code points, like we did in the for..of example.

We could use the spread operator, which relies on the iterator protocol, to split a string into an array made up of its conforming code points and then pull that array's length, getting the correct code point count, as seen next.

```
[...'🐴🐌🖤'].length
// <- 3
```

Keep in mind that splitting strings into code points isn't enough if you want to be 100% precise about string length. Take for instance the combining overline Unicode code unit, represented with \u0305. On its own, this code unit is just an overline, as shown next.

```
'\u0305'
// <- '‾'
```

When preceded by another code unit, however, they are combined together into a single glyph.

```
function overlined(text) {
  return '${ text }\u0305'
}

overlined('o')
// <- 'ō'
'hello world'.split('').map(overlined).join('')
// <- 'h̄ēl̄l̄ō w̄ōr̄l̄d̄'
```

Attempts to näively figure out the actual length by counting code points prove insufficient, just like when using String#length to count code points, as shown next.

```
'ō'.length
// <- 2
[...'ō'].length
// <- 2, should be 1
[...'hello world'].length
// <- 22, should be 11
[...'hello world'].length
// <- 16, should be 11
```

As Unicode expert Mathias Bynens points out, splitting by code points isn't enough. Unlike surrogate pairs like the emojis we've used in our earlier examples, other grapheme clusters aren't taken into account by the string iterator.[6] In those cases we're out of luck, and have to fall back to regular expressions or utility libraries to correctly calculate string length.

7.3.8 A Proposal to Split Grapheme Segments

Multiple code points that combine into a single visual glyph are getting more common.[7] There is a new proposal in the works (currently in stage 2) that may settle the matter of iterating over grapheme clusters once and for all. It introduces an Intl.Segmenter built-in, which can be used to split a string into an iterable sequence.

To use the Segmenter API, we start by creating an instance of Intl.Segmenter specifying a locale and the granularity level we want: per grapheme, word, sentence, or line. The segmenter instance can be used to produce an iterator for any given string, splitting it by the specified granularity. Note that the segmenting algorithm may vary depending on the locale, which is why it is a part of the API.

The following example defines a getGraphemes function that produces an array of grapheme clusters for any given locale and piece of text.

```
function getGraphemes(locale, text) {
  const segmenter = new Intl.Segmenter(locale, {
    granularity: 'grapheme'
  })
  const sequence = segmenter.segment(text)
```

---

6 I recommend you read "JavaScript has a Unicode problem" (*https://mjavascript.com/out/unicode-mathias*) from Mathias Bynens. In the article, Mathias analyzes JavaScript's relationship with Unicode.

7 Emoji popularize this with glyphs sometimes made up of four code points. See this list of emoji (*https://mjavascript.com/out/emoji*) made up of several code points.

```
  const graphemes = [...sequence].map(item => item.segment)
  return graphemes
}
getGraphemes('es', 'Esto está bien bueno!')
```

Using the `Segmenter` (*https://mjavascript.com/out/segmenter*) proposal, we wouldn't have any trouble splitting strings containing emoji or other combining code units.

Let's look at more Unicode-related methods introduced in ES6.

7.3.9 String#codePointAt

We can use `String#codePointAt` to get the numeric representation of a code point at a given position in a string. Note that the expected start position is indexed by code unit, not by code point. In the following example we print the code points for each of the three emoji in our demo 🐎 🦳 💜 string.

```
const text = '\ud83d\udc0e\ud83d\udc71\u2764'
text.codePointAt(0)
// <- 0x1f40e
text.codePointAt(2)
// <- 0x1f471
text.codePointAt(4)
// <- 0x2764
```

Identifying the indices that need to be provided to `String#codePoin tAt` may prove cumbersome, which is why you should instead loop through a string iterator that can identify them on your behalf. You can then call `.codePointAt(0)` for each code point in the sequence, and 0 will always be the correct start index.

```
const text = '\ud83d\udc0e\ud83d\udc71\u2764'
for (const codePoint of text) {
  console.log(codePoint.codePointAt(0))
  // <- 0x1f40e
  // <- 0x1f471
  // <- 0x2764
}
```

We could also reduce our example to a single line of code by using a combination of the spread operator and `Array#map`.

```
const text = '\ud83d\udc0e\ud83d\udc71\u2764'
[...text].map(cp => cp.codePointAt(0))
// <- [0x1f40e, 0x1f471, 0x2764]
```

You can take the base-16 representation of those base-10 code points, and use them to create a string with the new Unicode code point escape syntax of \u{codePoint}. This syntax allows you to represent Unicode code points that are beyond the BMP. That is, code points outside the [U+0000, U+FFFF] range that are typically represented using the \u1234 syntax.

Let's start by updating our example to print the hexadecimal version of our code points.

```
const text = '\ud83d\udc0e\ud83d\udc71\u2764'
[...text].map(cp => cp.codePointAt(0).toString(16))
// <- ['1f40e', '1f471', '2764']
```

We could wrap those base-16 values in '\u{codePoint}' and voilá: you'd get the emoji values once again.

```
'\u{1f40e}'
// <- '🐎'
'\u{1f471}'
// <- '👱'
'\u{2764}'
// <- '❤'
```

7.3.10 String.fromCodePoint

This method takes in a number and returns a code point. Note how I can use the 0x prefix with the terse base-16 code points we got from String#codePointAt moments ago.

```
String.fromCodePoint(0x1f40e)
// <- '🐎'
String.fromCodePoint(0x1f471)
// <- '👱'
String.fromCodePoint(0x2764)
// <- '❤'
```

You can just as well use plain base-10 literals and achieve the same results.

```
String.fromCodePoint(128014)
// <- '🐎'
String.fromCodePoint(128113)
// <- '👱'
String.fromCodePoint(10084)
// <- '❤'
```

You can pass in as many code points as you'd like to String.fromCodePoint.

```
String.fromCodePoint(0x1f40e, 0x1f471, 0x2764)
// <- '🐎👱❤'
```

As an exercise in futility, we could map a string to their numeric representation of code points, and back to the code points themselves.

```
const text = '\ud83d\udc0e\ud83d\udc71\u2764'
[...text]
  .map(cp => cp.codePointAt(0))
  .map(cp => String.fromCodePoint(cp))
  .join('')
// <- '🐎👱❤'
```

Reversing a string has potential to cause issues as well.

7.3.11 Unicode-Aware String Reversal

Consider the following piece of code.

```
const text = '\ud83d\udc0e\ud83d\udc71\u2764'
text.split('').map(cp => cp.codePointAt(0))
// <- [55357, 56334, 55357, 56433, 10084]
text.split('').reverse().map(cp => cp.codePointAt(0))
// <- [10084, 56433, 128014, 55357]
```

The problem is that we're reversing individual code units, while we'd have to reverse code points for a correct solution. If, instead, we were to use the spread operator to split the string by its code points, and then reversed that, the code points would be preserved and the string would be properly reversed.

```
const text = '\ud83d\udc0e\ud83d\udc71\u2764'
[...text].reverse().join('')
// <- '❤👱🐎'
```

This way we avoid breaking up code points. Once again, keep in mind that this won't work for all grapheme clusters.

```
[...'hello\u0305'].reverse().join('')
// <- `̅olleh`
```

The last Unicode-related method we'll be addressing is .normalize.

7.3.12 String#normalize

There are different ways of representing strings that look identical to humans even though their code points differ. Consider the following example, where two seemingly identical strings aren't deemed equal by any JavaScript runtime.

```
'mañana' === 'mañana'
// <- false
```

What's going on here? We have an ñ on the left version, while the version on the right has a combining tilde character +˜ ` and an n. The two are visually identical, but if we take a look at the code points, we'll notice they're different.

```
[...'mañana'].map(cp => cp.codePointAt(0).toString(16))
// <- ['6d', '61', 'f1', '61', '6e', '61']
[...'mañana'].map(cp => cp.codePointAt(0).toString(16))
// <- ['6d', '61', '6e', '303', '61', '6e', '61']
```

Just like with the `'hellō'` examples, the second string has a length of 7, even though visually it is also 6 glyphs long.

```
[...'mañana'].length
// <- 6
[...'mañana'].length
// <- 7
```

If we normalize the second version, using `String#normalize`, we'll get back the same code points we had in the first version.

```
const normalized = 'mañana'.normalize()
[...normalized].map(cp => cp.codePointAt(0).toString(16))
// <- ['6d', '61', 'f1', '61', '6e', '61']
normalized.length
// <- 6
```

Note that we should use `String#normalize` on both strings when comparing them if we want to test for equality.

```
function compare(left, right) {
  return left.normalize() === right.normalize()
}
const normal = 'mañana'
const irregular = 'mañana'
normal === irregular
// <- false
compare(normal, irregular)
// <- true
```

7.4 Regular Expressions

In this section we'll take a look at regular expressions in and after ES6. There are a couple of regular expressions flags that were introduced in ES6: the /y, or sticky flag, and the /u, or Unicode flag. Then we'll discuss five proposals that are making their way through the ECMAScript specification development process at TC39.

7.4.1 Sticky Matching Flag /y

The sticky matching y flag introduced in ES6 is similar to the global g flag. Like global regular expressions, sticky ones are typically used to match several times until the input string is exhausted. Sticky regular expressions move `lastIndex` to the position after the last match, just like global regular expressions. The only difference is that a sticky regular expression must start matching where the previous match left off, unlike global regular expressions that move onto the rest of the input string when the regular expression goes unmatched at any given position.

The following example illustrates the difference between the two. Given an input string like `'haha haha haha'` and the `/ha/` regular expression, the global flag will match every occurrence of `'ha'`, while the sticky flag will only match the first two, since the third occurrence doesn't match starting at index 4, but rather at index 5.

```
function matcher(regex, input) {
  return () => {
    const match = regex.exec(input)
    const lastIndex = regex.lastIndex
    return { lastIndex, match }
  }
}
const input = 'haha haha haha'
const nextGlobal = matcher(/ha/g, input)
console.log(nextGlobal()) // <- { lastIndex: 2, match: ['ha'] }
console.log(nextGlobal()) // <- { lastIndex: 4, match: ['ha'] }
console.log(nextGlobal()) // <- { lastIndex: 7, match: ['ha'] }
const nextSticky = matcher(/ha/y, input)
console.log(nextSticky()) // <- { lastIndex: 2, match: ['ha'] }
console.log(nextSticky()) // <- { lastIndex: 4, match: ['ha'] }
console.log(nextSticky()) // <- { lastIndex: 0, match: null }
```

We can verify that the sticky matcher would work if we forcefully moved `lastIndex` with the next piece of code.

```
const rsticky = /ha/y
const nextSticky = matcher(rsticky, input)
console.log(nextSticky()) // <- { lastIndex: 2, match: ['ha'] }
console.log(nextSticky()) // <- { lastIndex: 4, match: ['ha'] }
rsticky.lastIndex = 5
console.log(nextSticky()) // <- { lastIndex: 7, match: ['ha'] }
```

Sticky matching was added to JavaScript as a way of improving the performance of lexical analyzers in compilers, which heavily rely on regular expressions.

7.4.2 Unicode Flag /u

ES6 also introduced a u flag. The u stands for Unicode, but this flag can also be thought of as a more strict version of regular expressions.

Without the u flag, the following snippet has a regular expression containing an 'a' character literal that was unnecessarily escaped.

```
/\a/.test('ab')
// <- true
```

Using an escape sequence for an unreserved character such as a in a regular expression with the u flag results in an error, as shown in the following bit of code.

```
/\a/u.test('ab')
// <- SyntaxError: Invalid escape: /\a/
```

The following example attempts to embed the horse emoji in a regular expression by way of the \u{1f40e} notation that ES6 introduced for strings like '\u{1f40e}', but the regular expression fails to match against the horse emoji. Without the u flag, the \u{...} pattern is interpreted as having an unnecessarily escaped u character followed by the rest of the sequence.

```
/\u{1f40e}/.test('🐎') // <- false
/\u{1f40e}/.test('u{1f40e}') // <- true
```

The u flag introduces support for Unicode code point escapes, like the \u{1f40e} horse emoji, within regular expressions.

```
/\u{1f40e}/u.test('🐎')
// <- true
```

Without the u flag, the . pattern matches any BMP symbol except for line terminators. The following example tests U+1D11E MUSICAL SYMBOL G CLEF, an astral symbol that doesn't match the dot pattern in plain regular expressions.

```
const rdot = /^.$/
rdot.test('a') // <- true
rdot.test('\n') // <- false
rdot.test('\u{1d11e}') // <- false
```

When using the u flag, Unicode symbols that aren't on the BMP are matched as well. The next snippet shows how the astral symbol matches when the flag is set.

```
const rdot = /^.$/u
rdot.test('a') // <- true
rdot.test('\n') // <- false
rdot.test('\u{1d11e}') // <- true
```

When the u flag is set, similar Unicode awareness improvements can be found in quantifiers and character classes, both of which treat each Unicode code point as a single symbol, instead of matching on the first code unit only. Insensitive case matching with the i flag performs Unicode case folding when the u flag is set as well, which is used to normalize code points in both the input string and the regular expression.[8]

7.4.3 Named Capture Groups

Up until now, JavaScript regular expressions could group matches in numbered capturing groups and noncapturing groups. In the next snippet we're using a couple of groups to extract a key and value from an input string containing a key/value pair delimited by '='.

```
function parseKeyValuePair(input) {
  const rattribute = /([a-z]+)=([a-z]+)/
  const [, key, value] = rattribute.exec(input)
  return { key, value }
}
parseKeyValuePair('strong=true')
// <- { key: 'strong', value: 'true' }
```

There' are also noncapturing groups, which are discarded and not present in the final result, but are still useful for matching. The following example supports input with key/value pairs delimited by ' is ' in addition to '='.

```
function parseKeyValuePair(input) {
  const rattribute = /([a-z]+)(?:=|\sis\s)([a-z]+)/
  const [, key, value] = rattribute.exec(input)
  return { key, value }
}
parseKeyValuePair('strong is true')
// <- { key: 'strong', value: 'true' }
parseKeyValuePair('flexible=too')
// <- { key: 'flexible', value: 'too' }
```

---

8 For more details around the u flag in regular expressions, read "Unicode-aware regular expressions in ECMAScript 6" (*https://mjavascript.com/out/regexp-unicode*) from Mathias Bynens.

While array destructuring in the previous example hid our code's reliance on magic array indices, the fact remains that matches are placed in an ordered array regardless. The named capture groups proposal[9] (in stage 3 at the time of this writing) adds syntax like (?<groupName>) to Unicode-aware regular expressions, where we can name capturing groups which are then returned in a groups property of the returned match object. The groups property can then be destructured from the resulting object when calling RegExp#exec or String#match.

```
function parseKeyValuePair(input) {
  const rattribute = (
    /(?<key>[a-z]+)(?:=|\sis\s)(?<value>[a-z]+)/
  )
  const { groups } = rattribute.exec(input)
  return groups
}
parseKeyValuePair('strong=true')
// <- { key: 'strong', value: 'true' }
parseKeyValuePair('flexible=too')
// <- { key: 'flexible', value: 'too' }
```

JavaScript regular expressions support backreferences, where captured groups can be reused to look for duplicates. The following snippet uses a backreference for the first capturing group to identify cases where a username is the same as a password in a piece of 'user:password' input.

```
function hasSameUserAndPassword(input) {
  const rduplicate = /([^:]+):\1/
  return rduplicate.exec(input) !== null
}
hasSameUserAndPassword('root:root') // <- true
hasSameUserAndPassword('root:pF6GGlyPhoy1!9i') // <- false
```

The named capture groups proposal adds support for named backreferences, which refer back to named groups.

```
function hasSameUserAndPassword(input) {
  const rduplicate = /(?<user>[^:]+):\k<user>/u
  return rduplicate.exec(input) !== null
}
hasSameUserAndPassword('root:root') // <- true
hasSameUserAndPassword('root:pF6GGlyPhoy1!9i') // <- false
```

---

9 Check out the named capture groups proposal document (*https://mjavascript.com/out/ regexp-named-groups*).

The \k<groupName> reference can be used in tandem with numbered references, but the latter are better avoided when already using named references.

Lastly, named groups can be referenced from the replacement passed to String#replace. In the next code snippet we use String#replace and named groups to change an American date string to use Hungarian formatting.

```
function americanDateToHungarianFormat(input) {
  const ramerican = (
    /(?<month>\d{2})\/(?<day>\d{2})\/(?<year>\d{4})/
  )
  const hungarian = input.replace(
    ramerican,
    '$<year>-$<month>-$<day>'
  )
  return hungarian
}
americanDateToHungarianFormat('06/09/1988')
// <- '1988-09-06'
```

If the second argument to String#replace is a function, then the named groups can be accessed via a new parameter called groups that is at the end of the parameter list. The signature for that function now is (match, ...captures, groups). In the following example, note how we're using a template literal that's similar to the replacement string found in the last example. The fact that replacement strings follow a $<groupName> syntax as opposed to a ${ group Name } syntax means we can name groups in replacement strings without having to resort to escape codes if we were using template literals.

```
function americanDateToHungarianFormat(input) {
  const ramerican = (
    /(?<month>\d{2})\/(?<day>\d{2})\/(?<year>\d{4})/
  )
  const hungarian = input.replace(ramerican, (...rest) => {
    const groups = rest[rest.length - 1]
    const { month, day, year } = groups
    return `${ year }-${ month }-${ day }`
  })
  return hungarian
}
americanDateToHungarianFormat('06/09/1988') // <- '1988-09-06'
```

7.4.4 Unicode Property Escapes

The proposed Unicode property escapes[10] (currently in stage 3) are a new kind of escape sequence that's available in regular expressions marked with the u flag. This proposal adds an escape in the form of \p{LoneUnicodePropertyNameOrValue} for binary Unicode properties and \p{UnicodePropertyName=UnicodePropertyValue} for nonbinary Unicode properties. In addition, \P is the negated version of a \p escape sequence.

The Unicode standard defines properties for every symbol. Armed with these properties, one may make advanced queries about Unicode characters. For example, symbols in the Greek alphabet have a Script property set to Greek. We could use the new escapes to match any Greek Unicode symbol.

```
function isGreekSymbol(input) {
  const rgreek = /^\p{Script=Greek}$/u
  return rgreek.test(input)
}
isGreekSymbol('π')
// <- true
```

Or, using \P, we could match non-Greek Unicode symbols.

```
function isNonGreekSymbol(input) {
  const rgreek = /^\P{Script=Greek}$/u
  return rgreek.test(input)
}
isNonGreekSymbol('π')
// <- false
```

When we need to match every Unicode decimal number symbol, and not just [0-9] like \d does, we could use \p{Decimal_Number} as shown next.

```
function isDecimalNumber(input) {
  const rdigits = /^\p{Decimal_Number}+$/u
  return rdigits.test(input)
}
isDecimalNumber('1234567890123456')
// <- true
```

---

10 Check out the Unicode property escapes proposal document (*https:// mjavascript.com/out/unicode-property-escapes*).

Check out this exhaustive overview of supported Unicode properties and values (*https://mjavascript.com/out/unicode-property-list*).

7.4.5 Lookbehind Assertions

JavaScript has had positive lookahead assertions for a long time. That feature allows us to match an expression but only if it's followed by another expression. These assertions are expressed as (?=...). Regardless of whether a lookahead assertion matches, the results of that match are discarded and no characters of the input string are consumed.

The following example uses a positive lookahead to test whether an input string has a sequence of letters followed by .js, in which case it returns the filename without the .js part.

```
function getJavaScriptFilename(input) {
  const rfile = /^(?<filename>[a-z]+)(?=\.js)\.[a-z]+$/u
  const match = rfile.exec(input)
  if (match === null) {
    return null
  }
  return match.groups.filename
}
getJavaScriptFilename('index.js') // <- 'index'
getJavaScriptFilename('index.php') // <- null
```

There are also negative lookahead assertions, which are expressed as (?!...) as opposed to (?=...) for positive lookaheads. In this case, the assertion succeeds only if the lookahead expression isn't matched. The next bit of code uses a negative lookahead and we can observe how the results are flipped: now any expression other than '.js' results in a passed assertion.

```
function getNonJavaScriptFilename(input) {
  const rfile = /^(?<filename>[a-z]+)(?!\.js)\.[a-z]+$/u
  const match = rfile.exec(input)
  if (match === null) {
    return null
  }
  return match.groups.filename
}
getNonJavaScriptFilename('index.js') // <- null
getNonJavaScriptFilename('index.php') // <- 'index'
```

The proposal for lookbehind[11] (stage 3) introduces positive and negative lookbehind assertions, denoted with (?<=…) and (?<!…), respectively. These assertions can be used to ensure a pattern we want to match is or isn't preceded by another given pattern. The following snippet uses a positive lookbehind to match the digits in dollar amounts, but not for amounts in euros.

```
function getDollarAmount(input) {
  const rdollars = /^(?<=\$)(?<amount>\d+(?:\.\d+)?)$/u
  const match = rdollars.exec(input)
  if (match === null) {
    return null
  }
  return match.groups.amount
}
getDollarAmount('$12.34') // <- '12.34'
getDollarAmount('€12.34') // <- null
```

On the other hand, a negative lookbehind could be used to match numbers that aren't preceded by a dollar sign.

```
function getNonDollarAmount(input) {
  const rnumbers = /^(?<!\$)(?<amount>\d+(?:\.\d+)?)$/u
  const match = rnumbers.exec(input)
  if (match === null) {
    return null
  }
  return match.groups.amount
}
getNonDollarAmount('$12.34') // <- null
getNonDollarAmount('€12.34') // <- '12.34'
```

7.4.6 A New /s "dotAll" Flag

When using the . pattern, we typically expect to match every single character. In JavaScript, however, a . expression doesn't match astral characters (which can be fixed by adding the u flag) nor line terminators.

```
const rcharacter = /^.$/
rcharacter.test('a') // <- true
rcharacter.test('\t') // <- true
rcharacter.test('\n') // <- false
```

---

11 Check out the lookbehind assertions proposal document (*https://mjavascript.com/out/regexp-lookbehind*).

This sometimes drives developers to write other kinds of expressions to synthesize a pattern that matches any character. The expression in the next bit of code matches any character that's either a whitespace character or a nonwhitespace character, delivering the behavior we'd expect from the . pattern matcher.

```
const rcharacter = /^[\s\S]$/
rcharacter.test('a') // <- true
rcharacter.test('\t') // <- true
rcharacter.test('\n') // <- true
```

The dotAll proposal[12] (stage 3) adds an s flag, which changes the behavior of . in JavaScript regular expressions to match any single character.

```
const rcharacter = /^.$/s
rcharacter.test('a') // <- true
rcharacter.test('\t') // <- true
rcharacter.test('\n') // <- true
```

7.4.7 String#matchAll

Often, when we have a regular expression with a global or sticky flag, we want to iterate over the set of captured groups for each match. Currently, it can be a bit of a hassle to produce the list of matches: we need to collect the captured groups using String#match or RegExp#exec in a loop, until the regular expression doesn't match the input starting at the lastIndex position property. In the following piece of code, the parseAttributes generator function does just that for a given regular expression.

```
function* parseAttributes(input) {
  const rattributes = /(\w+)="([^"]+)"\s/ig
  while (true) {
    const match = rattributes.exec(input)
    if (match === null) {
      break
    }
    const [ , key, value] = match
    yield [key, value]
  }
}
const html = '<input type="email"
placeholder="hello@mjavascript.com" />'
```

---

12 Check out the dotAll flag proposal document (*https://mjavascript.com/out/regexp-dotall*).

```
console.log(...parseAttributes(html))
// [
//   ['type', 'email']
//   ['placeholder', 'hello@mjavascript.com']
// ]
```

One problem with this approach is that it's tailor-made for our regular expression and its capturing groups. We could fix that issue by creating a `matchAll` generator that is only concerned about looping over matches and collecting sets of captured groups, as shown in the following snippet.

```
function* matchAll(regex, input) {
  while (true) {
    const match = regex.exec(input)
    if (match === null) {
      break
    }
    const [ , ...captures] = match
    yield captures
  }
}
function* parseAttributes(input) {
  const rattributes = /(\w+)="([^"]+)"\s/ig
  yield* matchAll(rattributes, input)
}
const html = '<input type="email"
placeholder="hello@mjavascript.com" />'
console.log(...parseAttributes(html))
// [
//   ['type', 'email']
//   ['placeholder', 'hello@mjavascript.com']
// ]
```

A bigger source of confusion is that `rattributes` mutates its `lastIndex` property on each call to `RegExp#exec`, which is how it can track the position after the last match. When there are no matches left, `lastIndex` is reset back to 0. A problem arises when we don't iterate over all possible matches for a piece of input in one go—which would reset `lastIndex` to 0—and then we use the regular expression on a second piece of input, obtaining unexpected results.

While it looks like our `matchAll` implementation wouldn't fall victim of this given it loops over all matches, it'd be possible to iterate over the generator by hand, meaning that we'd run into trouble if we reused the same regular expression, as shown in the next bit of code. Note how the second matcher should report `['type', 'text']` but instead starts at an index much further ahead than 0, even misreporting the 'placeholder' key as 'laceholder'.

```
const rattributes = /(\w+)="([^"]+)"\s/ig
const email = '<input type="email"
placeholder="hello@mjavascript.com" />'
const emailMatcher = matchAll(rattributes, email)
const address = '<input type="text"
placeholder="Enter your business address" />'
const addressMatcher = matchAll(rattributes, address)
console.log(emailMatcher.next().value)
// <- ['type', 'email']
console.log(addressMatcher.next().value)
// <- ['laceholder', 'Enter your business address']
```

One solution would be to change matchAll so that lastIndex is always 0 when we yield back to the consumer code, while keeping track of lastIndex internally so that we can pick up where we left off in each step of the sequence.

The following piece of code shows that indeed, that'd fix the problems we're observing. Reusable global regular expressions are often avoided for this very reason: so that we don't have to worry about resetting lastIndex after every use.

```
function* matchAll(regex, input) {
  let lastIndex = 0
  while (true) {
    regex.lastIndex = lastIndex
    const match = regex.exec(input)
    if (match === null) {
      break
    }
    lastIndex = regex.lastIndex
    regex.lastIndex = 0
    const [ , ...captures] = match
    yield captures
  }
}
const rattributes = /(\w+)="([^"]+)"\s/ig
const email = '<input type="email"
placeholder="hello@mjavascript.com" />'
const emailMatcher = matchAll(rattributes, email)
const address = '<input type="text"
placeholder="Enter your business address" />'
const addressMatcher = matchAll(rattributes, address)
console.log(emailMatcher.next().value)
// <- ['type', 'email']
console.log(addressMatcher.next().value)
// <- ['type', 'text']
```

```
console.log(emailMatcher.next().value)
// <- ['placeholder', 'hello@mjavascript.com']
console.log(addressMatcher.next().value)
// <- ['placeholder', 'Enter your business address']
```

The String#matchAll proposal[13] (in stage 1 at the time of this writing) introduces a new method for the string prototype that would behave in a similar fashion as our matchAll implementation, except the returned iterable is a sequence of match objects as opposed to just the captures in the preceding example. Note that the String#matchAll sequence contains entire match objects, and not just numbered captures. This means we could access named captures through match.groups for each match in the sequence.

```
const rattributes = /(?<key>\w+)="(?<value>[^"]+)"\s/igu
const email = '<input type="email"
placeholder="hello@mjavascript.com" />'
for (const match of email.matchAll(rattributes)) {
  const { groups: { key, value } } = match
  console.log(`${ key }: ${ value }`)
}
// <- type: email
// <- placeholder: hello@mjavascript.com
```

7.5 Array

Over the years, libraries like Underscore and Lodash spoke loudly of missing features when it came to arrays. As a result, ES5 brought in heaps of functional methods to arrays: Array#filter, Array#map, Array#reduce, Array#reduceRight, Array#forEach, Array#some, and Array#every.

ES6 brings a few more methods that will help manipulate, fill, and filter arrays.

7.5.1 Array.from

Before ES6, JavaScript developers often needed to cast arguments to a function into an array.

```
function cast() {
  return Array.prototype.slice.call(arguments)
```

---

13 Check out the String#matchAll proposal document (*https://mjavascript.com/out/ string-matchall*).

```
}
cast('a', 'b')
// <- ['a', 'b']
```

We've already explored more terse ways of doing this in Chapter 2, when we first learned about rest and spread. You could, for instance, use the spread operator. As you no doubt remember, the spread operator leverages the iterator protocol to produce a sequence of values in arbitrary objects. The downside is that the objects we want to cast with spread must adhere to the iterator protocol by having implemented Symbol.iterator. Luckily for us, arguments does implement the iterator protocol in ES6.

```
function cast() {
  return [...arguments]
}
cast('a', 'b')
// <- ['a', 'b']
```

Using the function rest parameter would be better for this particular case as it wouldn't involve the arguments object, nor any added logic in the function body.

```
function cast(...params) {
  return params
}
cast('a', 'b')
// <- ['a', 'b']
```

You may also want to cast NodeList DOM element collections, like those returned from document.querySelectorAll, through the spread operator. This can be helpful when we need access to native array methods like Array#map or Array#filter. This is possible because the DOM standard upgraded NodeList to an iterable, after ES6 defined the iterator protocol.

```
[...document.querySelectorAll('div')]
// <- [<div>, <div>, <div>, …]
```

What happens when we try to cast a jQuery collection through the spread operator? If you're on a modern version of jQuery that implements the iterator protocol, spreading a jQuery object will work, otherwise you may get an exception.

```
[...$('div')]
// <- [<div>, <div>, <div>, …]
```

The new Array.from method is a bit different. It doesn't only rely on the iterator protocol to figure out how to pull values from an object.

It has support for array-likes out the box, unlike the spread operator. The following code snippet will work with any version of jQuery.

```
Array.from($('div'))
// <- [<div>, <div>, <div>, …]
```

The one thing you cannot do with either `Array.from` nor the spread operator is to pick a start index. Suppose you wanted to pull every `<div>` after the first one. With `Array#slice`, you could do the following.

```
[].slice.call(document.querySelectorAll('div'), 1)
```

Of course, there's nothing stopping you from using `Array#slice` after casting. This is a bit easier to read than the previous example, as it keeps the slice call closer to the index at which we want to slice the array.

```
Array.from(document.querySelectorAll('div')).slice(1)
```

`Array.from` has three arguments, although only the `input` is required. To wit:

- `input`—the array-like or iterable object you want to cast
- `map`—a mapping function that's executed on every item of `input`
- `context`—the `this` binding to use when calling `map`

With `Array.from` you cannot slice, but you can dice. The `map` function will efficiently map the values into something else as they're being added to the array that results from calling `Array.from`.

```
function typesOf() {
  return Array.from(arguments, value => typeof value)
}
typesOf(null, [], NaN)
// <- ['object', 'object', 'number']
```

Do note that, for the specific case of dealing with `arguments`, you could also combine rest parameters and `Array#map`. In this case in particular, we may be better off just doing something like the snippet of code found next. It's not as verbose as the previous example. Like with the `Array#slice` example we saw earlier, the mapping is more explicit in this case.

```
function typesOf(...all) {
  return all.map(value => typeof value)
}
```

```
typesOf(null, [], NaN)
// <- ['object', 'object', 'number']
```

When dealing with array-like objects, it makes sense to use
Array.from if they don't implement Symbol.iterator.

```
const apple = {
  type: 'fruit',
  name: 'Apple',
  amount: 3
}
const onion = {
  type: 'vegetable',
  name: 'Onion',
  amount: 1
}
const groceries = {
  0: apple,
  1: onion,
  length: 2
}
Array.from(groceries)
// <- [apple, onion]
Array.from(groceries, grocery => grocery.type)
// <- ['fruit', 'vegetable']
```

7.5.2 Array.of

The Array.of method is exactly like the cast function we played
around with earlier. Next is a code snippet that shows how Array.of
might be ponyfilled.

```
function arrayOf(...items) {
  return items
}
```

The Array constructor has two overloads: ...items, where you provide the items for the new array; and length, where you provide its
numeric length. You can think about Array.of as a flavor of new
Array that doesn't support a length overload. In the following code
snippet, you'll find some of the unexpected ways in which new
Array behaves, thanks to its single-argument length overloaded
constructor. If you're confused about the undefined x ${ count }
notation in the browser console, that's indicating there are array
holes in those positions. This is also known as a *sparse array*.

```
new Array() // <- []
new Array(undefined) // <- [undefined]
new Array(1) // <- [undefined x 1]
```

```
new Array(3) // <- [undefined x 3]
new Array('3') // <- ['3']
new Array(1, 2) // <- [1, 2]
new Array(-1, -2) // <- [-1, -2]
new Array(-1) // <- RangeError: Invalid array length
```

In contrast, Array.of has more consistent behavior because it doesn't have the special length case. This makes it a more desirable way of consistently creating new arrays programmatically.

```
console.log(Array.of()) // <- []
console.log(Array.of(undefined)) // <- [undefined]
console.log(Array.of(1)) // <- [1]
console.log(Array.of(3)) // <- [3]
console.log(Array.of('3')) // <- ['3']
console.log(Array.of(1, 2)) // <- [1, 2]
console.log(Array.of(-1, -2)) // <- [-1, -2]
console.log(Array.of(-1)) // <- [-1]
```

7.5.3 Array#copyWithin

Let's start with the signature of Array#copyWithin.

```
Array.prototype.copyWithin(target, start = 0, end = this.length)
```

The Array#copyWithin method copies a sequence of array elements within an array instance to the "paste position" starting at target. The elements to be copied are taken from the [start, end) range. The Array#copyWithin method returns the array instance itself.

Let's lead with a simple example. Consider the items array in the following code snippet.

```
const items = [1, 2, 3, , , , , , , , ]
// <- [1, 2, 3, undefined x 7]
```

The function call shown next takes the items array and determines that it'll start "pasting" items in the sixth position (zero-based). It further determines that the items to be copied will be taken starting in the second position, until the third position (not inclusive).

```
const items = [1, 2, 3, , , , , , , , ]
items.copyWithin(6, 1, 3)
// <- [1, 2, 3, undefined × 3, 2, 3, undefined × 2]
```

Reasoning about Array#copyWithin is hard. Let's break it down.

If we consider that the items to be copied were taken from the [start, end) range, then we could express that using an

---

Array#slice call. These are the items that were pasted at the target position. We can use .slice to grab the copy.

```
const items = [1, 2, 3, , , , , , , , ]
const copy = items.slice(1, 3)
// <- [2, 3]
```

We could also consider the pasting part of the operation as an advanced usage of Array#splice. The next code snippet does just that, passing the paste position to splice, telling it to remove as many items as we want to copy, and inserting the pasted items. Note that we're using the spread operator so that elements are inserted individually, and not as an array, through .splice.

```
const items = [1, 2, 3, , , , , , , , ]
const copy = items.slice(1, 3)
// <- [2, 3]
items.splice(6, 3 - 1, ...copy)
console.log(items)
// <- [1, 2, 3, undefined × 3, 2, 3, undefined × 2]
```

Now that we better understand the internals of Array#copyWithin, we can generalize the example in order to implement the custom copyWithin function shown in the following code snippet.

```
function copyWithin(
  items,
  target,
  start = 0,
  end = items.length
) {
  const copy = items.slice(start, end)
  const removed = end - start
  items.splice(target, removed, ...copy)
  return items
}
```

The example we've been trying so far would work just as well with our custom copyWithin function.

```
copyWithin([1, 2, 3, , , , , , , , ], 6, 1, 3)
// <- [1, 2, 3, undefined × 3, 2, 3, undefined × 2]
```

7.5.4 Array#fill

A convenient utility method to replace all items in an array with the provided value. Note that sparse arrays will be filled in their entirety, while existing items will be replaced by the fill value.

```
['a', 'b', 'c'].fill('x') // <- ['x', 'x', 'x']
new Array(3).fill('x') // <- ['x', 'x', 'x']
```

You could also specify the starting index and end index. In this case, as shown next, only the items in those positions would be filled.

```
['a', 'b', 'c', , ,].fill('x', 2)
// <- ['a', 'b', 'x', 'x', 'x']
new Array(5).fill('x', 0, 1)
// <- ['x', undefined x 4]
```

The provided value can be anything, and is not just limited to primitive values.

```
new Array(3).fill({})
// <- [{}, {}, {}]
```

You can't fill arrays using a mapping method that takes an index parameter or anything like that.

```
const map = i => i * 2
new Array(3).fill(map)
// <- [map, map, map]
```

7.5.5 Array#find and Array#findIndex

The Array#find method runs a callback for each item in an array until the first one that returns true, and then returns that item. The method follows the signature of (callback(item, i, array), context) that's also present in Array#map, Array#filter, and others. You can think of Array#find as a version of Array#some that returns the matching element instead of just true.

```
['a', 'b', 'c', 'd', 'e'].find(item => item === 'c')
// <- 'c'
['a', 'b', 'c', 'd', 'e'].find((item, i) => i === 0)
// <- 'a'
['a', 'b', 'c', 'd', 'e'].find(item => item === 'z')
// <- undefined
```

There's an Array#findIndex method as well, and it leverages the same signature. Instead of returning a Boolean value, or the element itself, Array.findIndex returns the index of the matching element, or -1 if no matches occur. Here are a few examples.

```
['a', 'b', 'c', 'd', 'e'].findIndex(item => item === 'c')
// <- 2
['a', 'b', 'c', 'd', 'e'].findIndex((item, i) => i === 0)
// <- 0
```

```
['a', 'b', 'c', 'd', 'e'].findIndex(item => item === 'z')
// <- -1
```

7.5.6 Array#keys

Array#keys returns an iterator that yields a sequence holding the keys for the array. The returned value is an iterator, meaning you can iterate over it with for..of, the spread operator, or by manually calling .next().

```
['a', 'b', 'c', 'd'].keys()
// <- ArrayIterator {}
```

Here's an example using for..of.

```
for (const key of ['a', 'b', 'c', 'd'].keys()) {
  console.log(key)
  // <- 0
  // <- 1
  // <- 2
  // <- 3
}
```

Unlike Object.keys, and most methods that iterate over arrays, this sequence doesn't ignore array holes.

```
Object.keys(new Array(4))
// <- []
[...new Array(4).keys()]
// <- [0, 1, 2, 3]
```

Now onto values.

7.5.7 Array#values

Array#values is the same as Array#keys(), but the returned iterator is a sequence of values instead of keys. In practice, you'll want to iterate over the array itself most of the time, but getting an iterator can come in handy sometimes.

```
['a', 'b', 'c', 'd'].values()
// <- ArrayIterator {}
```

You can use for..of or any other methods like a spread operator to pull out the iterable sequence. The following example uses the spread operator on an array's .values() to create a copy of that array.

```
[...['a', 'b', 'c', 'd'].values()]
// <- ['a', 'b', 'c', 'd']
```

Note that omitting the `.values()` method call would still produce a copy of the array: the sequence is iterated and spread over a new array.

7.5.8 Array#entries

Similar to both preceding methods, except `Array#entries` returns an iterator with a sequence of key/value pairs.

```
['a', 'b', 'c', 'd'].entries()
// <- ArrayIterator {}
```

Each item in the sequence is a two-dimensional array with the key and the value for an item in the array.

```
[...['a', 'b', 'c', 'd'].entries()]
// <- [[0, 'a'], [1, 'b'], [2, 'c'], [3, 'd']]
```

Great, one last method left!

7.5.9 Array.prototype[Symbol.iterator]

This is exactly the same as the `Array#values` method.

```
const list = ['a', 'b', 'c', 'd']
list[Symbol.iterator] === list.values
// <- true
[...list[Symbol.iterator]()]
// <- ['a', 'b', 'c', 'd']
```

The following example combines a spread operator, an array, and `Symbol.iterator` to iterate over its values. Can you follow the code?

```
[...['a', 'b', 'c', 'd'][Symbol.iterator]()]
// <- ['a', 'b', 'c', 'd']
```

Let's break it down. First, there's the array.

```
['a', 'b', 'c', 'd']
// <- ['a', 'b', 'c', 'd']
```

Then we get an iterator.

```
['a', 'b', 'c', 'd'][Symbol.iterator]()
// <- ArrayIterator {}
```

Last, we spread the iterator over a new array, creating a copy.

```
[...['a', 'b', 'c', 'd'][Symbol.iterator]()]
// <- ['a', 'b', 'c', 'd']
```

CHAPTER 8

JavaScript Modules

Over the years, we've seen multiple different ways in which to split code into more manageable units. For the longest time we've had the module pattern, where you simply wrapped pieces of code in self-invoking function expressions. You had to be careful to sort your scripts so that each script came after all of its dependencies.

A while later, the RequireJS library was born. It provided a way of defining the dependencies of each module programmatically, so that a dependency graph is created and you wouldn't have to worry about sorting your scripts anymore. RequireJS demands that you provide an array of strings used to identify your dependencies and also wrap modules in a function call, which would then receive those dependencies as parameters. Many other libraries provide similar functionality but offer a slightly different API.

Other complexity management mechanisms exist, such as the dependency injection mechanism in AngularJS, where you define named components using functions where you can, in turn, specify other named component dependencies. AngularJS carries the load of dependency injection on your behalf, so you only have to name components and specify dependencies.

CommonJS (CJS) surfaced as an alternative to RequireJS, and it was swiftly popularized by Node.js soon afterwards. In this chapter we'll take a look at CommonJS, which is still heavily in use today. We'll then cover the module system introduced to native JavaScript in ES6, and lastly we'll explore interoperability between CommonJS and native JavaScript modules—also known as ECMAScript modules (ESM).

8.1 CommonJS

Unlike other module formats where modules are declared programmatically, in CommonJS every file is a module. CommonJS modules have an implicit local scope, while the `global` scope needs to be accessed explicitly. CommonJS modules can dynamically export a public interface consumers can interact with. CommonJS modules import their dependencies dynamically as well, resolving dependencies through `require` function calls. These `require` function calls are synchronous and return the interface exposed by required modules.

Interpreting the definition of a module format without looking at some code can be confusing. The following code snippet shows what a reusable CommonJS module file may look like. Both the `has` and `union` functions are local to our module's scope. Given that we've assigned `union` to `module.exports`, that'll be the public API for our module.

```
function has(list, item) {
  return list.includes(item)
}
function union(list, item) {
  if (has(list, item)) {
    return list
  }
  return [...list, item]
}
module.exports = union
```

Suppose we take that snippet of code and save it as *union.js*. We can now consume *union.js* in another CommonJS module. Let's call that one *app.js*. In order to consume *union.js*, we call `require` passing in a relative path to the *union.js* file.

```
const union = require('./union.js')
console.log(union([1, 2], 3))
// <- [1, 2, 3]
console.log(union([1, 2], 2))
// <- [1, 2]
```

We can omit the file extension as long as it's *.js* or *.json*, but this is discouraged.

While the file extension is optional for `require` statements and when using the `node` CLI, we should strongly consider getting into the habit of including it nevertheless. Browser implementations of ESM (*https://html.spec.whatwg.org/multipage/webappapis.html#integration-with-the-javascript-module-system*) won't have this luxury, since that'd entail extra roundtrips to figure out the correct endpoint for a JavaScript module HTTP resource.

We could run _app.js_ in its current state through the CLI for Node.js, `node`, as seen in the next snippet.

```
» node app.js
# [1, 2, 3]
# [1, 2]
```

After installing Node.js (*https://mjavascript.com/out/node*), you'll be able to use the `node` program in your terminal.

The `require` function in CJS can be treated dynamically, just like any other JavaScript function. This aspect of `require` is sometimes leveraged to dynamically `require` different modules that conform to one interface. As an example, let's conjure up a *templates* directory with a number of view template functions. Our templates will take a model and return an HTML string.

The template found in the following code snippet renders an item of a grocery shopping list by reading its attributes from a `model` object.

```
// views/item.js
module.exports = model => `<li>
  <span>${ model.amount }</span>
  <span>x </span>
  <span>${ model.name }</span>
</li>`
```

Our application could print a `<li>` by leveraging the *item.js* view template.

```
// app.js
const renderItem = require('./views/item.js')
const html = renderItem({
  name: 'Banana bread',
  amount: 3
})
console.log(html)
```

Figure 8-1 shows our tiny application in action.

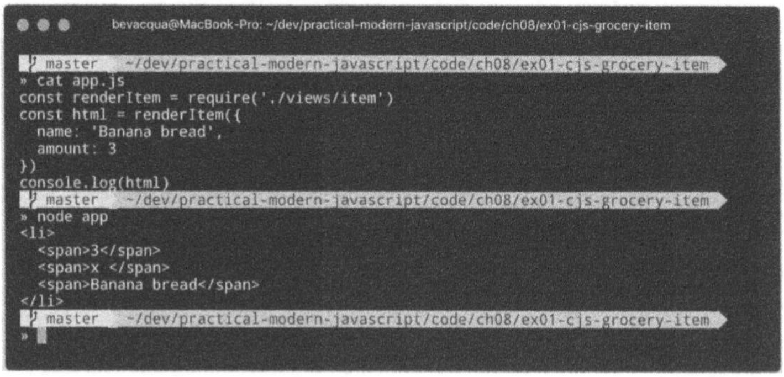

Figure 8-1. Rendering a model as HTML is as easy as saying template literal expression interpolation!

The next template we'll make renders the grocery list itself. It receives an array of items, and renders each of them by reusing the *item.js* template from the previous code snippet.

```
// views/list.js
const renderItem = require('./item.js')

module.exports = model => `<ul>
  ${ model.map(renderItem).join('\n') }
</ul>`
```

We can consume the *list.js* template in a very similar way to what we did before, but we'll need to adjust the model passed into the template so that we provide a collection of items instead of a single one.

```
// app.js
const renderList = require('./views/list.js')
const html = renderList([{
  name: 'Banana bread',
  amount: 3
}, {
  name: 'Chocolate chip muffin',
  amount: 2
```

```
}])
console.log(html)
```

Figure 8-2 shows our updated application in all its glory.

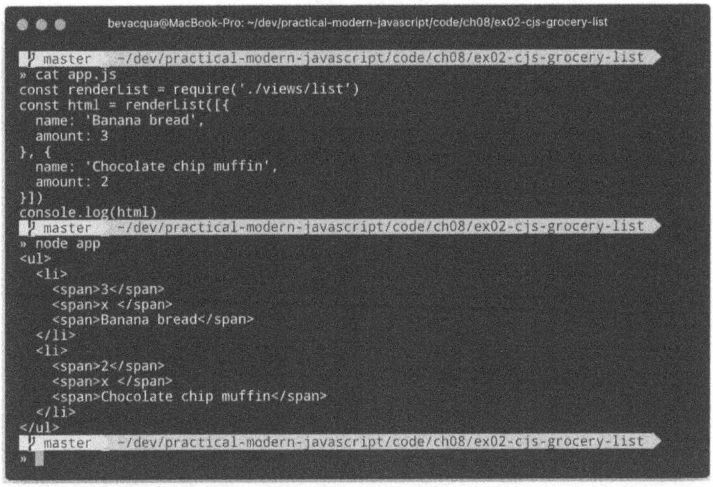

Figure 8-2. Composing components made with template literals can be as simple as we choose to make them

In the examples so far, we've written short modules that are only concerned with producing an HTML view after matching a `model` object with the corresponding view template. A simple API encourages reusability, which is why we're easily able to render the items for a list by mapping their models to the *item.js* templating function, and joining their HTML representations with newlines.

Given that the views all have a similar API where they take a model and return an HTML string, we can treat them uniformly. If we wanted a `render` function that could render any template, we could easily do that, thanks to the dynamic nature of `require`. The next example shows how we can construct the path to a template module. An important distinction is how `require` calls don't necessarily need to be on the top level of a module. Calls to `require` can be anywhere, even embedded within other functions.

```
// render.js
module.exports = function render(template, model) {
  return require(`./views/${ template }`.js)(model)
}
```

Once we had such an API, we wouldn't have to worry about carefully constructing `require` statements that match the directory structure of our view templates, because the *render.js* module could take care of that. Rendering any template becomes a matter of calling the `render` function with the template's name and the model for that template, as demonstrated in the following code and Figure 8-3.

```
// app.js
const render = require('./render.js')
console.log(render('item', {
  name: 'Banana bread',
  amount: 1
}))
console.log(render('list', [{
  name: 'Apple pie',
  amount: 2
}, {
  name: 'Roasted almond',
  amount: 25
}]))
```

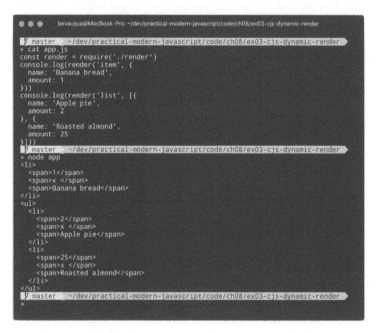

Figure 8-3. Creating a bare bones HTML rendering application is made easy by template literals

Moving on, you'll notice that ES6 modules are somewhat influenced by CommonJS. In the next few sections we'll look at `export` and `import` statements, and learn how ESM is compatible with CJS.

8.2 JavaScript Modules

As we explored the CommonJS module system, you might've noticed how the API is simple but powerful and flexible. ES6 modules offer an even simpler API that's almost as powerful at the expense of some flexibility.

8.2.1 Strict Mode

In the ES6 module system, strict mode is turned on by default. Strict mode is a feature[1] that disallows bad parts of the language, and turns some silent errors into loud exceptions being thrown. Taking into account these disallowed features, compilers can enable optimizations, making JavaScript runtime faster and safer.

- Variables must be declared
- Function parameters must have unique names
- Using `with` statements is forbidden
- Assignment to read-only properties results in errors being thrown
- Octal numbers like `00740` are syntax errors
- Attempts to `delete` undeletable properties throw an error
- `delete prop` is a syntax error, instead of assuming `delete global.prop`
- `eval` doesn't introduce new variables into its surrounding scope
- `eval` and `arguments` can't be bound or assigned to
- `arguments` doesn't magically track changes to method parameters
- `arguments.callee` is no longer supported, throws a `TypeError`
- `arguments.caller` is no longer supported, throws a `TypeError`

---

1 Read this comprehensive article about strict mode on Mozilla's MDN (*https://mjava script.com/out/strict-mode*).

- Context passed as `this` in method invocations is not "boxed" into an `Object`
- No longer able to use `fn.caller` and `fn.arguments` to access the JavaScript stack
- Reserved words (e.g., `protected`, `static`, `interface`, etc.) cannot be bound

Let's now dive into the `export` statement.

8.2.2 export Statements

In CommonJS modules, you export values by exposing them on `module.exports`. You can expose anything from a value type to an object, an array, or a function, as seen in the next few code snippets.

```
module.exports = 'hello'
module.exports = { hello: 'world' }
module.exports = ['hello', 'world']
module.exports = function hello() {}
```

ES6 modules are files that may expose an API through `export` statements. Declarations in ESM are scoped to the local module, just like we observed about CommonJS. Any variables declared inside a module aren't available to other modules unless they're explicitly exported as part of that module's API and then imported in the module that wants to access them.

Exporting a default binding

You can mimic the CommonJS code we just saw by replacing `module.exports =` with `export default` statements.

```
export default 'hello'
export default { hello: 'world' }
export default ['hello', 'world']
export default function hello() {}
```

In CommonJS, `module.exports` can be assigned-to dynamically.

```
function initialize() {
  module.exports = 'hello!'
}
initialize()
```

In contrast with CJS, export statements in ESM can only be placed at the top level. "Top-level only" export statements is a good constraint to have, as there aren't many good reasons to dynamically define and expose an API based on method calls. This limitation also helps compilers and static analysis tools parse ES6 modules.

```
function initialize() {
  export default 'hello!' // SyntaxError
}
initialize()
```

There are a few other ways of exposing an API in ESM, besides export default statements.

Named exports

When you want to expose multiple values from CJS modules you don't necessarily need to explicitly export an object containing every one of those values. You could simply add properties onto the implicit module.exports object. There's still a single binding being exported, containing all properties the module.exports object ends up holding. While the following example exports two individual values, both are exposed as properties on the exported object.

```
module.exports.counter = 0
module.exports.count = () => module.exports.counter++
```

We can replicate this behavior in ESM by using the named exports syntax. Instead of assigning properties to an implicit module.exports object like with CommonJS, in ES6 you declare the bindings you want to export, as shown in the following code snippet.

```
export let counter = 0
export const count = () => counter++
```

Note that the last bit of code cannot be refactored to extract the variable declarations into standalone statements that are later passed to export as a named export, as that'd be a syntax error.

```
let counter = 0
const count = () => counter++
export counter // SyntaxError
export count
```

By being rigid in how its declarative module syntax works, ESM favors static analysis, once again at the expense of flexibility. Flexibility inevitably comes at the cost of added complexity, which is a good reason not to offer flexible interfaces.

Exporting lists

ES6 modules let you `export` lists of named top-level members, as seen in the following snippet. The syntax for export lists is easy to parse, and presents a solution to the problem we observed in the last code snippet from the previous section.

```
let counter = 0
const count = () => counter++
export { counter, count }
```

If you'd like to export a binding but give it a different name, you can use the aliasing syntax: `export { count as increment }`. In doing so, we're exposing the count binding from the local scope as a public method under the `increment` alias, as the following snippet shows.

```
let counter = 0
const count = () => counter++
export { counter, count as increment }
```

Finally, we can specify a default export when using the named member list syntax. The next bit of code uses `as default` to define a default export at the same time as we're enumerating named exports.

```
let counter = 0
const count = () => counter++
export { counter as default, count as increment }
```

The following piece of code is equivalent to the previous one, albeit a tad more verbose.

```
let counter = 0
const count = () => counter++
export default counter
export { count as increment }
```

It's important to keep in mind that we are exporting bindings, and not merely values.

Bindings, not values

ES6 modules export bindings, not values or references. This means that a `fungible` binding exported from a module would be bound into the `fungible` variable on the module, and its value would be subject to changes made to `fungible`. While unexpectedly changing the public interface of a module after it has initially loaded can lead to confusion, this can indeed be useful in some cases.

In the next code snippet, our module's `fungible` export would be initially bound to an object and be changed into an array after five seconds.

```
export let fungible = { name: 'bound' }
setTimeout(() => fungible = [0, 1, 2], 5000)
```

Modules consuming this API would see the `fungible` value changing after five seconds. Consider the following example, where we print the consumed binding every two seconds.

```
import { fungible } from './fungible.js'

console.log(fungible) // <- { name: 'bound' }
setInterval(() => console.log(fungible), 2000)
// <- { name: 'bound' }
// <- { name: 'bound' }
// <- [0, 1, 2]
// <- [0, 1, 2]
// <- [0, 1, 2]
```

This kind of behavior is best suited for counters and flags, but is best avoided unless its purpose is clearly defined, since it can lead to confusing behavior and API surfaces changing unexpectedly from the point of view of a consumer.

The JavaScript module system also offers an `export..from` syntax, where you can expose another module's interface.

Exporting from another module

We can expose another module's named exports using by adding a `from` clause to an `export` statement. The bindings are not imported into the local scope: our module acts as a pass-through where we expose another module's bindings without getting direct access to them.

```
export { increment } from './counter.js'
increment()
// ReferenceError: increment is not defined
```

You can give aliases to named exports, as they pass through your module. If the module in the following example were named `aliased`, then consumers could `import { add } from './`

aliased.js' to get a reference to the `increment` binding from the counter module.

```
export { increment as add } from './counter.js'
```

An ESM module could also expose every single named export found in another module by using a wildcard, as shown in the next snippet. Note that this wouldn't include the default binding exported by the counter module.

```
export * from './counter.js'
```

When we want to expose another module's `default` binding, we'll have to use the named export syntax adding an alias.

```
export { default as counter } from './counter.js'
```

We've now covered every way in which we can expose an API in ES6 modules. Let's jump over to `import` statements, which can be used to consume other modules.

8.2.3 import Statements

We can load a module from another one using `import` statements. The way modules are loaded is implementation-specific; that is, it's not defined by the specification. We can write spec-compliant ES6 code today while smart people figure out how to deal with module loading in browsers.

Compilers like Babel are able to concatenate modules with the aid of a module system like CommonJS. That means `import` statements in Babel mostly follow the same semantics as `require` statements in CommonJS.

Let's suppose we have the following code snippet in a *./counter.js* module.

```
let counter = 0
const increment = () => counter++
const decrement = () => counter--
export { counter as default, increment, decrement }
```

The statement in the following code snippet could be used to load the counter module into our app module. It won't create any variables in the app scope. It will execute any code in the top level of the counter module, though, including that module's own `import` statements.

```
import './counter.js'
```

In the same fashion as export statements, import statements are only allowed in the top level of your module definitions. This limitation helps compilers simplify their module loading capabilities, as well as help other static analysis tools parse your codebase.

Importing default exports

CommonJS modules let you import other modules using require statements. When we need a reference to the default export, all we'd have to do is assign that to a variable.

```
const counter = require('./counter.js')
```

To import the default binding exported from an ES6 module, we'll have to give it a name. The syntax and semantics are a bit different than what we use when declaring a variable, because we're importing a binding and not just assigning values to variables. This distinction also makes it easier for static analysis tools and compilers to parse our code.

```
import counter from './counter.js'
console.log(counter)
// <- 0
```

Besides default exports, you could also import named exports and alias them.

Importing named exports

The following bit of code shows how we can import the increment method from our counter module. Reminiscent of assignment destructuring, the syntax for importing named exports is wrapped in braces.

```
import { increment } from './counter.js'
```

To import multiple bindings, we separate them using commas.

```
import { increment, decrement } from './counter.js'
```

The syntax and semantics are subtly different from destructuring. While destructuring relies on colons to create aliases, import statements use an as keyword, mirroring the syntax in export statements. The following statement imports the increment method as add.

```
import { increment as add } from './counter.js'
```

You can combine a default export with named exports by separating them with a comma.

```
import counter, { increment } from './counter.js'
```

You can also explicitly name the `default` binding, which needs an alias.

```
import { default as counter, increment } from './counter.js'
```

The following example demonstrates how ESM semantics differ from those of CJS. Remember: we're exporting and importing bindings, and not direct references. For practical purposes, you can think of the `counter` binding found in the next example as a property getter that reaches into the `counter` module and returns its local `counter` variable.

```
import counter, { increment } from './counter.js'
console.log(counter) // <- 0
increment()
console.log(counter) // <- 1
increment()
console.log(counter) // <- 2
```

Lastly, there are also namespace imports.

Wildcard import statements

We can import the namespace object for a module by using a wildcard. Instead of importing the named exports or the default value, it imports everything at once. Note that the * must be followed by an alias where all the bindings will be placed. If there was a `default` export, it'll be placed in the namespace binding as well.

```
import * as counter from './counter.js'
counter.increment()
counter.increment()
console.log(counter.default) // <- 2
```

8.2.4 Dynamic import()

At the time of this writing, a proposal for dynamic `import()`Check out the proposal specification draft (*https://mjavascript.com/out/dynamic-import*). expressions is sitting at stage 3 of the TC39 proposal review process. Unlike `import` statements, which are statically analyzed and linked, `import()` loads modules at runtime, returning a promise for the module namespace object after fetching, parsing, and executing the requested module and all of its dependencies.

The module specifier can be any string, like with `import` statements. Keep in mind `import` statements only allow statically defined plain string literals as module specifiers. In contrast, we're able to use template literals or any valid JavaScript expression to produce the module specifier string for `import()` function calls.

Imagine you're looking to internationalize an application based on the language provided by user agents. You might statically import a `localizationService`, and then dynamically import the localized data for a given language using `import()` and a module specifier built using a template literal that interpolates `navigator.language`, as shown in the following example.

```
import localizationService from './localizationService.js'
import(`./localizations/${ navigator.language }.json`)
  .then(module => localizationService.use(module))
```

Note that writing code like this is generally a bad idea for a number of reasons:

- It can be challenging to statically analyze, given that static analysis is executed at build time, when it can be hard or impossible to infer the value of interpolations such as `${ navigator.language }`.

- It can't be packaged up as easily by JavaScript bundlers, meaning the module would probably be loaded asynchronously while the bulk of our application has been loaded.

- It can't be tree-shaken by tools like Rollup, which can be used to remove module code that's never imported anywhere in the codebase—and thus never used—reducing bundle size and improving performance.

- It can't be linted by `eslint-plugin-import` or similar tools that help identify module import statements where the imported module file doesn't exist.

Just like with `import` statements, the mechanism for retrieving the module is unspecified and left up to the host environment.

The proposal does specify that once the module is resolved, the promise should fulfill with its namespace object. It also specifies that whenever an error results in the module failing to load, the promise should be rejected.

This allows for loading noncritical modules asynchronously, without blocking page load, and being able to gracefully handle failure scenarios when such a module fails to load, as demonstrated next.

```
import('./vendor/jquery.js')
  .then($ => {
    // use jquery
  })
  .catch(() => {
    // failed to load jquery
  })
```

We could load multiple modules asynchronously using Promise.all. The following example imports three modules and then leverages destructuring to reference them directly in the .then clause.

```
const specifiers = [
  './vendor/jquery.js',
  './vendor/backbone.js',
  './lib/util.js'
]
Promise
  .all(specifiers.map(specifier => import(specifier)))
  .then(([$, backbone, util]) => {
    // use modules
  })
```

In a similar fashion, you could load modules using synchronous loops or even async/await, as demonstrated next.

```
async function load() {
  const { map } = await import('./vendor/jquery.js')
  const $ = await import('./vendor/jquery.js')
  const response = await fetch('/cats')
  const cats = await response.json()
  $('<div>')
    .addClass('container cats')
    .html(map(cats, cat => cat.htmlSnippet))
    .appendTo(document.body)
}
load()
```

Using await import() makes dynamic module loading look and feel like static import statements. We need to watch out and remind ourselves that the modules are asynchronously loaded one by one, though.

Keep in mind that import is function-like, but it has different semantics from regular functions: import is not a function definition, it can't be extended, it can't be assigned properties, and it can't be destructured. In this sense, import() falls in a similar category as the super() call that's available in class constructors.

8.3 Practical Considerations for ES Modules

When using a module system, any module system, we gain the ability of explicitly publishing an API while keeping everything that doesn't need to be public in the local scope. Perfect information hiding like this is a sought-out feature that was previously hard to reproduce: you'd have to rely on deep knowledge of JavaScript scoping rules, or blindly follow a pattern inside which you could hide information, as shown next. In this case, we create a random module with a locally scoped calc function, which computes a random number in the [0, n) range; and a public API with the range method, which computes a random number in the [min, max] range.

```
const random = (function() {
  const calc = n => Math.floor(Math.random() * n)
  const range = (max = 1, min = 0) => calc(max + 1 - min) + min
  return { range }
})()
```

Compare that to the following piece of code, used in an ESM module called random. The Immediately Invoked Function Expression (IIFE) wrapper trick went away, along with the name for our module, which now resides in its filename. We've regained the simplicity from back in the day, when we wrote raw JavaScript inside plain HTML <script> tags.

```
const calc = n => Math.floor(Math.random() * n)
const range = (max = 1, min = 0) => calc(max + 1 - min) + min
export { range }
```

While we don't have the problem of having to wrap our modules in an IIFE anymore, we still have to be careful about how we define, test, document, and use each module.

Deciding what constitutes a module is difficult. A lot of factors come into play, some of which I've outlined in the form of questions below:

- Is it highly complex?
- Is it too large?
- How well-defined is its API?
- Is said API properly documented?
- Is it easy to write tests for the module?
- How hard is it to add new features?
- Is it difficult to remove existing functionality?

Complexity is a more powerful metric to track than length. A module can be several thousand lines long but simple, such as a dictionary that maps identifiers to localized strings in a particular language; or it could be a couple dozen lines long but very hard to reason about, such as a data model that also includes domain validation and business logic rules. Complexity can be mitigated by splitting our code up into smaller modules that are only concerned with one aspect of the problem we're trying to solve. As long as they're not highly complex, large modules are not as much of an issue.

Having a well-defined API that's also properly documented is a key aspect of effective modular application design. A module's API should be focused, and follow information hiding principles. That is: only reveal what is necessary for consumers to interact with it. By not exposing internal aspects of a module, which may be undocumented and prone to change, we keep a simple interface overall and avoid unintended usage patterns. By documenting the public API, even if it's documented in code or self-documenting, we reduce the barrier of entry for humans looking to utilize the module.

Tests should only be written against the public interface to a module, while its internals must be treated as uninteresting implementation details. Tests need to cover the different aspects of a module's public interface, but changes to the internal implementation shouldn't break our test coverage as long as the API remains the same in terms of inputs and outputs.

Ease of adding or removing functionality from a module is yet another useful metric:

- How hard would it be to add a new feature?
- Do you have to edit several different modules in order to implement something?

- Is this a repetitive process? Maybe you could abstract those changes behind a higher-level module that hides that complexity, or maybe doing so would mostly add indirection and make following the codebase harder to read, but with little added benefit or justification.

- From the other end of the spectrum, how deeply entrenched is the API?

- Would it be easy to remove a portion of the module, delete it entirely, or even replace it with something else?

- If modules become too co-dependent, then it can be hard to make edits as the codebase ages, mutates, and grows in size.

We'll plunge deeper into proper module design, effective module interaction, and module testing over the next three books in this series.

Browsers are only scratching the surface of native JavaScript modules. At the time of this writing, some browsers already implement `import` and `export` statements. Some browsers have already implemented `<script type='module'>`, enabling them to consume modules when specifying the `module` script type. The module loader specification isn't finalized yet, and you can track its current status (*https://mjavascript.com/out/loader*).

Meanwhile, Node.js hasn't yet shipped a working implementation of the JavaScript module system. Given that JavaScript ecosystem tooling relies on node, it's not yet clear how cross-compatibility will be attained. The dilemma of how to know whether a file is written in CJS or ESM is what's delaying a working implementation. A proposal to infer whether a file was ESM based on the presence of at least one `import` or `export` statement was abandoned, and it seems like the current course of action is to introduce a new file extension specifically tailored toward ESM modules. There is quite a bit of nuance given the variety of use cases and platforms Node.js runs on, making it tough to arrive at a solution that remains elegant, performant, and correct for every use case.

With that said, let's turn over to the last chapter, on leveraging all of these new language features and syntax effectively.

CHAPTER 9

Practical Considerations

JavaScript is an ever-evolving language. Its development rhythm has had different paces throughout the years, entering a high-velocity phase with the introduction of ES5. Thus far, this book has taught you about dozens of language features and syntax changes introduced in ES6, and a few that came out afterwards, in ES2016 and ES2017.

Reconciling all of these new features with our existing ES5 knowledge may seem like a daunting task: what features should we take advantage of, and how? This chapter aims to rationalize the choices we have to make when considering whether to use specific ES6 features.

We'll take a look at a few different features, the use cases where they shine, and the situations where we might be better off using features that were already available in the language. Let's go case by case.

9.1 Variable Declarations

When developing software, most of our time is spent reading code, instead of writing it. ES6 offers `let` and `const` as new flavors of variable declaration, and part of the value in these statements is that they can signal how a variable is used. When reading a piece of code, others can take cues from these signals in order to better understand what we did. Cues like these are crucial to reducing the amount of time someone spends interpreting what a piece of code does, and as such we should try and leverage them whenever possible.

A `let` statement indicates that a variable can't be used before its declaration, due to the Temporal Dead Zone rule. This isn't a convention, it is a fact: if we tried accessing the variable before its declaration statement was reached, the program would fail. These statements are block-scoped and not function-scoped; this means we need to read less code in order to fully grasp how a `let` variable is used.

The `const` statement is block-scoped as well, and it follows TDZ semantics too. The upside is that a `const` binding can only be assigned during declaration.

Note that this means that the variable binding can't change, but it doesn't mean that the value itself is immutable or constant in any way. A `const` binding that references an object can't later reference a different value, but the underlying object can indeed mutate.

In addition to the signals offered by `let`, the `const` keyword indicates that a variable binding can't be reassigned. This is a strong signal. You know what the value is going to be; you know that the binding can't be accessed outside of its immediately containing block, due to block scoping; and you know that the binding is never accessed before declaration, because of TDZ semantics.

You know all of this just by reading the `const` declaration statement and without scanning for other references to that variable.

Constraints such as those offered by `let` and `const` are a powerful way of making code easier to understand. Try to accrue as many of these constraints as possible in the code you write. The more declarative constraints that limit what a piece of code could mean, the easier and faster it is for humans to read, parse, and understand a piece of code in the future.

Granted, there are more rules to a `const` declaration than to a `var` declaration: block-scoped, TDZ, assign at declaration, no reassignment, whereas `var` statements only signal function scoping. Rule-counting, however, doesn't offer a lot of insight. It is better to weigh these rules in terms of complexity: does the rule add or subtract complexity? In the case of `const`, block scoping means a narrower scope than function scoping, TDZ means that we don't need to scan the scope backward from the declaration in order to spot usage before declaration, and assignment rules mean that the binding will always preserve the same reference.

The more constrained statements are, the simpler a piece of code becomes. As we add constraints to what a statement might mean, code becomes less unpredictable. This is one of the reasons why statically typed programs are, generally speaking, a bit easier to read than their dynamically typed counterparts. Static typing places a big constraint on the program writer, but it also places a big constraint on how the program can be interpreted, making its code easier to understand.

With these arguments in mind, it is recommended that you use const where possible, as it's the statement that gives us the fewest possibilities to think about.

```
if (condition) {
  // can't access `isReady` before declaration is reached
  const isReady = true
  // `isReady` binding can't be reassigned
}
// can't access `isReady` outside of its containing block scope
```

When const isn't an option, because the variable needs to be reassigned later, we may resort to a let statement. Using let carries all the benefits of const, except that the variable can be reassigned. This may be necessary in order to increment a counter, flip a Boolean flag, or defer initialization.

Consider the following example, where we take a number of megabytes and return a string such as 1.2 GB. We're using let, as the values need to change if a condition is met.

```
function prettySize(input) {
  let value = input
  let unit = 'MB'
  if (value >= 1024) {
    value /= 1024
    unit = 'GB'
  }
  if (value >= 1024) {
    value /= 1024
    unit = 'TB'
  }
  return `${ value.toFixed(1) } ${ unit }`
}
```

Adding support for petabytes would involve a new if branch before the return statement.

```
if (value >= 1024) {
  value /= 1024
```

```
    unit = 'PB'
  }
```

If we were looking to make `prettySize` easier to extend with new units, we could consider implementing a `toLargestUnit` function that computes the `unit` and `value` for any given `input` and its current unit. We could then consume `toLargestUnit` in `prettySize` to return the formatted string.

The following code snippet implements such a function. It relies on a list of supported `units` instead of using a new branch for each unit. When the input `value` is at least `1024` and there are larger units, we divide the input by `1024` and move to the next unit. Then we call `toLargestUnit` with the updated values, which will continue recursively reducing the `value` until it's small enough or we reach the largest unit.

```
function toLargestUnit(value, unit = 'MB') {
  const units = ['MB', 'GB', 'TB']
  const i = units.indexOf(unit)
  const nextUnit = units[i + 1]
  if (value >= 1024 && nextUnit) {
    return toLargestUnit(value / 1024, nextUnit)
  }
  return { value, unit }
}
```

Introducing petabyte support used to involve a new `if` branch and repeating logic, but now it's only a matter of adding the `'PB'` string at the end of the `units` array.

The `prettySize` function becomes concerned only with how to display the string, as it can offload its calculations to the `toLargestU` `nit` function. This separation of concerns is also instrumental in producing more readable code.

```
function prettySize(input) {
  const { value, unit } = toLargestUnit(input)
  return `${ value.toFixed(1) } ${ unit }`
}
```

Whenever a piece of code has variables that need to be reassigned, we should spend a few minutes thinking about whether there's a better pattern that could resolve the same problem without reassignment. This is not always possible, but it can be accomplished most of the time.

Once you've arrived at a different solution, compare it to what you used to have. Make sure that code readability has actually improved and that the implementation is still correct. Unit tests can be instrumental in this regard, as they'll ensure you don't run into the same shortcomings twice. If the refactored piece of code seems worse in terms of readability or extensibility, carefully consider going back to the previous solution.

Consider the following contrived example, where we use array concatenation to generate the result array. Here, too, we could change from let to const by making a simple adjustment.

```
function makeCollection(size) {
  let result = []
  if (size > 0) {
    result = result.concat([1, 2])
  }
  if (size > 1) {
    result = result.concat([3, 4])
  }
  if (size > 2) {
    result = result.concat([5, 6])
  }
  return result
}
makeCollection(0) // <- []
makeCollection(1) // <- [1, 2]
makeCollection(2) // <- [1, 2, 3, 4]
makeCollection(3) // <- [1, 2, 3, 4, 5, 6]
```

We can replace the reassignment operations with Array#push, which accepts multiple values. If we had a dynamic list, we could use the spread operator to push as many ...items as necessary.

```
function makeCollection(size) {
  const result = []
  if (size > 0) {
    result.push(1, 2)
  }
  if (size > 1) {
    result.push(3, 4)
  }
  if (size > 2) {
    result.push(5, 6)
  }
  return result
}
makeCollection(0) // <- []
makeCollection(1) // <- [1, 2]
```

```
makeCollection(2) // <- [1, 2, 3, 4]
makeCollection(3) // <- [1, 2, 3, 4, 5, 6]
```

When you do need to use `Array#concat`, you might prefer to use
`[...result, 1, 2]` instead, to make the code shorter.

The last case we'll cover is one of refactoring. Sometimes, we write
code like the next snippet, usually in the context of a larger function.

```
let completionText = 'in progress'
if (completionPercent >= 85) {
  completionText = 'almost done'
} else if (completionPercent >= 70) {
  completionText = 'reticulating splines'
}
```

In these cases, it makes sense to extract the logic into a pure function. This way we avoid the initialization complexity near the top of
the larger function, while clustering all the logic about computing
the completion text in one place.

The following piece of code shows how we could extract the completion text logic into its own function. We can then move `getCom`
`pletionText` out of the way, making the code more linear in terms
of readability.

```
const completionText = getCompletionText(completionPercent)
// …
function getCompletionText(progress) {
  if (progress >= 85) {
    return 'almost done'
  }
  if (progress >= 70) {
    return 'reticulating splines'
  }
  return 'in progress'
}
```

9.2 Template Literals

For the longest time, JavaScript users have resorted to utility libraries to format strings, as that was never a part of the language until
now. Creating a multiline string was also a hassle, as was escaping
single or double quotes—depending on which quote style you were
using. Template literals are different, and they fix all of these incon-
veniences.

With a template literal, you can use expression interpolation, which enables you to inline variables, function calls, or any other arbitrary JavaScript expressions in a string without relying on concatenation.

```
'Hello, ' + name + '!' // before
`Hello, ${ name }!` // after
```

Multiline strings such as the one shown in the following snippet involve one or more of array concatenation, string concatenation, or explicit \n line feeds. The code is a typical example for writing an HTML string in the pre-ES6 era.

```
'<div>' `
  '<p>' `
    '<span>Hello</span>' `
    '<span>' + name + '</span>' `
    '<span>!</span>' `
  '</p>' `
'</div>'
```

Using template literals, we can avoid all of the extra quotes and concatenation, focusing on the content. The interpolation certainly helps in these kinds of templates, making multiline strings one of the most useful aspects of template literals.

```
`<div>
  <p>
    <span>Hello</span>
    <span>${ name }</span>
    <span>!</span>
  </p>
</div>`
```

When it comes to quotes, ' and " are more likely to be necessary when writing a string than ` is. For the average English phrase, you're less likely to require backticks than single or double quotes. This means that backticks lead to less escaping.[1]

```
'Alfred\'s cat suit is "slick".'
"Alfred's cat suit is \"slick\"."
`Alfred's cat suit is "slick".`
```

---

1 Typography enthusiasts will be quick to point out that straight quotes are typographically incorrect, meaning we should be using " " ' ', which don't lead to escaping. The fact remains that in practice we use straight quotes in code simply because they're easier to type. Meanwhile, typographic beautification is usually offloaded to utility libraries or a compilation step such as within a Markdown compiler.

As we discovered in Chapter 2, there are also other features such as tagged templates, which make it easy to sanitize or otherwise manipulate interpolated expressions. While useful, tagged templates are not as pervasively beneficial as multiline support, expression interpolation, or reduced escaping.

The combination of all of these features warrants considering template literals as the default string flavor over single- or double-quoted strings. There are a few concerns usually raised when template literals are proposed as the default style. We'll go over each concern and address each individually. You can then decide for yourself.

Before we begin, let's set a starting point everyone agrees on: using template literals when an expression has to be interpolated in a string is better than using quoted string concatenation.

Performance is often one of the cited concerns: is using template literals everywhere going to harm my application's performance? When using a compiler like Babel, template literals are transformed into quoted strings and interpolated expressions are concatenated amid those strings.

Consider the following example using template literals.

```
const suitKind = `cat`
console.log(`Alfred's ${ suitKind } suit is "slick".`)
// <- Alfred's cat suit is "slick".
```

A compiler such as Babel would transform our example into code similar to this, relying on quoted strings.

```
const suitKind = 'cat'
console.log('Alfred\'s ' + suitKind + ' suit is "slick".')
// <- Alfred's cat suit is "slick".
```

We've already settled that interpolated expressions are better than quoted string concatenation, in terms of readability, and the compiler turns those into quoted string concatenation, maximizing browser support.

When it comes to the suitKind variable, a template literal with no interpolation, no newlines, and no tags, the compiler simply turns it into a plain quoted string.

Once we stop compiling template literals down to quoted strings, we can expect optimizing compilers to be able to interpret them as such with negligible slowdown.

Another often-cited concern is syntax: as of this writing, we can't use backtick strings in JSON, object keys, import declarations, or strict mode directives.

The first statement in the following snippet of code demonstrates that a serialized JSON object couldn't represent strings using backticks. As shown on the second line, we can certainly declare an object using template literals and then serialize that object as JSON. By the time JSON.stringify is invoked, the template literal has evaluated to a quoted string.

```
JSON.parse('{ "payload": `message` }')
// <- SyntaxError
JSON.stringify({ payload: `message` })
// <- '{"payload":"message"}'
```

When it comes to object keys, we're out of luck. Attempting to use a template literal would result in a syntax error.

```
const alfred = { `suit kind`: `cat` }
```

Object property keys accept value types, which are then cast into plain strings, but template literals aren't value types, and thus it's not possible to use them as property keys.

As you might recall from Chapter 2, ES6 introduces computed property names, as seen in the following code snippet. In a computed property key we can use any expression we want to produce the desired property key, including template literals.

```
const alfred = { [`suit kind`]: `cat` }
```

The preceding is far from ideal due to its verbosity, though, and in these cases it's best to use regular quoted strings.

As always, the rule is to never take rules such as "template literals are the best option" too literally, and be open to use your best judgment as necessary and break the rules a little bit, if they don't quite fit your use cases, conventions, or view of how an application is best structured. Rules are often presented as such, but what may be a rule to someone need not be a rule to everyone. This is the main reason why modern linters make every rule optional: the rules we use should be enforced, but not every rule may fit every project.

Perhaps someday we might get a flavor of computed property keys that doesn't rely on square brackets for template literals, saving us a couple of characters when we need to interpolate a string. For the foreseeable future, the following code snippet will result in a syntax error.

```
const brand = `Porsche`
const car = {
  `wheels`: 4,
  `has fuel`: true,
  `is ${ brand }`: `you wish`
}
```

Attempts to import a module using template literals will also result in a syntax error. This is one of those cases where we might expect to be able to use template literals, if we were to adopt them extensively throughout our codebase, but can't.

```
import { SayHello } from `./World`
```

Strict mode directives have to be single- or double-quoted strings. As of this writing, there's no plan to allow template literals for 'use strict' directives. The following piece of code does not result in a syntax error, but it also does not enable strict mode. This is the biggest caveat when heavily using template literals.

```
'use strict' // enables strict mode
"use strict" // enables strict mode
`use strict` // nothing happens
```

Lastly, it could be argued that turning an existing codebase from single-quoted strings to template literals would be error-prone and a waste of time that could be otherwise used to develop features or fix bugs.

Fortunately, we have eslint at our disposal, as discussed in Chapter 1. To switch our codebase to backticks by default, we can set up an .eslintrc.json configuration similar to the one in the following piece of code. Note how we turn the quotes rule into an error unless the code uses backticks.

```
{
  "env": {
    "es6": true
  },
  "extends": "eslint:recommended",
  "rules": {
    "quotes": ["error", "backtick"]
  }
}
```

With that in place, we can add a lint script to our *package.json*, like the one in the next snippet. The --fix flag ensures that any style errors found by the linter, such as using single quotes over backticks, are autocorrected.

```
{
  "scripts": {
    "lint": "eslint --fix ."
  }
}
```

Once we run the following command, we're ready to start experimenting with a codebase that uses backticks by default!

```
» npm run lint
```

In conclusion, there are trade-offs to consider when using template literals. You're invited to experiment with the backtick-first approach and gauge its merits. Always prefer convenience, over convention, over configuration.

9.3 Shorthand Notation and Object Destructuring

Chapter 1 introduced us to the concept of shorthand notation. Whenever we want to introduce a property and there's a binding by the same name in scope, we can avoid repetition.

```
const unitPrice = 1.25
const tomato = {
  name: 'Tomato',
  color: 'red',
  unitPrice
}
```

This feature becomes particularly useful in the context of functions and information hiding. In the following example we leverage object destructuring for a few pieces of information from a grocery item and return a model that also includes the total price for the items.

```
function getGroceryModel({ name, unitPrice }, units) {
  return {
    name,
    unitPrice,
    units,
    totalPrice: unitPrice * units
  }
}
```

```
getGroceryModel(tomato, 4)
/*
{
  name: 'Tomato',
  unitPrice: 1.25,
  units: 4,
  totalPrice: 5
}
*/
```

Note how well shorthand notation works in tandem with destructuring. If you think of destructuring as a way of pulling properties out of an object, then you can think of shorthand notation as the analog for placing properties onto an object. The following example shows how we can leverage the getGroceryModel function to pull the totalPrice of a grocery item when we know how many the customer is buying.

```
const { totalPrice } = getGroceryModel(tomato, 4)
```

While counterintuitive at first, usage of destructuring in function parameters results in a convenient and implicitly contract-based solution, where we know that the first parameter to getGroceryModel is expected to be an object containing name and unitPrice properties.

```
function getGroceryModel({ name, unitPrice }, units) {
  return {
    name,
    unitPrice,
    units,
    totalPrice: unitPrice * units
  }
}
```

Conversely, destructuring a function's output gives the reader an immediate feel for what aspect of that output a particular piece of code is interested in. In the next snippet, we'll use only the product name and total price so that's what we destructure out of the output.

```
const { name, totalPrice } = getGroceryModel(tomato, 4)
```

Compare the last snippet with the following line of code, where we don't use destructuring. Instead, we pull the output into a model binding. While subtle, the key difference is that this piece communicates less information explicitly: we need to dig deeper into the code to find out which parts of the model are being used.

```
const model = getGroceryModel(tomato, 4)
```

Destructuring can also help avoid repeating references to the host object when it comes to using several properties from the same object.

```
const summary = `${ model.units }x ${ model.name }
($${ model.unitPrice }) = $${ model.totalPrice }`
// <- '4x Tomato ($1.25) = $5'
```

However, there's a trade-off here: we avoid repeating the host object when referencing properties, but at the expense of repeating property names in our destructuring declaration statement.

```
const { name, units, unitPrice, totalPrice } = model
const summary = `${ units }x ${ name } ($${ unitPrice }) =
$${ totalPrice }`
```

Whenever there are several references to the same property, it becomes clear that we should avoid repeating references to the host object, by destructuring it.

When there's a single reference to a single property, it's clear we should avoid destructuring, as it mostly generates noise.

```
const { name } = model
const summary = `This is a ${ name } summary`
```

Having a reference to `model.name` directly in the `summary` code is less noisy.

```
const summary = `This is a ${ model.name } summary`
```

When we have two properties to destructure (or two references to one property), things change a bit.

```
const summary = `This is a summary for ${ model.units }x
${ model.name }`
```

Destructuring does help in this case. It reduces the character count in the `summary` declaration statement, and it explicitly announces the `model` properties we're going to be using.

```
const { name, units } = model
const summary = `This is a summary for ${ units }x ${ name }`
```

If we have two references to the same property, similar conditions apply. In the next example, we have one less reference to `model` and one more reference to `name` than we'd have without destructuring. This case could go either way, although the value in explicitly declaring the future usage of `name` could be incentive enough to warrant destructuring.

```
const { name } = model
const summary = `This is a ${ name } summary`
const description = `${ name } is a grocery item`
```

Destructuring is as valuable as the amount of references to host objects it eliminates, but the amount of properties being referenced can dilute value, because of increased repetition in the destructuring statement. In short, destructuring is a great feature but it doesn't necessarily lead to more readable code every time. Use it judiciously, especially when there aren't that many host references being removed.

9.4 Rest and Spread

Matches for regular expressions are represented as an array. The matched portion of the input is placed in the first position, while each captured group is placed in subsequent elements in the array. Often, we are interested in specific captures such as the first one.

In the following example, array destructuring helps us omit the whole match and place the integer and fractional parts of a number into corresponding variables. This way, we avoid resorting to magic numbers pointing at the indices where captured groups will reside in the match result.

```
function getNumberParts(number) {
  const rnumber = /(\d+)\.(\d+)/
  const matches = number.match(rnumber)
  if (matches === null) {
    return null
  }
  const [ , integer, fractional] = number.match(rnumber)
  return { integer, fractional }
}
getNumberParts('1234.56')
// <- { integer: '1234', fractional: '56' }
```

The spread operator could be used to pick up every captured group, as part of destructuring the result of .match.

```
function getNumberParts(number) {
  const rnumber = /(\d+)\.(\d+)/
  const matches = number.match(rnumber)
  if (matches === null) {
    return null
  }
  const [ , ...captures] = number.match(rnumber)
  return captures
```

```
}
getNumberParts('1234.56')
// <- ['1234', '56']
```

When we need to concatenate lists, we use .concat to create a new array. The spread operator improves code readability by making it immediately obvious that we want to create a new collection comprising each list of inputs, while preserving the ease of adding new elements declaratively in array literals.

```
administrators.concat(moderators)
[...administrators, ...moderators]
[...administrators, ...moderators, bob]
```

Similarly, the object spread feature[2] introduced in Section 3.3.1, "Extending Objects with Object.assign," on page 76 allows us to merge objects onto a new object. Consider the following snippet where we programmatically create a new object comprising base defaults, user-provided options, and some important override property that prevails over previous properties.

```
Object.assign({}, defaults, options, { important: true })
```

Compare that to the equivalent snippet using object spread declaratively. We have the object literal, the defaults and options being spread, and the important property. Not using the Object.assign function has greatly improved our code's readability, even letting us inline the important property in the object literal declaration.

```
{
  ...defaults,
  ...options,
  important: true
}
```

Being able to visualize object spread as an Object.assign helps internalize how the feature works. In the following example we've replaced the defaults and options variables with object literals. Since object spread relies on the same operation as Object.assign for every property, we can observe how the options literal overrides speed with the number 3, and why important remains true even when the options literal attempts to override it, due to precedence.

```
{
  ...{ // defaults
```

---

2 Currently in stage 3 of the ECMAScript standard development process.

```
      speed: 1,
      type: 'sports'
    },
    ...{ // options
      speed: 3,
      important: false
    },
    important: true
  }
```

Object spread comes in handy when we're dealing with immutable structures, where we're supposed to create new objects instead of editing existing ones. Consider the following bit of code where we have a player object and a function call that casts a healing spell and returns a new, healthier, player object.

```
const player = {
  strength: 4,
  luck: 2,
  mana: 80,
  health: 10
}
castHealingSpell(player) // consumes 40 mana, gains 110 health
```

The following snippet shows an implementation of castHealing Spell where we create a new player object without mutating the original player parameter. Every property in the original player object is copied over, and we can update individual properties as needed.

```
const castHealingSpell = player => ({
  ...player,
  mana: player.mana - 40,
  health: player.health + 110
})
```

As we explained in Chapter 3, we can use object rest properties while destructuring objects. Among other uses, such as listing unknown properties, object rest can be used to create a shallow copy of an object.

In the next snippet, we'll look at three of the simplest ways in which we can create a shallow copy of an object in JavaScript. The first one uses Object.assign, assigning every property of source to an empty object that's then returned; the second example uses object spread and is equivalent to using Object.assign, but a bit more gentle on the eyes; the last example relies on destructuring the rest parameter.

```
const copy = Object.assign({}, source)
const copy = { ...source }
const { ...copy } = source
```

Sometimes we need to create a copy of an object, but omit some properties in the resulting copy. For instance, we may want to create a copy of person while omitting their name, so that we only keep their metadata.

One way to achieve that with plain JavaScript would be to destructure the name property while placing other properties in a metadata object, using the rest parameter. Even though we don't need the name, we've effectively "removed" that property from the metadata object, which contains the rest of the properties in person.

```
const { name, ...metadata } = person
```

In the following bit of code, we map a list of people to a list of person models, excluding personally identifiable information such as their name and Social Security number, while placing everything else in the person rest parameter.

```
people.map(({ name, ssn, ...person }) => person)
```

9.5 Savoring Function Flavors

JavaScript already offered a number of ways in which we can declare functions before ES6.

Function declarations are the most prominent kind of JavaScript function. The fact that declarations aren't hoisted means we can sort them based on how to improve code readability, instead of worrying about sorting them in the exact order they are used.

The following snippet displays three function declarations arranged in such a way that the code is more linear to read.

```
printSum(2, 3)
function printSum(x, y) {
  return print(sum(x, y))
}
function sum(x, y) {
  return x + y
}
function print(message) {
  console.log(`printing: ${ message }`)
}
```

Function expressions, in contrast, must be assigned to a variable before we can execute them. Keeping with the preceding example, this means we would necessarily need to have all function expressions declared before any code can use them.

The next snippet uses function expressions. Note that if we were to place the printSum function call anywhere other than after all three expression assignments, our code would fail because of a variable that hasn't been initialized yet.

```
var printSum = function (x, y) {
  return print(sum(x, y))
}
var sum = function (x, y) {
  return x + y
}
// a `printSum()` statement would fail: print is not defined
var print = function (message) {
  console.log(`printing: ${ message }`)
}
printSum(2, 3)
```

For this reason, it may be better to sort function expressions as a LIFO (last-in-first-out) stack: placing the last function to be called first, the second to last function to be called second, and so on. The rearranged code is shown in the next snippet.

```
var sum = function (x, y) {
  return x + y
}
var print = function (message) {
  console.log(`printing: ${ message }`)
}
var printSum = function (x, y) {
  return print(sum(x, y))
}
printSum(2, 3)
```

While this code is a bit harder to follow, it becomes immediately obvious that we can't call printSum before the function expression is assigned to that variable. In the previous piece of code this wasn't obvious because we weren't following the LIFO rule. This is reason enough to prefer function declarations for the vast majority of our code.

Function expressions can have a name that can be used for recursion, but that name is not accessible in the outer scope. The following example shows a function expression that's named sum and assigned to a sumMany variable. The sum reference is used for recursion in the inner scope, but we get an error when trying to use it from the outer scope.

```
var sumMany = function sum(accumulator = 0, ...values) {
  if (values.length === 0) {
    return accumulator
  }
  const [value, ...rest] = values
  return sum(accumulator + value, ...rest)
}
console.log(sumMany(0, 1, 2, 3, 4))
// <- 10
console.log(sum())
// <- ReferenceError: sum is not defined
```

Arrow functions, introduced in Section 2.2, "Arrow Functions," on page 24, are similar to function expressions. The syntax is made shorter by dropping the function keyword. In arrow functions, parentheses around the parameter list are optional when there's a single parameter that's not destructured nor the rest parameter. It is possible to implicitly return any valid JavaScript expression from an arrow function without declaring a block statement.

The following snippet shows an arrow function explicitly returning an expression in a block statement, one that implicitly returns the expression, one that drops the parentheses around its only parameter, and one that uses a block statement but doesn't return a value.

```
const sum = (x, y) => { return x + y }
const multiply = (x, y) => x * y
const double = x => x * 2
const print = x => { console.log(x) }
```

Arrow functions can return arrays using tiny expressions. The first example in the next snippet implicitly returns an array comprising two elements, while the second example discards the first parameter and returns all other parameters held in the rest operator's bag.

```
const makeArray = (first, second) => [first, second]
const makeSlice = (discarded, ...items) => items
```

Implicitly returning an object literal is a bit tricky because they're hard to tell apart from block statements, which are also wrapped in curly braces. We'll have to add parentheses around our object literal, turning it into an expression that evaluates into the object. This bit of indirection is just enough to help us disambiguate and tell JavaScript parsers that they're dealing with an object literal.

Consider the following example, where we implicitly return an object expression. Without the parentheses, the parser would interpret our code as a block statement containing a label and the literal expression 'Nico'.

```
const getPerson = name => ({
  name: 'Nico'
})
```

Explicitly naming arrow functions isn't possible, due to their syntax. However, if an arrow function expression is declared in the right-hand side of a variable or property declaration, then its name becomes the name for the arrow function.

Arrow function expressions need to be assigned before use, and thus suffer from the same ordering ailments as regular function expressions. In addition, since they can't be named, they must be bound to a variable for us to reference them in recursion scenarios.

Using function declarations by default should be preferred. They are less limited in terms of how they can be ordered, referenced, and executed, leading to better code readability and maintainability. In future refactors, we won't have to worry about keeping function declarations in the same order in fear of breaking dependency chains or LIFO representations.

That said, arrow functions are a terse and powerful way of declaring functions in short form. The smaller the function, the more valuable using arrow syntax becomes, as it helps avoid a situation where we spend more code on form than we spend on function. As a function grows larger, writing it in arrow form loses its appeal due to the aforementioned ordering and naming issues.

Arrow functions are invaluable in cases where we would've otherwise declared an anonymous function expression, such as in test cases, functions passed to new Promise() and setTimeout, or array mapping functions.

Consider the following example, where we use a nonblocking wait promise to print a statement after five seconds. The wait function takes a delay in milliseconds and returns a Promise, which resolves after waiting for the specified time with setTimeout.

```
wait(5000).then(function () {
  console.log('waited 5 seconds!')
})
```

```
function wait(delay) {
  return new Promise(function (resolve) {
    setTimeout(function () {
      resolve()
    }, delay)
  })
}
```

When switching to arrow functions, we should stick with the top-level wait function declaration so that we don't need to hoist it to the top of our scope. We can turn every other function into arrows to improve readability, thus removing many function keywords that got in the way of interpreting what those functions do.

The next snippet shows what that code would look like using arrow functions. With all the keywords out of the way after refactoring, it's easier to understand the relationship between the delay parameter of wait and the second argument to setTimeout.

```
wait(5000).then(
  () => console.log('waited 5 seconds!')
)

function wait(delay) {
  return new Promise(resolve =>
    setTimeout(() => resolve(), delay)
  )
}
```

Another large upside in using arrow functions lies in their lexical scoping, where they don't modify the meaning of this or argu ments. If we find ourselves copying this to a temporary variable—typically named self, context, or _this—we may want to use an arrow function for the inner bit of code instead. Let's take a look at an example of this.

```
const pistol = {
  caliber: 50,
  trigger() {
    const self = this
    setTimeout(function () {
      console.log(`Fired caliber ${ self.caliber } pistol`)
    }, 1000)
  }
}
pistol.trigger()
```

If we tried to use this directly in the previous example, we'd get a caliber of undefined instead. With an arrow function, however, we can avoid the temporary self variable. We not only removed the function keyword but we also gained functional value due to lexical scoping, since we don't need to work our way around the language's limitations anymore in this case.

```
const pistol = {
  caliber: 50,
  trigger() {
    setTimeout(() => {
      console.log(`Fired caliber ${ self.caliber } pistol`)
    }, 1000)
  }
}
pistol.trigger()
```

As a general rule of thumb, think of every function as a function declaration by default. If that function doesn't need a meaningful name, requires several lines of code, or involves recursion, then consider an arrow function.

9.6 Classes and Proxies

Most modern programming languages have classes in one form or another. JavaScript classes are syntactic sugar on top of prototypal inheritance. Using classes turns prototypes more idiomatic and easier for tools to statically analyze.

When writing prototype-based solutions the constructor code is the function itself, while declaring instance methods involves quite a bit of boilerplate code, as shown in the following code snippet.

```
function Player() {
  this.health = 5
}
Player.prototype.damage = function () {
  this.health--
}
Player.prototype.attack = function (player) {
  player.damage()
}
```

In contrast, classes normalize the constructor as an instance method, thus making it clear that the constructor is executed for every instance. At the same time, methods are built into the class literal and rely on a syntax that's consistent with methods in object literals.

```
class Player {
  constructor() {
    this.health = 5
  }
  damage() {
    this.health--
  }
  attack(player) {
    player.damage()
  }
}
```

Grouping instance methods under an object literal ensures class declarations aren't spread over several files, but rather unified in a single location describing their whole API.

Declaring any static methods as part of a class literal, as opposed to dynamically injecting them onto the class, also helps centralize API knowledge. Keeping this knowledge in a central location helps code readability because developers need to go through less code to learn the Player API. At the same time, when we define a convention of declaring instance and static methods on the class literal, coders know not to waste time looking elsewhere for methods defined dynamically. The same applies to getters and setters, which we can also define on the class literal.

```
class Player {
  constructor() {
    Player.heal(this)
  }
  damage() {
    this.health--
  }
  attack(player) {
    player.damage()
  }
  get alive() {
    return this.health > 0
  }
  static heal(player) {
    player.health = 5
  }
}
```

Classes also offer extends, simple syntactic sugar on top of prototypal inheritance. This, again, is more convenient than prototype-based solutions. With `extends`, we don't have to worry about choosing a library or otherwise dynamic method of inheriting from another class.

```
class GameMaster extends Player {
  constructor(...rest) {
    super(...rest)
    this.health = Infinity
  }
  kill(player) {
    while (player.alive) {
      player.damage()
    }
  }
}
```

Using that same syntax, classes can extend native built-ins such as `Array` or `Date` without relying on an `<iframe>` or shallow copying. Consider the `List` class in the following code snippet, which skips the default `Array` constructor in order to avoid the often-confusing single number parameter overload. It also illustrates how we could implement our own methods on top of the native `Array` prototype.

```
class List extends Array {
  constructor(...items) {
    super()
    this.push(...items)
  }
  get first() {
    return this[0]
  }
  get last() {
    return this[this.length - 1]
  }
}
const number = new List(2)
console.log(number.first)
// <- 2
const items = new List('a', 'few', 'examples')
console.log(items.last)
// <- 'examples'
```

JavaScript classes are less verbose than their prototype-based equivalents. Class sugar is thus a most welcome improvement over raw prototypal inheritance. As for the merits of using JavaScript classes, it depends. Even though classes may be compelling to use due to their improved syntax, sugar alone doesn't instantly promote classes to a wider variety of use cases.

Statically typed languages typically offer and enforce the use of classes.[3] In contrast, due to the highly dynamic nature of JavaScript, classes aren't mandatory. Almost every scenario that would typically demand classes can be addressed using plain objects.

Plain objects are simpler than classes. There's no need for special constructor methods, their only initialization is the declaration, they're easy to serialize via JSON, and they're more interoperable. Inheritance is seldom the right abstraction to use, but when it is desirable we might switch to classes or stick with plain objects and `Object.create`.

Proxies empower many previously unavailable use cases, but we need to tread lightly. Solutions that involve a `Proxy` object may also be implemented using plain objects and functions without resorting to an object that behaves as if by magic.

There may indeed be cases where using a `Proxy` is warranted, particularly when it comes to developer tooling meant for development environments, where a high degree of code introspection is desirable and complexity is hidden away in the developer tool's codebase. Using `Proxy` in application-level codebases is easily avoided, and leads to less enigmatic code.

Readability hinges on code that has a clear purpose. Declarative code is readable: upon reading a piece of code, it becomes clear what it is intended to do. In contrast, using layers of indirection such as a `Proxy` on top of an object can result in highly complex access rules that may be hard to infer when reading a piece of code. It's not that a solution involving a `Proxy` is impossible to understand, but the fact remains that more code needs to be read and carefully considered before we fully understand the nuances of how the proxy layer behaves.

If we're considering proxies, then maybe objects aren't the tool for what we're trying to accomplish. Instead of going straight to a `Proxy` indirection layer, consider whether a simple function offers just enough indirection without causing an object to behave in a manner that's inconsistent with how plain objects typically behave in JavaScript.

---

3 An exception should be made for most functional programming languages.

As such, always prefer boring, static, and declarative code over smart and elegant abstractions. Boring code might be a little more repetitive than using an abstraction, but it will also be simpler, easier to understand, and decidedly a safer bet in the short term.

Abstractions are costly. Once an abstraction is in place, it is often hard to go back and eliminate it. If an abstraction is created too early, it might not cover all common use cases, and we may end up having to handle special cases separately.

When we prefer boring code, patterns flourish gradually and naturally. Once a pattern emerges, then we can decide whether an abstraction is warranted and refactor our code fittingly. A time-honed well-placed abstraction is likely to cover more use cases than it might have covered if we had gone for an abstraction as soon as we had two or three functionally comparable pieces of code.

9.7 Asynchronous Code Flows

In Chapter 4 we discussed how many of the different ways in which we can manage complexity in asynchronous operations work, and how we can use them. Callbacks, events, promises, generators, async functions and async iterators, external libraries, and the list goes on. You should now be comfortable with how these constructs work, but when should you use them?

Callbacks are the most primitive solution. They require little knowledge beyond basic JavaScript, making callback-based code some of the easiest to read. Callbacks should be approached with care in cases where the flow of operations involves a long dependency chain, as a series of deeply nested asynchronous operations can lead to callback hell.

When it comes to callbacks, libraries like `async` can help reduce complexity when we have three or more related tasks that need to be executed asynchronously.[4] Another positive aspect of these libraries is how they unobtrusively interoperate with plain callbacks, which is useful when we have a mix of complex flows that need to be abstrac-

---

4 A popular flow control library. You can find `async` on GitHub (*https:// mjavascript.com/out/async-library*).

ted through the library and simpler flows that you can articulate with plain callbacks.

Events are a cheap way of introducing extensibility into code flows, asynchronous or otherwise. Events don't lend themselves well to managing the complexity of asynchronous tasks, however.

The following example shows how convoluted our code could become if we wanted to handle asynchronous tasks using events. Half of the lines of code are spent on defining the code flow, and even then the flow is quite hard to understand. This means we probably chose the wrong tool for the job.

```
const tracker = emitter()
tracker.on('started', multiply)
tracker.on('multiplied', print)
start(256, 512, 1024)
function start(...input) {
  const sum = input.reduce((a, b) => a + b, 0)
  tracker.emit('started', { sum, input })
}
function multiply({ sum, input }) {
  const message = `The sum of ${ input.join('`') } is ${ sum }`
  tracker.emit('multiplied', message)
}
function print(message) {
  console.log(message)
}
```

Promises were around for a long time, in user libraries, before TC39 decided to bring them into the core JavaScript language. They serve a similar purpose as callback libraries, offering an alternative way of writing asynchronous code flows.

Promises are a bit more expensive than callbacks in terms of commitment, because promise chains involve more promises, so they are hard to interleave with plain callbacks. At the same time, you don't want to interleave promises with callback-based code, because that leads to complex applications. For any given portion of code, it's important to pick one paradigm and stick with it. Relying on a single paradigm produces code that doesn't focus as much on the mechanics as it does on task processing.

Committing to promises isn't inherently bad; however, it's merely a cost you need to be aware of. As more and more of the web platform relies on promises as a fundamental building block, they only get better. Promises underlie generators, async functions, async iterators, and async generators. The more we use those constructs, the more synergistic our applications become, and while it could be argued that plain callbacks are already synergistic by nature, they certainly don't compare to the sheer power of async functions and all promise-based solutions that are now native to the JavaScript language.

Once we commit to promises, the variety of tools at our disposal is comparable to using a library that offers solutions to common flow control problems by relying on callbacks. The difference is that, for the most part, promises don't require any libraries because they're native to the language.

We could use iterators to lazily describe sequences that don't necessarily need to be finite. Further, their asynchronous counterpart could be used to describe sequences that require out-of-band processing, such as GET requests, to produce elements. Those sequences can be consumed by using a for await..of loop, hiding away the complexity of their asynchronous nature.

An iterator is a useful way of describing how an object is iterated to produce a sequence. When there isn't an object to describe, generators offer a way of describing standalone sequences. Implementing an iterator is the ideal way of describing how a Movie object should be iterated, perhaps using Symbol.asyncIterator and fetching information about each actor and their roles for every credited actor in a movie. Without the context of a Movie object, however, such an iterator would make more sense as a generator.

Another case where generators are useful is infinite sequences. Consider the following iterator, where we produce an infinite stream of integer numbers.

```
const integers = value => ({
  value,
  [Symbol.iterator]() {
    return {
      next: () => ({
        value: this.value++
      })
    }
  }
})
```

You probably remember generators are inherently iterable, meaning they follow the iterator protocol without the need for us to supply an iterator. Now compare the iterable `integers` object to the equivalent generator function found in the next piece of code.

```
function* integers(value = 0) {
  while (true) {
    yield value++
  }
}
```

Not only is the generator code shorter, but it's also far more readable. The fact that it produces an infinite sequence becomes immediately obvious due to the `while` loop. The iterable requires us to understand that the sequence is infinite because the code never returns an element with the `done: true` flag. Setting the seed `value` is more natural and doesn't involve wrapping the object in a function that receives the initial parameters.

Promises were originally hailed as a cure to callback hell ailments. Programs that rely heavily on promises can fall into the callback hell trap when we have deeply nested asynchronous series flows. Async functions present an elegant solution to this problem, where we can describe the same promise-based code using `await` expressions.

Consider the following piece of code.

```
Promise
  .resolve(2)
  .then(x => x * 2)
  .then(x => x * 2)
  .then(x => x * 2)
```

When we use an `await` expression, the expression on its righthand side is coerced into a promise. When an `await` expression is reached, the async function will pause execution until the promise—coerced or otherwise—has been settled. When the promise is fulfilled, then execution in the async function continues, but if the promise is rejected then the rejection will bubble up to the promise returned by the async function call, unless that rejection is suppressed by a `catch` handler.

```
async function calculate() {
  let x = 2
  x = await x * 2
  x = await x * 2
  x = await x * 2
  return x
}
```

The beauty of async/await lies in the fact that it fixes the biggest problem with promises, where you can't easily mix synchronous code into your flows. At the same time, async functions let you use try/catch, a construct we are unable to leverage when using callbacks. Meanwhile, async/await manages to stay synergistic with promises by using them under the hood, always returning a Promise from every async function and coercing awaited expressions into promises. Moreover, async functions accomplish all of the above while turning asynchronous code into synchronous-looking code.

While using await expressions optimizes toward reducing complexity in serial asynchronous code, it becomes hard to reason about concurrent asynchronous code flows when replacing promises with async/await. This can be mitigated by using await Promise.all(tasks) and firing those tasks concurrently before the await expression is reached. Given, however, that async functions don't optimize for this use case, reading this kind of code can be confusing, so this is something to look out for. If our code is highly concurrent, we might want to consider a callback-based approach.

Once again, this leads us to critical thinking. New language features aren't always necessarily better for all use cases. While sticking to conventions is important so that our code remains consistent and we don't spend most of our time deciding on how to better represent a small portion of a program, it is also important to have a fine balance.

When we don't spend at least some of our time figuring out what feature or flow style is the most appropriate for the code we're writing, we risk treating every problem as a nail because all we have is a hammer. Picking the right tool for the problem at hand is even more important than being a stickler for conventions and hard rules.

9.8 Complexity Creep, Abstractions, and Conventions

Picking the right abstractions is hard: we want to reduce complexity in our code flows by introducing complexity that's hidden away behind the constructs we use. Async functions borrow their foundation from generators. Generator objects are iterable. Async iterators use promises. Iterators are implemented using symbols. Promises use callbacks.

Consistency is an important theme when it comes to maintainable code. An application might mostly use callbacks, or mostly use promises. Individually, both callbacks and promises can be used to reduce complexity in code flows. When mixing them together, however, we need to make sure we don't introduce context switching where developers reading different pieces of a codebase need to enter different mindsets to understand them.

This is why conventions exist. A strong convention such as "use promises where possible" goes a long way toward augmenting consistency across a codebase. Conventions, more than anything, are what drive readability and maintainability in a codebase. Code is, after all, a communication device used to convey a message. This message is not only relevant to the computers executing the code, but most importantly to developers reading the code, maintaining and improving the application over time.

Without strong conventions, communication breaks down and developers have a hard time understanding how a program works, ultimately leading to reduced productivity.

The vast majority of the time spent working as a software developer is spent reading code. It's only logical, then, that we pay careful attention to how to write code in such a way that's optimized for readability.

Index

BMP (basic multilinual plane), 231

u flag, 240-241
Unicode-Aware String Reversal,
    237
Unicode property escapes, 244
util.inherits, 64

V

validator handler, 184
value, 155
.values(), 165
var versus let, 49
variable declarations, 279-284

W

WeakMap, 69, 168-170, 199
WeakSet, 173-175, 206
WHATWG, 4
wildcard import statements, 272

Y

y flag, 239
yield, 121, 126, 134-135
yield*, 123-125

About the Author

Nicolás Bevacqua is the author of *JavaScript Application Design* (Manning). He's a JavaScript hacker based in Buenos Aires, Argentina. An avid writer, Nicolás is an open source advocate working at Elastic as a UI engineer. You can find his essays about the web on ponyfoo.com (*https://ponyfoo.com*).

He enjoys travelling around the world and speaking at tech conferences.

Colophon

The cover fonts are Helvetica Inserat and DIN. The text font is Adobe Minion Pro; the heading font is Adobe Myriad Condensed; and the code font is Dalton Maag's Ubuntu Mono.

Learn from experts.
Find the answers you need.

Sign up for a **10-day free trial** to get **unlimited access** to all of the content on Safari, including Learning Paths, interactive tutorials, and curated playlists that draw from thousands of ebooks and training videos on a wide range of topics, including data, design, DevOps, management, business—and much more.

Start your free trial at:
oreilly.com/safari

(No credit card required.)